To Dad at Xmas.
1944.

Love.
Charlie

ONWARDS TO VICTORY

BY THE RIGHT HON.
WINSTON S. CHURCHILL

THE UNRELENTING STRUGGLE
THE END OF THE BEGINNING
ONWARDS TO VICTORY

ONWARDS
TO VICTORY

—————*War Speeches by the*—————

RIGHT HON.
WINSTON S. CHURCHILL
C.H., M.P.

Compiled by CHARLES EADE

McCLELLAND AND STEWART, LIMITED
PUBLISHERS   TORONTO
1944

Printed in Canada
by
THE HUNTER-ROSE CO. LIMITED, TORONTO

Introduction

BY January the First, 1943, the initiative in the War had passed to the United Nations. The enemy armies sprawled over vast territories. Bitter, resentful peoples suffered by scores of millions under the oppression and cruelties of Axis invaders. The map showed vast gains for the aggressors. But the tide had turned. The new year opened with a brighter, hopeful vista for the democratic nations.

In the North African desert, Britain's Eighth Army, under General Alexander and General Montgomery, was pursuing Rommel's beaten and battered German Afrika Corps and Italian Army across Libya to the West and was about 250 miles from Tripoli. In the South, a small French force under General Leclerc was moving steadily Northwards from the Chad towards Tripolitania and had just attacked an aerodrome about 400 miles from Tripoli itself.

In French North Africa, General Giraud had, a few days earlier, assumed the leadership of the French Colonial Empire following the assassination of Admiral Darlan, but the political situation remained confused by the failure of the Giraud–de Gaulle elements to reach agreement and unity. Meanwhile, the United Nations military operations in Tunisia proceeded slowly. The surprise landings by American and British forces some eight weeks earlier had brought the whole of Algeria and Morocco and part of Tunisia under Allied control, but the Germans, pouring troops across the narrow sea from Sicily, were daily strengthening the hold on Tunis, Bizerta and the coastline down to Tripolitania.

In the Far East, too, the Japanese had been halted and were on the defensive in the island outposts of their Pacific conquests. Heavy Allied blows were being struck in New Guinea, and American naval successes had restored to the United Nations the predominant position in the Solomons.

Introduction

British troops under General Wavell were advancing from India into Burma, their progress being hailed as a preparation for greater and more active aid to the sorely-pressed forces of General Chiang Kai-Shek in China. All these movements were evidence of the growing Allied strength in the Far East as well as in the West.

But the brightest scene of all on New Year's Day, 1943, was in Russia. The Soviet armies, having trapped some 300,000 Germans at Stalingrad, were sweeping forward along the caravan trails of the Kalmuck Steppes, past Kotchnikov and on towards the Sea of Azov and Rostov. Along the whole vast front the Red Army was on the offensive. Britain and America had helped the Soviet to arm for this gigantic recovery and by this date had sent 6,200 tanks, 5,600 'planes and 85,000 trucks to Russia.

In the West, Germany was facing ever-increasing pressure in the air. Devastating raids had shattered the industrial cities of the Rhineland and the U-boats' home ports. Every week the power of the British and American air offensive was growing in intensity. The Luftwaffe could not hit back. The raids on Britain had dwindled to insignificant proportions and the British people, armed, organised, and equipped for war as never before, found the prospect of the New Year full of hope. Health was good. The birth-rate was the highest for twelve years. Only the shadow of the ever-present, ever-growing U-boat menace darkened the outlook in the British Isles.

Such, briefly, was the war situation at the opening of the year 1943.

CHARLES EADE

Contents

Contents

Contents

ix

Contents

x

Contents

ONWARDS TO VICTORY

January 1.   Russians captured Veliki Luki and developed an offensive along the Black Sea coast.

   The Eighth Army massed West of El Kebir.

January 2.   General de Gaulle proposed a meeting between himself and General Giraud on French soil.

January 3.   Russians captured Mozdok and other towns in the Caucasus.

January 6.   Four thousand people arrested in Roumania following discovery of Iron Guard plot against Antonescu Government.

January 7.   President Roosevelt, in a speech to Congress, declared: "We shall strike in Europe and strike hard."

January 12.   Russian advance in Caucasus reported to have covered 100 miles in nine days.

January 14.   Mr. Churchill and President Roosevelt met in secret at Casablanca, North Africa, but the meeting was not announced to the world until January 26.

January 16 and 17.   R.A.F. made heavy raids on Berlin on two successive nights. On the second night the Germans attempted a reprisal raid on London, but were beaten off by a great barrage, and ten raiders were destroyed.

January 18.   Russians captured Schlusselburg and raised the siege of Leningrad which had lasted for eighteen months. On the South-Western front Soviet troops forced the Donetz and captured Kamensk.

   Eighth Army reached to within 40 miles of Tripoli by capturing Misurata.

January 19. Announced that Marcel Peyrouton, former Vichy Minister of Interior, had been appointed Governor-General of Algiers.

January 20. In a surprise daylight raid on London a school was hit and 45 children and six teachers killed. Fourteen raiders were destroyed.

Russians made advances all along the front from Voronezh to the Caucasus.

January 22. Salsk, important railway junction south-east of Rostov, was captured by the Russians.

Japanese troops in the Sanananda sector of North Papua were overwhelmed and all enemy resistance in Papua was ended.

January 23. The Eighth Army captured Tripoli and started pursuit of Rommel's forces towards Tunisia.

Russians, continuing their advance, took Armavir, pivot of the German position south-east of Rostov.

January 26. The world learned that Mr. Churchill and President Roosevelt, with their chiefs of staffs, had conferred for ten days at Casablanca, drawing up plans for the 1943 offensive. "Unconditional surrender" was the name Mr. Roosevelt gave to the conference, as it was decided that this was the only peace term ever to be offered to the Axis.

General Giraud and General de Gaulle also met at Casablanca in an effort to unify the French war effort.

The Soviet announced the final stage of the Battle of Stalingrad, stating that the surrounded German troops were being liquidated.

January 27. American heavy bombers made their first daylight attack on Germany with a raid on Wilhelmshaven.

January 28. An order was made in Germany requiring all men from 16 to 65 and women from 17 to 45 to register for national defence work.

4

> *The Russians made a 50-mile advance to capture Kastornaya and threatened Kursk, a German key base.*

January 30. *R.A.F. Mosquito bombers made two daylight attacks on Berlin and disturbed celebrations of the 10th Anniversary of Hitler's accession to power.*

January 31. *Battle of Stalingrad ended with the capture of Field-Marshal Paulus, commander of the German forces, 16 generals and the remnants of the Axis forces.*

February 1. *Announced that Mr. Churchill had visited Turkey and conferred with President Inönü.*

February 2. *First news of a series of important sea and air actions between America and Japan in the Solomons area.*

February 3. *Mr. Churchill visited British troops in Tripoli.*

February 5. *Mussolini dismissed his son-in-law, Count Ciano, from the post of Foreign Minister, and Count Grandi from his position of Minister of Justice. Ciano subsequently became Italian Minister to the Vatican.*

February 7. *Russians captured Azov at the mouth of the Don, and cut the main road from Kursk to Orel and the railway from Kursk to Byelgorod.*

> *Mr. Churchill arrived back in London from his visit to N. Africa and the Middle East.*

In January and February, 1943, Mr. Churchill made an extensive tour of North Africa and the Middle East. The primary purpose of his journey was to confer with President Roosevelt at Casablanca, a meeting which was to be known to the world as the "Unconditional Surrender" conference.

From Casablanca, the Prime Minister travelled to Turkey, Egypt and Cyprus and also visited the men of the fighting forces in Tripoli. During his journey he made several speeches, which are printed in the following pages.

Visit to Cyprus

In Cyprus, the Prime Minister made speeches to a representative gathering of islanders and to the men of his old regiment, the 4th Hussars, who were stationed in the island at that time.

[*February 1, 1943*

THIS is my third visit to your beautiful island, and I descended upon it rather suddenly yesterday evening. I hope that this has caused no undue perturbation. My first visit was a very long time ago, 36 years ago, when I came here as Under-Secretary of State for the Colonies and spent two or three days in this capital of Nicosia, and also in riding about the whole island, and seeing as many people as I could. In those days I began to work for the abolition of the Tribute, which I considered was an undue burden upon the island; but things worked very slowly, and it was not until I became Chancellor of the Exchequer, 20 years afterwards, that I was in a position to bring that system to an end.*

In the time which has passed the island has prospered and progressed, and now, I am glad to say, in consequence of the very powerful forces that are now gathered here to join the Cypriots in the defence of their island home, that for a period considerable, though temporary, prosperity has come to pass. I would respectfully give my advice to the islanders to be careful not to spend the additional money which comes in under the

---

* The "Turkish Tribute" referred to by the Prime Minister in the above speech arose from the taking over by Britain of the administration of Cyprus in 1878. Turkey remained nominally sovereign and received an annual payment of £92,800. After the annexation of Cyprus in 1914 the Tribute was continued for a time under the name of the "Cyprus share of the Turkish debt charge."

strange workings of war-time, and to save it for the rainy days which may well follow; because, after the war is over, there will be a great effort needed to rebuild the world, and that will be the time when it will be a good thing to have savings to use.

Now I come to you from Turkey, where I have had a most agreeable meeting with President Inönü and with the Chiefs of the Turkish State, and I am glad to tell you that our relations with the Turks are of a most friendly character. Their views are very much like our own, and we intend to help their own general defensive security in every way in our power. Our hearts all go out to gallant Greece, heroic Greece, who in these modern days has revived her fame of ancient times. The sufferings of Greece are terrible, but one can already see the light breaking in the sky which will herald a day when she will be delivered from the foul bondage and tyranny by which she is now overpressed, and will take her place restored and proud in the ranks of the victorious nations.

We have seen some very dangerous and dark times during this war, which was forced upon us by those whom we had beaten a generation ago, and whom we foolishly allowed to prepare their deadly plans again. We have passed through many dark, several very dark, phases, but now, I am able to assure you, the United Nations represent incomparably the strongest group of human beings that has ever been marshalled in arms in the whole history of the world; not only in their numbers, not only in the great armaments that are now being prepared on a scale hitherto unexampled, not only in material force, but in their unity of purpose and in their comradeship and in their inflexible resolution. They are strong, and they will march forward from strength to strength until unconditional surrender is extorted from those who have laid the world in havoc and in ruins.

Now I am glad to tell you in Cyprus how much admired in the Motherland, in old England, is the sturdy spirit in which you have prepared to defend your island, and the vigilance with which you guard it, aided by the troops of the British Empire.

Believe me, after the war is over, the name of Cyprus will be included in the list of those who have deserved well, not only of the British Commonwealth of Nations, not only of the united peoples now in arms, but, as I firmly believe, of future generations of mankind.

Speech to the 4th Hussars

FEBRUARY 1, 1943

[*February 1, 1943*

THE last time I saw the 4th Hussars was during the dark days in the Western Desert. Since then there has been hard fighting for all of you. I watched on the map which the War Office makes every day for the War Cabinet your positions in that grim fighting. This Regiment was here, was there, was apparently everywhere. You were constantly in the picture.

What a change there has been in the past few months! Rommel, who was just about to advance, has been hurled back fifteen or sixteen hundred miles, and will be harried by the Eighth Army, that great Desert Army, to the end. The First Army, too, is on the other side.

I cannot doubt that within a reasonable time the whole pack of Germans and Italians will be driven into the sea, and Africa relieved. One continent will then be freed from the enemy. Egypt has been defended and secured against attack.

In all this dramatic story you have played your part, but the Germans have suffered even greater losses than those you inflicted on them in Egypt. In the recent battles in Russia we have seen how grievous those losses are, for the German army has had more maimed and killed at the hands of the Russians than they lost in the whole of the last war. The German army entered Russia already haggard and worn, and they are still suffering. They have received very grave injuries which I daresay will prove mortal.

During my visit to North Africa I have seen those powerful armies of British and American troops. We have poured half a million men into that area. And that is not all. They will soon be turning North, across the Mediterranean, carrying the war to a tense climax.

I am glad to see so many of you carrying on the fine traditions of the Regiment, for it has many glorious traditions. Those who now have the honour to carry on have added names to those famous battles of the past. The battle honours which you have won in this war will be treasured by those of the Regiment who come after you. I give you the heartiest wishes for your future. You will not weary or falter.

From the bottom of my heart I thank you. God bless you.

A Cairo Press Conference

STATEMENT TO THE NEWSPAPER REPRESENTATIVES
STATIONED IN CAIRO, AFTER THE VISITS
TO TURKEY AND CYPRUS
FEBRUARY 1, 1943

[February 1, 1943

LADIES and Gentlemen,

You have read the communiqué, and therefore you know the news which will be broken to the world to-morrow in the morning papers. Nothing that I say here is secret. It can all be used as you may desire. I thought that as I was again in Cairo it would be very nice to see you, gentlemen, if only for the satisfaction of drawing a contrast with the position when I was last here and met, I will not say the same audience, but a largely similar audience, in the closing days of August.

Then the enemy was but a morning's motor drive from this great city. Rommel was preparing his offensive. We now know it was his last desperate thrust, but we had no right at that time to assume that his forces would not have at any rate initial success. There was always the possibility, which was fully contemplated and prepared for by our Commanders, that the Eighth Army, in order to retain its liberty of manœuvre, might for a number of hours, or days even, have left open the approaches to the Capital for the defence of which and of the line of the Nile another considerable army was in existence. Of course in advancing on Cairo Rommel would have exposed himself to the vengeance of the Eighth Army, who would have been between him and his lines of supply. He did not dare in the event to by-pass the Eighth Army. He endeavoured to carry out on its southern flank a manœuvre very similar to that at the battle of Gazala in the spring. But he was met by the full strength of our forces and by an immensely powerful artillery, and after three or four days of sharp fighting, he found himself overweighted and outmatched, and fell back on the defensive.

Then, after a pause in which General Alexander and his brilliant lieutenant, General Montgomery, created a mass of manœuvre — the great thunderbolt of assault — there began the third battle of Alamein, or, as perhaps it would be better to call it, the battle of Egypt, since it has effectively delivered Egypt from all danger of invasion from the Western Desert in any period which we can imagine or foresee. You have told to the world the tale of that fierce battle, which lasted for eleven days before the artillery had blasted the path and the infantry had cleared the mines, thus enabling the very powerful armoured forces and the very excellent American tanks to break through the gap and begin that memorable, unparalleled pursuit which has now driven the enemy completely out of Egypt, out of Cyrenaica, and at this very moment forced him to withdraw into Tunisia. The enemy is now, I suppose, 1,500 miles away from Cairo, and the Eighth Army will follow Rommel wherever he goes. The fugitive from Egypt and Libya is endeavouring to present himself as the deliverer of Tunis. We shall see how that new character fits him and fits the circumstances.

You know I always avoid prophesying beforehand, because it is much better policy to prophesy after the event has already taken place. Therefore I say we have very much to be thankful for in what has occurred, and I should like to remind you that I declared here to you in this room that Egypt would be effectively defended, that Cairo would be defended, that the soil of Egypt would be swept clear of those who had affronted it with invasion, and that Britain would be found not to have failed in any jot or tittle of her long-standing engagement of friendship to this historic land, and to have successfully kept the horrors of war away from the population of this vast city, and guarded faithfully the Valley of the Nile. These are words I am entitled to speak to you, and I feel that you on your part will render justice, all of you, to the work which our troops have done, and to the great results that have been derived from that work.

Meanwhile on that other flank by which Egypt might be approached — from the North — the prodigious victories of the Russian armies have entirely altered the situation which we were bound to contemplate as a possibility and to prepare against when I saw you here in August. We were then forming the Tenth Army in Persia and Iraq under the distinguished command of Sir Henry Maitland Wilson in order to be ready should the enemy fall upon us from the North. But all has been brushed aside by the tremendous feat of arms performed by our Russian Ally under the general command and direction of Premier Stalin, a great warrior, and a name which will rank with those most honoured and most lasting in the history of the Russian people. Only now when I arrive in Cairo again from across the sea, I find the news of the surrender of the last remnants of the very well-equipped and formidable German Sixth Army under Field-Marshal Paulus, which Hitler had declared, since I saw you here, would certainly take Stalingrad. These are very important events, and they have altered altogether the position in the East, have altered it, I think, in a way which may well prove to be permanent and favourable.

A third event of first importance in the war has been the American and British landing in French North-West Africa, and the occupation with very large forces, well-equipped and growing in numbers and in power with every week that passes — the occupation of Morocco, Algeria and Tunisia except for the eastern coastal strip. There we must expect very considerable fighting to take place in the next few months or weeks. For my part I have confidence in the result, and I have also the belief that the Desert Army which started from Cairo when we were last together will play a noteworthy part in achieving the final result, namely the redemption of the African Continent from all stain or insult from the foot of an armed German or Italian. I felt myself entitled to survey this scene, although details of it are familiar to you, in view of the talk we had together in the anxious days of August.

The communiqué which you have read opens another topic. I was very glad indeed to be able to travel, after the Casablanca conference with President Roosevelt, to the shores of Turkey, where I had the pleasure of meeting President Inönü, the principal Ministers of his Government, and Marshal Chakmak and his military assistants. I have just returned from Turkey, and this communiqué, which has been agreed upon by the British and Turkish representatives, will, I am sure, show you that we have had an important and agreeable discussion, and that a conference has taken place which has undoubtedly relation to the general world position as it is now disclosed. Following a habit inculcated by experience, and learning always by the process of trial and error as I have tried to do in my long life, I would say that it would not be wise to try to read more into this important document than it bears on its face. Let us see how the course of events develops, and let us not endeavour to pry too closely or speculate too audaciously upon those mysteries of the future which are veiled from our eyes, and which, if they were not veiled from our eyes by the wisdom of Providence, would confront us with a state of existence here below very much less interesting and exciting than that in which we find ourselves. I never admire the habit which some people follow of always skipping the pages of a book and looking on to see how it ends. The authors must be permitted to tell their tale in their own way, and to unfold the story chapter by chapter. In the same way, with a drama or a film, it is a great mistake not to give it a chance to work out in its fullness and in its setting, and therefore I give this word of caution about not jumping to conclusions and not trying to strain the interpretation of any phrase which has been used in this public document. Certainly it is clear that the old friendship between Great Britain and Turkey, which was so grievously slashed across by the tragedies of the last war, is now in its fullest strength and sincerity, and I cannot doubt that advantages will come to both the British and Turkish peoples from this fact, and that friendship and mutual trust, goodwill and sympathy and understanding of each other's difficulties, are now in full vitality again.

I thank you very much indeed for coming here to meet me. The war having rolled so far away from Cairo may, to some extent, have lessened your burden, and maybe you have not recently had so much part to play as in the critical days of June, July and August. But nevertheless the Press, accredited and otherwise, has played a very helpful and useful role in sustaining the defence of Egypt, and the spirit of the Army. I should not like the fact that the danger is now so far removed to prevent me in any way from expressing to you my sincere thanks for your help in this remarkable series of events. I read with great pleasure the Egyptian papers which are published here, full of excellent information, most readable, and most admirably conceived from the point of view of upholding the common cause. Though Egypt has been and still is a neutral country, it would never be true to say that Egypt has not played an important, valuable and honourable part, not only in her own defence but also in the world struggle which is proceeding with gathering momentum towards its climax. As to when that climax will be reached, as to whether further unexpected vicissitudes may lie before us, I shall attempt to say nothing to-day. But at any rate so far as we have gone we have every reason to rejoice, and in that rejoicing you are fully entitled to take your part.

The Desert Army

[February 3, 1943

GENERAL MONTGOMERY and men of the Joint Headquarters of the Eighth Army.

The last time I saw this army was in the closing days of August
on those sandy and rocky bluffs near Alamein and the Ruweisat
ridge, when it was apparent from all the signs that Rommel was
about to make his final thrust on Alexandria and Cairo. Then
all was to be won or lost. Now I come to you a long way from
Alamein, and I find this army and its famous commander with
a record of victory behind it which has undoubtedly played a
decisive part in altering the whole character of the war.

The fierce and well-fought battle of Alamein, the blasting
through of the enemy's seaward flank, and the thunderbolt of
the armoured attack, irretrievably broke the army which Rommel
had boasted would conquer Egypt, and upon which the German
and Italian peoples had set their hopes. Thereafter and ever since,
in these remorseless three months, you have chased this hostile
army and driven it from pillar to post over a distance of more
than 1,400 miles — in fact, as far as from London to Moscow.
You have altered the face of the war in a most remarkable way.

What it has meant in the skill and organisation of movement
and manœuvres, what it has meant in the tireless endurance and
self-denial of the troops and in the fearless leadership displayed
in action, can be appreciated only by those who were actually on
the spot. But I must tell you that the fame of the Desert Army
has spread throughout the world.

After the surrender of Tobruk, there was a dark period when
many people, not knowing us, not knowing the British and the
nations of the British Empire, were ready to take a disparaging

15

view. But now everywhere your work is spoken of with respect and admiration. When I was with the Chief of the Imperial General Staff at Casablanca and with the President of the United States, the arrival of the Desert Army in Tripoli was a new factor which influenced the course of our discussions and opened up hopeful vistas for the future. You are entitled to know these things, and to dwell upon them with that satisfaction which men in all modesty feel when a great work has been finally done. You have rendered a high service to your country and the common cause.

It must have been a tremendous experience driving forward day after day over this desert which it has taken me this morning more than six hours to fly at 200 miles an hour. You were pursuing a broken enemy, dragging on behind you this ever-lengthening line of communications, carrying the whole art of desert warfare to perfection. In the words of the old hymn, you have "nightly pitched your moving tents a day's march nearer home." Yes, not only in the march of the army but in the progress of the war you have brought home nearer. I am here to thank you on behalf of His Majesty's Government of the British Isles and of all our friends the world over.

Hard struggles lie ahead. Rommel, the fugitive of Egypt, Cyrenaica, and Tripolitania, in a non-stop race of 1,400 miles, is now trying to present himself as the deliverer of Tunisia. Along the Eastern coast of Tunisia are large numbers of German and Italian troops, not yet equipped to their previous standard, but growing stronger. On the other side, another great operation, planned in conjunction with your advance, has carried the First British Army, our American comrades, and the French armies to within 30 or 40 miles of Bizerta and Tunis. Therefrom a military situation arises which everyone can understand.

The days of your victories are by no means at an end, and with forces which march from different quarters we may hope to achieve the final destruction or expulsion from the shores of Africa of every armed German or Italian. You must have felt relief when, after those many a hundred miles of desert, you came once more into a green land with trees and grass, and I do not think you will lose that advantage. As you go forward on further missions that will fall to your lot, you will fight in countries which will present undoubtedly serious tactical difficulties, but which none the less will not have that grim character of desert war which you have known how to endure and how to overcome.

Let me then assure you, soldiers and airmen, that your fellow-countrymen regard your joint work with admiration and gratitude, and that after the war when a man is asked what he did it will be quite sufficient for him to say, "I marched and fought with the Desert Army." And when history is written and all the facts are known, your feats will gleam and glow and will be a source of song and story long after we who are gathered here have passed away.

New Zealand's Part

[February 4, 1943

WHEN I last saw your General Bernard Freyberg, my friend
of so many years of war and peace, the Salamander, as he may
be called, of the British Empire, it was on those bare and rocky
slopes to the South of Alamein where you were then preparing
to receive what was expected to be a most dangerous and deadly
thrust by the hitherto victorious Rommel. At that time, also, we
had great doubts and anxieties as to the position in Russia, and
what would happen in the Caucasus and in the approaches to
the great oilfields without which the plight of Germany is grave.

But what a change has taken place since then! By the immortal
victory of the battle of Egypt, the Axis Powers, who had fondly
hoped and loudly boasted they would take Egypt and the Nile
Valley, found their Army broken — shattered; and ever since then,
by a march unexampled in history for the speed and force of its
advance, you have been driving the remnants of the enemy before
you until now the would-be conqueror of Egypt is endeavouring
to pass himself off as the "Deliverer of Tunisia." These events
will long live in the annals of war, and will be studied minutely
by other generations than our own. These feats of arms entitle
the Army of the Desert to feel a deep-founded sense of comfort
and pride based on valiant duty faithfully done.

Now I come and find you here 1,400 miles from where I saw
you last. And you may all feel that in that period a decisive
change has taken place in the war, and that we now have a right
to say that a term will be fixed to its intense exertions and sor-
rows. A transformation has come upon the scene. Just as after all
those hundreds and hundreds of miles of desert you suddenly

18

came again into green and fertile land, so there has been a vast improvement in the fortunes of the whole world cause with its twenty-nine United Nations. Struggles and victories lie ahead. You will march into fairer lands. You will march into lands where the grim and severe conditions of the desert will be but memories; but having endured those conditions, the fighting qualities which you have displayed will only shine brighter and be turned to greater advantage.

Far away in New Zealand homes at the other side of the globe all hearts are swelling with pride at your deeds. It is the same throughout our small island of Britain, which stood alone for a year championed only by its children from overseas, and against dire odds. All are filled with admiration for the Desert Army. All are full of gratitude to the people of New Zealand who have sent this splendid Division to win fame and honour across the oceans.

The enemy has been driven out of Egypt; out of Cyrenaica; out of Tripolitania. He is now coming towards the end of his means of running, and in the corner of Tunisia a decisive battle has presently to be fought. Other great forces are coming in from the West, but I am sure the Desert Army and the New Zealand Division will play a prime part. The good cause will not be trampled down. Justice and freedom will reign among men.

On behalf of His Majesty's Government, on behalf of all the peoples of the homeland, I give you our expression of earnest warm-hearted thanks. We cherish the memory of all you have done. We wish you Godspeed and God's assistance in your further conquests. You can be sure that as your duty will not fail, so your success will be achieved.

The War Situation

A SPEECH IN THE HOUSE OF COMMONS
FEBRUARY 11, 1943

February 8.   *Russians captured Kursk, one of the Germans' key bases.*

February 9.   *Officially announced that all Japanese resistance on Guadalcanal was ended.*

    Russians, still maintaining their great offensive, captured Byelgorod.

February 10.   *General Alexander, C.-in-C. Middle East, stated that the German defeats in Russia and North Africa made it unlikely that they would ever be strong enough to mount another offensive.*

February 11.   *Mr. Churchill, in a review of the War in the House of Commons, announced that General Eisenhower had been appointed Commander-in-Chief in North Africa.*

[February 11, 1943

THE dominating aim which we set before ourselves at the Conference at Casablanca was to engage the enemy's forces on land, on sea, and in the air on the largest possible scale and at the earliest possible moment. The importance of coming to ever closer grips with the enemy and intensifying the struggle outweighs a number of other considerations which ordinarily would be decisive in themselves. We have to make the enemy burn and bleed in every way that is physically and reasonably possible, in the same way as he is being made to burn and bleed along the vast Russian front from the White Sea to the Black Sea. But this is not so simple as it sounds. Great Britain and the United States were formerly peaceful countries, ill-armed and unprepared. They are now warrior nations, walking in the fear of the Lord, very heavily armed, and with an increasingly clear view of their salvation. We are actually possessed of very powerful and growing forces, with great masses of munitions coming along. The problem is to bring these forces into action. The United States has vast oceans to cross in order to close with her enemies. We also have seas or oceans to cross in the first instance, and then for both of us there is the daring and complicated enterprise of landing on defended coasts, and also the building-up of all the supplies and communications necessary for vigorous campaigning when once a landing has been made.

It is because of this that the U-boat warfare takes the first place in our thoughts. There is no need to exaggerate the danger of the U-boats or to worry our merchant seamen by harping upon it unduly, because the British and American Governments have known for some time past that there were these U-boats about, and have given the task of overcoming them the first priority in all their plans. This was reaffirmed most explicitly by the Combined Staffs at Casablanca. The losses we suffer at sea are very heavy, and they hamper us and delay our operations. They prevent us from coming into action with our full strength, and thus they prolong the war, with its certain waste and loss and all its unknowable hazards.

Progress is being made in the war against the U-boats. We are holding our own, and more than holding our own. Before the United States came into the war, we made our calculations on the basis of British building and guaranteed Lend-Lease, which assured us of a steady and moderate improvement in our position by the end of 1943 on a very high scale of losses. There never was a moment in which we did not see our way through, provided that what the United States promised us was made good.

Since then various things have happened. The United States have entered the war, and their shipbuilding has been stepped-up to the present prodigious levels, mounting for the year 1943 to over 13,000,000 gross tons, or, as they would express it in American nomenclature, 18,000,000 or 19,000,000 dead weight tons. When the United States entered the war she brought with her a Mercantile Marine, American and American-controlled, of perhaps 10,000,000 gross tons, as compared with our then existing tonnage, British and British-controlled, of about — I am purposely not being precise — twice as much. On the other hand, the two Powers had more routes to guard, more jobs to do, and they therefore of course presented more numerous targets to the U-boats. Very serious depredations were committed by the U-boats off the East coast of America, until the convoy system was put into proper order by the exertions of Admiral King. Heavy losses in the Far East were also incurred at the outset of the war against Japan, when the Japanese pounced upon large quantities of British and United States shipping there. The great operation of landing in North Africa and maintaining the armies ashore naturally exposed the Anglo-American fleets to further losses, though there is a compensation for that which I will refer to later; and the Arctic convoys to Russia have also imposed a heavy toll, the main part of both these operational losses having fallen upon the British.

In all these circumstances it was inevitable that the joint American and British losses in the past 15 months should exceed the limits for which we British ourselves, in the days when we were alone, had budgeted. However, when the vast expansion in the United States shipbuilding is added on the credit side, the position is very definitely improved. It is in my opinion desirable to leave the enemy guessing at our real figures, to let him be the victim of his own lies, and to deprive him of every means of checking the exaggerations of his U-boat captains or of associating particular losses with particular forms and occasions of attack. I therefore do not propose to give any exact figures. This, however, I may say, that in the last six months, which included some of those heavy operations which I have mentioned, the Anglo-American and the important Canadian new building, all taken together, exceeded all the losses of the United Nations by over 1,250,000 tons. That is to say, our joint fleet is 1,250,000 tons bigger to-day than it was six months ago. That is not much, but it is something, and something very important.

But that statement by no means does justice to the achievement of the two countries, because the great American flow of shipbuilding is leaping up month by month, and the losses in the last two months are the lowest sustained for over a year. The number of U-boats is increasing, but so are their losses, and so also are the means of attacking them and protecting the convoys. It is, however, a horrible thing to plan ahead in cold blood on the basis of losing hundreds of thousands of tons a month, even if you can show a favourable balance at the end of the year. The waste of precious cargoes, the destruction of so many noble ships, the loss of heroic crews, all combine to constitute a repulsive and sombre panorama. We cannot possibly rest content with losses on this scale, even though they are outweighed by new building, even if they are for that reason not mortal in their character. Nothing is more clearly proved than that well-escorted convoys, especially when protected by long-distance aircraft, beat the U-boats. I do not say that they are a complete protection, but they are an enormous mitigation of losses. We have had hardly any losses at sea in our heavily escorted troop convoys. Out of about 3,000,000 soldiers who have been moved under the protection of the British Navy about the world, to and fro across the seas and oceans, about 1,348 have been killed or drowned, including missing. It is about 2,200 to one against your being drowned if you travel in British troop convoys in this present war.

Even if the U-boats increase in number, there is no doubt that a superior proportion of increase in the naval and air escort will be a remedy. A ship not sunk is better than a new ship built. Therefore, in order to reduce the waste in the merchant shipping convoys, we have decided, by successive steps during the last six months, to throw the emphasis rather more on the production of escort vessels, even though it means some impingement on new building. Very great numbers of escort vessels are being constructed in Great Britain and the United States, equipped with every new device of anti-U-boat warfare in all its latest refinements. We pool our resources with the United States, and we have been promised, and the promise is being executed in due course, our fair allocation of American-built escort vessels.

There is another point. Everyone sees how much better it is to have fast ships than slow. This is also true of racehorses, as the Noble Lady (Viscountess Astor) was well aware in her unregenerate days. However, speed is a costly luxury. The most careful calculations are made and are repeatedly revised as between having fewer fast ships or more slow ones. The choice, however, is not entirely a free one. The moment you come into the sphere of fast ships, engine competition enters a new phase. It starts with the escort vessels, and also in the materials for the higher-speed engines there come other complicated factors. I should strongly advise the House to have confidence in the extremely capable people who, with full knowledge of all the facts, are working day in day out on all these aspects and who would be delighted to fit-in an additional line of fast ships, even at some loss in aggregate tonnage, provided they could be sure that the engines would not clash with other even more urgent needs. In all these matters I should like the House to realise that we do not have to aim at a maximum but rather an optimum, which is not quite the same thing.

On the offensive side the rate of killing U-boats has steadily improved. From January to October, 1942, inclusive, a period of ten months, the rate of sinkings, certain and probable, was the best we have seen so far in this war; but from November to the present day, a period of three months, that rate has improved more than half as much again.

At the same time, the destructive power of the U-boat has undergone a steady diminution since the beginning of the war. In the first year, each operational U-boat that was at work accounted for an average of 19 ships; in the second year, for an average of 12; and in the third year for an average of 7½. These figures, I think, are, in themselves, a tribute to the Admiralty and to all others concerned.

It is quite true that at the present time, as I said in answer to an inquiry the other day, we are making inroads upon the reserves of food and raw materials which we prudently built up in the earlier years of the war. We are doing this for the sake of the military operations in Africa and Asia and in the Far Pacific. We are doing it for the sake of the Russian convoys, and for the sake of giving aid and supplies to India and to Persia and other Middle Eastern countries. We are doing this on the faith of President Roosevelt's promise to me of large allocations of shipping coming to us, as the floods of American new building come upon the seas. Risks have to be run, but I can assure the House that these needs are not left to chance and to sudden and belated panic spurts.

Provided that the present intense efforts are kept up here and in the United States, and that anti-U-boat warfare continues to hold first place in our thoughts and energies, I take the responsibility of assuring the House — and I have not misled them so far — that we shall be definitely better off, so far as shipping is concerned, at the end of 1943 than we are now; and while it is imprudent to try to peer so far ahead, all the tendencies show that unless something entirely new and unexpected happens in this well-explored field, we shall be still better off at the end of 1944, assuming that the war continues until then. It may be disappointing to Herr Hitler to learn that we are upon a rising tide of tonnage and not upon an ebb or shrinkage, but it is the governing fact of the situation. Therefore, let everyone engaged in this sphere of operations bend to his or her task and try to get the losses down and try to get the launchings up, and let them do this, not under the spur of fear or gloom or patriotic jitters, but in the sure and exhilarating consciousness of a gigantic task which is forging steadily forward to a successful accomplishment. The more the sinkings are reduced, the more vehement our Anglo-American war effort can be. The margin, improving and widening, means the power to strike heavier blows against the enemy. The greater the weight we can take off Russia, the quicker the war will come to an end. All depends upon the margin of new building forging ahead over the losses, which, although decreasing, are still, as I have said, a lamentable and grievous fact to meditate upon. Meanwhile, let the enemy, if he will, nurse his vain hopes of averting his doom by U-boat warfare. He cannot avert it, but he may delay it, and it is for us to shorten that delay by every conceivable effort we can make.

It was only after full and cold, sober and mature consideration of all these facts, on which our lives and liberties certainly depend, that the President, with my full concurrence as agent of the War Cabinet, decided that the note of the Casablanca Conference should be the unconditional surrender of all our foes. Our inflexible insistence upon unconditional surrender does not mean that we shall stain our victorious arms by any cruel treatment of whole populations. But justice must be done upon the wicked and the guilty, and, within her proper bounds, justice must be stern and implacable. No vestige of the Nazi or Fascist power, no vestige of the Japanese war-plotting machine, will be left by us when the work is done, and done it certainly will be.

That disposes, I think, of two important features of the Casablanca Conference: the recognition that the defeat of the U-boat and the improvement of the margin of shipbuilding resources are the prelude to all effective aggressive operations; and secondly, after considering all those facts, the statement which the President wished to be made on the subject of unconditional surrender. But the Casablanca Conference was, in my not inconsiderable experience of these functions, in various ways unparalleled. There never has been, in all the inter-Allied Conferences I have known, anything like the prolonged professional examination of the whole scene of the world war in its military, its armament-production and its economic aspects. This examination was conducted through the whole day, and far into the night, by the military, naval and air experts, sitting by themselves, without political influence thrust upon them, although general guidance was given by the President and by myself. But they were sitting by themselves, talking all these matters out as experts and professionals. Some of these Conferences in the last war, I remember, lasted a day or two days, but this was eleven days. If I speak of decisions taken, I can assure the House that they are based upon professional opinion and advice in their integrity. There never has been anything like that.

When you have half a dozen theatres of war open in various parts of the globe, there are bound to be divergences of view when the problem is studied from different angles. There were many divergences of view before we came together, and it was for that reason that I had been pressing for so many months for the meeting of as many of the great Allies as possible. These divergences are of emphasis and priority rather than of principle. They can only be removed by the prolonged association of consenting and instructed minds. Human judgment is fallible. We may have taken decisions which will prove to be less good than we hoped, but at any rate anything is better than not having a plan. You must be able to answer every question in these matters of war, and have a good, clear, plain answer to the question: what is your plan, what is your policy? But it does not follow that we always give the answer. It would be foolish.

We have now a complete plan of action, which comprises the apportionment of forces as well as their direction, and the weight of the particular movements which have been decided upon; and this plan we are going to carry out according to our ability during the next nine months, before the end of which we shall certainly make efforts to meet again. I feel justified in asking the House to believe that their business is being conducted according to a definite design, and although there will surely be disappointments and failures — many disappointments and serious failures and frustrations — there is no question of drifting or indecision, or being unable to form a scheme or waiting for something to turn up. For good or for ill, we know exactly what it is that we wish to do. We have the united and agreed advice of our experts behind it, and there is nothing now to be done but to work these plans out in their detail and put them into execution one after the other.

I believe it was Bismarck who said in the closing years of his life that a dominating fact in the modern world was that the people of Britain and of the United States spoke the same language. If so, it was certainly a much more sensible remark than some that we have heard from those who now fill high positions in Germany. Certainly the British and American experts and their political chiefs gain an enormous advantage from the fact that they can interchange their thoughts so easily and freely and frankly by a common medium of speech.

This, however, did not in any way diminish our great regret that Premier Stalin and some of his distinguished generals could not be with us. The President, in spite of the physical disability which he has so heroically surmounted, was willing to go as far East as Khartoum in the hope that we could have a tripartite meeting. Premier Stalin is, however, the supreme director of the whole vast Russian offensive, which was already then in full swing and which is still rolling remorselessly and triumphantly forward. He could not leave his post, as he told us, even for a single day. But I can assure the House that although he was absent, our duty to aid to the utmost in our power the magnificent, tremendous effort of Russia and try to draw the enemy and the enemy's air force from the Russian front was accepted as the first of our objectives, once the needs of the anti-U-boat warfare were met in such a way as to enable us to act aggressively.

We have made no secret of the fact that British and American strategists and leaders are unanimous in adhering to their decision of a year ago, namely, that the defeat of Hitler and the breaking of the German power must have priority over the decisive phase of the war against Japan. I have already some two months ago indicated that the defeat of the enemy in Europe may be achieved before victory is won over Japan, and I made it clear that in that event all the forces of the British Empire, land, sea and air, will be moved to the Far Eastern theatre with the greatest possible speed, and that Great Britain will continue the war by the side of the United States with the utmost vigour until unconditional surrender has been enforced upon Japan. With the authority of the War Cabinet, I renewed this declaration in our Conference at Casablanca. I offered to make it in any form which might be desired, even embodying it in a special Treaty if that were thought advantageous. The President, however, stated that the word of Great Britain was quite enough for him. We have already, of course, bound ourselves, along with all the rest of the United Nations, to go on together to the end, however long it may take or however grievous the cost may be. I therefore think it only necessary to mention the matter to the House in order to give them the opportunity of registering their assent to that obvious and very necessary declaration.

We may now congratulate our American Allies upon their decisive victory at Guadalcanal, upon the taking of which the Japanese had expended a serious part of their limited strength and largely irreplaceable equipment. We must also express our admiration for the hard-won successes of the Australian and American Forces, who, under their brilliant commander General MacArthur, have taken Buna in New Guinea and slaughtered the last of its defenders. The ingenious use of aircraft to solve the intricate tactical problems, by the transport of reinforcements, supplies and munitions, including field guns, is a prominent feature of MacArthur's generalship, and should be carefully studied in detail by all concerned in the technical conduct of the war. In the meantime, while Hitler is being destroyed in Europe, every endeavour will be made to keep Japan thoroughly occupied, and force her to exhaust and expend her material strength against the far superior Allied and, above all, American resources. This war in the Pacific Ocean, although fought by both sides with comparatively small forces at the end of enormous distances, has already engaged a great part of the American resources employed overseas as well as those of Australia and New Zealand. The effort to hold the dumbbell at arms length is so exhausting and costly to both sides that it would be a great mistake to try to judge the effort by the actual numbers that come into contact at particular points. It is a tremendous effort to fight at four, five and six thousand miles across the ocean under these conditions. It is a kind of effort which is most injurious to Japan, whose resources in material are incomparably weaker than those of which we dispose.

For the time being, in the war against Japan the British effort is confined to the Indian theatre. Our Asiatic war effort is confined to operations to clear Burma, to open the Burma road, and to give what aid can be given to the Chinese. That is the task which we have before us. We have been in close correspondence with the Generalissimo Chiang Kai-shek, whom of course we should have been delighted to see at our Conference had it been possible for him to come. General Arnold, head of the United States Air Force, and Field-Marshal Dill are at present in Chungking concerting what we have in mind with the Chinese Generalissimo.

We have already received from him an expression of his satisfaction in the strong additional help that will be provided for China at this stage in her long-drawn, undaunted struggle. The Generalissimo also concurs in the plans for future action in the Far East which we have submitted to him as the result of our deliberations. A communiqué about this Conference, received only a few minutes ago, declares the complete accord between the three Powers in their plans for the co-ordination of their forces and in their determination in all their operations against Japan to ensure continued efforts and mutual assistance. Discussions between General MacArthur and Field-Marshal Wavell will follow in due course.

So much for the Casablanca decisions and their repercussions as far as they can be made public. I must, however, add this. When I look at all that Russia is doing and the vast achievements of the Soviet Armies, I should feel myself below the level of events if I were not sure in my heart and conscience that everything in human power is being done and will be done to bring British and American Forces into action against the enemy with the utmost speed and energy and on the largest scale. This the President and I have urgently and specifically enjoined upon our military advisers and experts. In approving their schemes and allocations of forces, we have asked for more weight to be put into the attacks and more speed into their dates. Intense efforts are now being made on both sides of the Atlantic for this purpose.

From the Conference at Casablanca, with the full assent of the President, I flew to Cairo and thence to Turkey. I descended upon a Turkish airfield at Adana, already well stocked with British Hurricane fighters manned by Turkish airmen, and out of the snow-capped Taurus Mountains there crawled like an enamelled caterpillar the Presidential train, bearing on board the head of the Turkish Republic, the Prime Minister, the Foreign Secretary, Marshal Chakmak, and the Party Leader — in fact, the High Executive of Turkey. I have already uttered a caution against reading anything into the communiqué which has already been published on this Conference, more than the communiqué conveys. It is no part of our policy to get Turkey into trouble. On the contrary, a disaster to Turkey would be a disaster to Britain and to all the United Nations. Hitherto, Turkey has maintained a solid barrier against aggression from any quarter, and by so doing, even in the darkest days, has rendered us invaluable service in preventing the spreading of the war through Turkey into Persia and Iraq, and in preventing the menace to the oilfields of Abadan, which are of vital consequence to the whole Eastern war.

It is an important interest of the United Nations, and especially of Great Britain, that Turkey should become well armed in all the apparatus of modern war, and that her brave infantry should not lack the essential weapons which play a decisive part on the battlefields of to-day. These weapons we and the United States are now for the first time in a position to supply to the full capacity of the Turkish railways and other communications. We can give them as much as they are able to take, and we can give these weapons as fast as and faster than the Turkish troops can be trained to use them. At our Conference I made no request of Turkey except to get this rearmament business thoroughly well organised, and a British and Turkish Joint Military Mission is now sitting in Ankara in order to press forward to the utmost the development of the general defensive strength of Turkey, the improvement of the communications, and, by the reception of the new weapons, the bringing of its army up to the highest pitch of efficiency. I am sure it would not be desirable to pry more closely into this part of our affairs. Turkey is our Ally. Turkey is our friend. We wish her well, and we wish to see her territory, rights, and interests effectively preserved. We wish to see, in particular, warm and friendly relations established between Turkey and her great Russian Ally to the North-West, to whom we are bound by the twenty-years Anglo-Russian Treaty. Whereas a little while ago it looked to superficial observers as if Turkey might be isolated by a German advance through the Caucasus on one side and by a German-Italian attack on Egypt on the other, a transformation scene has occurred. Turkey now finds on each side of her victorious Powers who are her friends. It will be interesting to see how the story unfolds chapter by chapter, and it would be very foolish to try to skip on too fast.

After discharging our business in Turkey I had to come home, and I naturally stopped at the interesting places on the way where I had people to see and things to do. I think that the story I have to tell follows very naturally stage by stage along my homeward journey. I have already mentioned to the House, at Question time the other day, my very pleasant stay during my return journey in Cyprus, which has played its part so well and is enjoying a period of war-time prosperity. But how different was the situation in Cairo from what I found it in the early days of last year! Then the Desert Army was bewildered and dispirited, feeling themselves better men than the enemy and wondering why they had had to retreat with heavy losses for so many hundreds of miles while Rommel pursued them on their own captured transport and with their own food, petrol and ammunition. Then the enemy was 60 miles from Alexandria, and I had to give orders for every preparation to be made to defend the line of the Nile, exactly as if we were fighting in Kent. I had also to make a number of drastic changes in the High Command. Those changes have been vindicated by the results. In a week an electrifying effect was produced upon the Desert Army by General Montgomery and by orders which he issued, and upon the whole situation by the appointment of General Alexander as Commander-in-Chief, Middle East. At the same time, great reinforcements, dispatched many weeks, even months, before round the Cape of Good Hope, were streaming up the Red Sea and pouring into the Nile Valley. The American Sherman tanks, which the President gave me in Washington on that dark morning when we learned of the fall of Tobruk and the surrender of its 25,000 defenders, came into the hands of troops thirsting to have good weapons to use against the enemy. As a consequence of those events and many others which could be cited, the enemy has been decisively defeated, first in the second Battle of Alamein, where Rommel's final thrust was repulsed, and, secondly, in the great battle near Alamein which will go down in history as the Battle of Egypt, for by it Egypt was delivered.

On arriving in Cairo I found that now the enemy, who had boasted that he would enter Cairo and Alexandria and cross and cut the Suez Canal, and had even struck a medal, of which I was handed a specimen, to commemorate the event, had been rolled back 1,500 miles, and it is probably 1,600 miles by now. What an amazing feat this has been! The battle is one story, the pursuit is another. So rapid an advance by such powerful, competent, heavily-equipped forces over distances so enormous is, as far as I am aware, without parallel in modern war; and the Ancients had not the advantages of locomotion which we possess, so they are out of it anyway.

Everywhere in Egypt there is a feeling that Britain has kept her word, that we have been a faithful and unfailing Ally, that we have preserved the Nile Valley and all its cities, villages and fertile lands from the horrors of invasion. It was always said that Egypt could never be successfully invaded across the Western Desert, and certainly that historical fact has now been established upon modern and far stronger foundations.

From Cairo I proceeded on my magic carpet to Tripoli, which ten days before had been in the possession of the enemy. Here I found General Montgomery. I must confess quite frankly that I had not realised how magnificent a city and harbour Tripoli has been made. It is the first Italian city to be delivered by British arms from the grip of the Huns. Naturally there was lively enthusiasm among the Italian population, and I can hardly do justice to the effusiveness of the demonstrations of which I was the fortunate object. I had the honour as your servant to review two of our forward divisions. The 51st Highland Division is the successor of that brave division that was overwhelmed on the coast of France in the tragedies of 1940. It has already more than equalised the account which Scotland had opened in this matter. In the afternoon I saw a mass of 10,000 New Zealanders, who, with a comparatively small portion of their vast equipment of cannon, tanks and technical vehicles, took one and a half hours to march past. On that day I saw at least 40,000 troops, and as representing His Majesty's Government I had the honour to receive their salutes and greetings.

Meanwhile, of course, the front had rolled nearly another hundred miles farther to the West, and the beaten enemy were being pursued back to the new positions in Tunisia on which it is said they intend to make a stand. I do not wish to encourage the House or the country to look for any very speedy new results. They may come, or they may not come. The enemy have carried out very heavy demolitions and blockings in Tripoli harbour. Therefore, supply from the sea is greatly hampered, and I cannot tell what time will be required to clear the port and begin the building-up of a new base for supplies. It is not the slightest use being impatient with these processes. Meanwhile General Montgomery's Army is feeding itself from its base at Cairo 1,500 miles away, through Tobruk, 1,000 miles away, and Benghazi, 750 miles away, by means of a prodigious mass of mechanical transport, all organised in a manner truly wonderful.

Presently we may be able to move forward again, but meanwhile the enemy may have time to consolidate his position and to bring in further reinforcements and further equipment. Let us just see how things go. But I should like to say this: I have never in my life, which from my youth up has been connected with military matters, seen troops who march with the style and air of those of the Desert Army. Talk about spit and polish! The Highland and New Zealand Divisions paraded after their immense ordeal in the desert as if they had come out of Wellington

Barracks. There was an air on the face of every private of that just and sober pride which comes from dear-bought victory and triumph after toil. I saw the same sort of marching smartness, and the same punctilio of saluting and discipline, in the Russian guard of honour which received me in Moscow six months ago. The fighting men of democracy feel that they are coming into their own.

Let me also pay my tribute to this vehement and formidable General Montgomery, a Cromwellian figure, austere, severe, accomplished, tireless, his life given to the study of war, who has attracted to himself in an extraordinary measure the confidence and the devotion of his Army. Let me also pay, in the name of the House, my tribute to General Alexander, on whom the overriding responsibility lay. I read to the House on 11th November the directive which in those critical days I gave to General Alexander. I may perhaps refresh the memory of hon. Members by reading it again: —

"1. Your prime and main duty will be to take or destroy at the earliest opportunity the German-Italian army commanded by Field-Marshal Rommel, together with all its supplies and establishments in Egypt and Libya.

"2. You will discharge, or cause to be discharged, such other duties as pertain to your Command without prejudice to the task described in paragraph 1, which must be considered paramount in His Majesty's interests."

I have now received, when, as it chanced, I visited the Army again, the following official communication from General Alexander, in which General Montgomery took great pleasure, and to which it will be necessary for us to send a reply: —

"Sir, The Orders you gave me on August 15, 1942, have been fulfilled. His Majesty's enemies, together with their impedimenta, have been completely eliminated from Egypt, Cyrenaica, Libya and Tripolitania. I now await your further instructions."

Well, obviously, we shall have to think of something else, and, indeed, this was one of the more detailed matters which we discussed in the Conference at Casablanca. I did not publish the original instructions to General Alexander until some months afterwards, when the Battle of Egypt had been won, and the House will naturally grant me a similar delay before I make public the reply to him which is now required.

I should, however, inform the House and the country of the various changes in the High Command which the marked improvement in our affairs and the movements of the Armies have rendered suitable and necessary.

This brings me to the general situation in French North-West Africa, on which I have a very few remarks to make. The descent upon North Africa by the British and American Forces will, I believe, be judged in the words which Premier Stalin used to me when I told him about it in August last. He said it was militarily correct. It certainly has altered the strategic axis of the war. By this very large-scale manœuvre, thought by many experts to be most hazardous before it was undertaken, we recovered the initiative in the West, and we recovered it at comparatively small cost of life and with less loss in shipping than we gained by what fell into our hands. Nearly half a million men have been landed successfully and safely in North-West Africa, and those fair and beautiful regions are now under the control of the United States. We agreed with the President many months ago that this should be an American enterprise, and I have gladly accepted, with the approval of the War Cabinet, the position of lieutenant in this sphere.

The Americans attach the greatest importance to unity of command between Allies, and to control over all three Services being in the hands of one supreme commander. We willingly and freely accepted this position, and we shall act loyally and faithfully up to it on all occasions and in every respect. Some people are busily concerned about the past records of various French functionaries whom the Americans have deemed it expedient to employ. For my part, I must confess that I am more interested in the safety of the Armies, and in the success of the operations which will soon be again advancing to an important climax. I shall therefore not take up the time of the House with the tales which can be told of how these various Frenchmen acted in the forlorn and hideous situation in which they found themselves when their country collapsed. What matters to General Eisenhower and to our troops, who, in great numbers, are serving under him, and what matters throughout this vast area, with its population of well over 16,000,000, 90 per cent. of whom are Moslems, is, first and foremost, a tranquil countryside, and, secondly, secure and unimpeded communications to the battle-front, which is now steadily developing on what I have called the Tunisian tip.

I have not seen this battle front, I am sorry to say, because it is 400 miles distant by road from Algiers, where I spent last Friday and Saturday with General Eisenhower and Admiral Cunningham, and also with our Minister-Resident, the right hon. Member for Stockton-on-Tees (Mr. Harold Macmillan), who is doing admirable work and becoming a real solver of problems — friends with everyone — and taking, with Mr. Murphy's co-operation, an increasingly heavy load off the shoulders of the Commander-in-Chief in regard to matters with which a military commander should not be burdened.

Although I did not have a chance to see this front — because one does get a number of communications from home from time to time — I can tell the House that conditions are absolutely different from those which the Desert Army has triumphantly surmounted. The Desert Army is the product of three years of trial and error and the continued perfecting of transport, communications, supplies and signals, and the rapid moving forward of airfields and the like. The Armies now fighting in Tunisia are still in a very early stage of building-up their communications. The enemy opposed to them, although largely an improvised army, have something like the advantage which we had over Rommel in front of Cairo, I mean the advantage of lying 30 to 40 miles in front of your bases; while we have to go over very long, slender, tightly stretched and heavily strained approaches, in order to get at them. Very nearly did General Anderson, under General Eisenhower's orders, clear the whole province at a run. A very little more, and we might have achieved everything. It was absolutely right to try, but it failed. The Germans effected their entry, and made good their bridge-heads. We had to fall back to gather strength, and to gather our resources for heavy battle. I cannot pretend not to be disappointed that the full result was not achieved at the first bound. Still, our main object is to fight the Germans, and one cannot be blind to the fact that we have made them fight us in a situation extremely costly to them and by no means disadvantageous to us. Although the enemy's lines of supply on land are short, they are under constant attack by sea. Before they reach the battlefield they lose one-quarter, or one-third even, of everything they bring across the sea. Our power of reinforcement is far greater and more secure than theirs.

The portentous apparition of the Desert Army, driving Rommel before them, is a new, most potent and possibly even decisive factor. Air fighting is developing on an ever-increasing scale, and this is, of course, greatly to our advantage, because it would pay us to lose two machines to one in order to wear down the German Air Force and draw it away from the Russian front. However, instead of losing two planes to one, the actual results are very nearly the other way round. Therefore, it seems to me that the House need not be unduly depressed because the fighting in North Africa is going to assume a very much larger scale and last a longer time than was originally anticipated and hoped. It is, indeed, quite remarkable that the Germans should have shown themselves ready to run the risk and pay the price required of them by their struggle to hold the Tunisian tip. While I always hesitate to say anything which might afterwards look like over-confidence, I cannot resist the remark that one seems to discern in this policy the touch of the master hand, the same master hand that planned the attack on Stalingrad, and that has brought upon the German armies the greatest disaster they have ever suffered in all their military history. However, I am making no predictions and no promises. Very serious battles will have to be fought. Including Rommel's army, there must be nearly a quarter of a million of the enemy in the Tunisian tip, and we must not in any way under-rate the hazards we have to dare or the burdens we have to carry. It is always folly to forecast the results of great trials of strength in war before they take place. I will say no more than this: All the disadvantages are not on one side, and certainly they are not all on our side. I think that conforms to the standards of anti-complacency opinion in this country.

French North-West Africa is, as I have said, a United States operation, under American command. We have agreed that the boundary between our respective spheres shall be the existing frontier between Tripolitania and Tunisia, but the Desert Army is now crossing that frontier and driving forward on its quest, which is Rommel. Its movements must, therefore, be combined with those of the First Army and with the various powerful forces coming from the West. For some weeks past, the commanders have been in close touch with one another; these contacts must now be formalised.

As the Desert Army passes into the American sphere it will naturally come under the orders of General Eisenhower. I have great confidence in General Eisenhower. I regard him as one of the finest men I have ever met. It was arranged at Casablanca that when this transfer of the Desert Army took place, General Alexander should become Deputy Commander-in-Chief under General Eisenhower. At the same time, Air Chief Marshal Tedder becomes Air Commander-in-Chief Mediterranean, responsible to General Eisenhower for all the air operations in this theatre. He will control also all the Air Forces throughout the whole of the Middle East. This is absolutely necessary, because our Air Forces of Egypt, Cyrenaica and Libya, and also our powerful Air Forces operating from Malta, are actually attacking the same targets, both by bomber and fighter aircraft, as the United States and British Air Forces now working from Algeria and Tunisia are attacking. You must have one control over all this, and that control must be exercised under the supreme command of one man — and who better, I ask, than the trusty and experienced Air Chief Marshal Tedder, for whom General Eisenhower so earnestly asked? Under him, Air Vice-Marshal Coningham, hitherto working with the Eighth Army, whose services have been so much admired, will concert the air operations in support of the British First and Eighth Armies and other troops on the Tunisian battlefield. At the same time, Admiral of the Fleet Sir Andrew Cunningham, who already commands all the British and American naval forces in this theatre, will extend his command Eastward so as to comprise effectively all the cognate operations inside the Mediterranean, and the present Commander-in-Chief in the Mediterranean will become, with his headquarters in Egypt, Commander-in-Chief of the Levant, dealing also with the Red Sea and all the approaches from that quarter. There is no need for me to announce exactly where the line of demarcation between those commands is drawn, but everything is arranged with precision.

The vacancy in the Command of the Middle East created by General Alexander's appointment as Deputy Commander-in-Chief to General Eisenhower, will be filled by General Sir Henry Maitland Wilson, now commanding in Persia and Iraq, where the Tenth Army, now become a very powerful force, is stationed. It is proposed to keep Persia and Iraq as a separate Command for the present, and the new Commander will shortly be appointed.

Meanwhile, General Eisenhower has already obtained the consent of General Giraud, who commands the French Army fighting on the Tunisian front, an army which is being raised by American equipment to a very powerful force, and which will play its part later on in liberating the French Motherland, to this Army being placed under the command of General Anderson, together with the strong United States Forces which have been moved forward into Tunisia. Thus we have a hierarchy established by international arrangement completely in accord with modern ideas of unity of command between various Allies and of the closest concert of the three Services.

I make an appeal to the House, the Press, and the country, that they will, I trust, be very careful not to criticise this arrangement. If they do so, I trust they will do it not on personal lines, or tc run one general against another, to the detriment of the smooth and harmonious relations which now prevail among this band of brothers who have got their teeth into the job. In General Eisenhower, as in General Alexander, you have two men remarkable for selflessness of character and disdain of purely personal advancement. Let them alone; give them a chance; and it is quite possible that one of these fine days the bells will have to be rung again. If not, we will address ourselves to the problem, in all loyalty and comradeship, and in the light of circumstances.

I have really tried to tell the House everything that I am sure the enemy knows and to tell them nothing that the enemy ought to know. [Hon. Members: "Ought not to know."] There was a joke in that. Still, I have been able to say something. At any rate, I appeal to all patriotic men on both sides of the Atlantic Ocean to stamp their feet on mischief-makers and sowers of tares wherever they may be found, and let the great machines roll into battle under the best possible conditions for our success. That is all I have to say at the present time.

I am most grateful for the extreme kindness with which I am treated by the House. I accept, in the fullest degree, the responsibility, as Minister of Defence and as the agent of the War Cabinet, for the plans we have devised. His Majesty's Government ask no favours for themselves. We desire only to be judged by results. We await the unfolding of events with sober confidence, and we are sure that Parliament and the British nation will display in these hopeful days, which may nevertheless be clouded o'er, the same qualities of steadfastness as they did in that awful period when the life of Britain and of our Empire hung by a thread.

Messages

ULSTER'S PART

[*January 2, 1943*

[A MESSAGE FROM THE PRIME MINISTER READ BY
MR. J. M. ANDREWS, PRIME MINISTER OF
NORTHERN IRELAND, AT A MEETING
IN BELFAST]

WHEN war broke out the resources of Ulster were pledged
in support, and this pledge has been observed with characteristic
loyalty and generosity in the field of battle, whether in the air,
on land, or on the high seas, as well as on the home front. Ulster-
men are to be found not only in the famous Northern Ireland
regiments, but also in every branch of His Majesty's Forces, and
in whatever quarter of the world they may be fighting. At least
three of our most distinguished military leaders — Dill, Brooke,
and Alexander, victor of Alamein — come from Ulster's shores.
Seamen from Ulster and Ulster ships, harbours, and airfields are
a determining factor in the Battle of the Atlantic, and in industry and agriculture alike your countrymen have played their part
in producing the sinews of war. I am confident that Ulster will
continue this unrelaxing effort with characteristic doggedness
through the stern days which still lie before us.

BRITAIN AND CHINA

[January 12, 1943

[A REPLY TO GENERAL CHIANG KAI–SHEK'S MESSAGE
ON THE OCCASION OF THE SIGNING OF THE
TREATY BETWEEN GREAT BRITAIN AND
CHINA]

THIS occasion will long be memorable for the opening of a
new chapter in our relations that holds great promise for the
future. Please be assured that His Majesty's Government and the
people of this country heartily welcome what we have done as
an earnest of ever closer collaboration between allies in a great
cause.

IRAQ DECLARES WAR

[January 16, 1943

[A MESSAGE TO GENERAL NURI SAID, PRIME MINISTER
OF IRAQ, WHEN THAT COUNTRY DECLARED WAR
ON GERMANY, ITALY AND JAPAN, AND AN–
NOUNCED THAT SHE WOULD ADHERE TO
THE UNITED NATIONS' DECLARATION]

THE news of the declaration of war by Iraq has been welcomed in this country. It has given us special satisfaction to
realise that the State which we helped to create during the first
World War will henceforth participate with us in the present
struggle.

When His Majesty's Government first accepted responsibility
for guiding the future of the new Kingdom of Iraq, they made her
complete and early independence their goal. That goal was

reached ten years ago, and since then the enemies of our two countries have spared no efforts to disturb our friendly relations. They have been lavish with falsehoods, and have even resorted to force. But they could achieve no lasting success.

The Iraqi Parliament, by the free and independent exercise of their constitutional powers, have now on their own initiative decided to show the world Iraq's adherence to the aims and ideals of the United Nations, and her fundamental opposition to the dark forces which seek to enslave humanity.

The struggle will be hard, but the end is sure, and we rejoice to have you at our side.

MR. GANDHI BLAMED

[February 24, 1943

[A REPLY TO SIR TEJ BAHADUR SAPRU AND OTHERS
WHO HAD REQUESTED THE IMMEDIATE AND
UNCONDITIONAL RELEASE OF MR. GANDHI
FROM PRISON, WHERE HE HAD STARTED
A FAST]

THE Government of India decided last August that Mr. Gandhi and other leaders of the Congress Party must be detained for reasons which have been fully explained and are well understood. The reasons for that decision have not ceased to exist, and His Majesty's Government endorse the determination of the Government of India not to be deflected from their duty towards the peoples of India and of the United Nations by Mr. Gandhi's attempt to secure his unconditional release by fasting.

The first duty of the Government of India and of His Majesty's Government is to defend the soil of India from the invasion by which it is still menaced, and to enable India to play her part in the general cause of the United Nations. There can be no justification for discriminating between Mr. Gandhi and other Congress leaders. The responsibility therefore rests entirely with Mr. Gandhi himself.

WINGS FOR VICTORY

[February 28, 1943

[A MESSAGE ON THE OPENING OF A GREAT WAR SAVINGS CAMPAIGN]

THE "Wings for Victory" campaign gives each one of us an opportunity of expressing our gratitude to the Royal Air Force, which has played so vital and heroic a part in every phase of the war. We can thus contribute our support to all those taking part in the great offensive of 1943, and so demonstrate our determination to help them to the utmost of our power to achieve final and complete victory. I wish the campaign every success.

A Four Years' Plan

A WORLD BROADCAST
MARCH 21, 1943

February 12. President Roosevelt stated that Allied troops were massing in Tunisia for one of the major battles of the war.

Russians captured Krasnodar, capital of the Kuban, and made more gains in the Ukraine.

February 14. Rostov and Voroshilovgrad fell to the advancing Russians.

Continuing their day-by-day offensive on the Continent, the R.A.F. made exceptionally heavy raids on Cologne, Milan and Spezia.

February 15. Rommel's forces launched a surprise attack against the Americans in Tunisia and captured Gafsa.

February 16. Russians captured Kharkov.

Officially announced in Washington that in recent operations off Guadalcanal an American cruiser, a destroyer and 22 aircraft were lost. The Japanese had 15 warships sunk or damaged and lost 61 aircraft.

February 17. Three airfields evacuated by American troops in Tunisia in face of renewed German attacks.

February 18. German advance in Tunisia was halted with the Americans holding a ridge of hills — the British Eighth Army advanced towards the Mareth Line.

February 20. General Alexander, appointed Deputy C.-in-C. to General Eisenhower, took over command of the field in Tunisia.

It was revealed that Britain and U.S. had sent to Russia 6,200 tanks and 5,600 aircraft in 15 months.

February 23.   *Tunisian battle took a favourable turn for the Allies, and Axis forces, which had advanced, were forced to fall back. There began a steady advance by British and American troops.*

February 28.   *R.A.F. completed their heaviest month of bombing by dropping 1,000 tons on St. Nazaire in just over half an hour.*

March 1.   *Berlin had its heaviest air raid of the war when a large force of R.A.F. bombers dropped many 8,000 and 4,000 lb. bombs.*

March 3.   *Russians took Rzhev.*

    A Japanese convoy off New Guinea, consisting of 10 warships and 12 transports, was completely destroyed, more than 15,000 being killed.

    Captain Fitzroy, Speaker of the House of Commons, died.

March 6.   *Rommel launched an offensive against the Eighth Army in Tunisia, but two days later withdrew, having suffered decisive defeat.*

    Russians captured Gshatsk, a great enemy bastion on the central sector.

    Total of Japanese warships sunk off the Solomons by U.S. naval forces in a week brought to 24.

March 9.   *Russians withdrew across the Donetz in face of concentration of 25 German divisions.*

March 12.   *Russians captured Vyasma, but the Germans recaptured Kharkov.*

    Announced that Mr. Anthony Eden, Foreign Secretary, had arrived in Washington.

March 13.   *President Roosevelt and Mr. Anthony Eden conferred in Washington.*

March 15.   *Germans recaptured Kharkov but the Russians continued to advance in the Vyasma and Bielyi areas.*

    General Giraud declared in a broadcast that he was ready to meet General de Gaulle.

March 18.   *Americans recaptured Gafsa in Southern*
            Tunisia and continued their advance towards
            El Guettar, which they took next day.
March 20.   *Announced that 787 British naval officers and*
            men were to be exchanged for a similar num-
            ber of Italians.
March 21.   *Mr. Churchill broadcast on post-war policy.*

[March 21, 1943

LET me first of all thank the very great numbers of people who have made kind inquiries about me during my recent illness. Although for a week I had a fairly stiff dose of fever, which but for modern science might have had awkward consequences, I wish to make it clear that I never for a moment had to relinquish the responsible direction of affairs. I followed attentively all the time what was happening in Parliament, and the lively discussions on our home affairs when peace comes.

It was very clear to me that a good many people were so much impressed by the favourable turn in our fortunes which has marked the last six months that they have jumped to the conclusion that the war will soon be over and that we shall soon all be able to get back to the politics and party fights of peace-time.

I am not able to share these sanguine hopes, and my earnest advice to you is to concentrate even more zealously upon the war effort, and if possible not to take your eye off the ball even for a moment. If to-night, contrary to that advice, I turn aside from the course of the war and deal with some post-war and domestic issues, that is only because I hope that by so doing I may simplify and mollify political divergences, and enable all our political forces to march forward to the main objective in unity and, so far as possible, in step.

First of all we must beware of attempts to over-persuade or even to coerce His Majesty's Government to bind themselves or their unknown successors, in conditions which no one can foresee and which may be years ahead, to impose great new expenditure on the State without any relation to the circumstances

47

which might prevail at that time, and to make them pledge themselves to particular schemes without relation to other extremely important aspects of our post-war needs.

The business of proposing expenditure rests ultimately with the responsible Government of the day, and it is their duty, and their duty alone, to propose to Parliament any new charges upon the public, and also to propose in the annual Budgets the means of raising the necessary funds.

The world is coming increasingly to admire our British parliamentary system and ideas. It is contrary to those ideas that Ministers or members should become pledge-bound delegates. They are a band of men who undertake certain honourable duties, and they would be dishonoured if they allowed their right and duty to serve the public as well as possible on any given occasion to be prejudiced by the enforced, premature contraction of obligations. Nothing would be easier for me than to make any number of promises and to get the immediate response of cheap cheers and glowing leading articles. I am not in any need to go about making promises in order to win political support or to be allowed to continue in office.

It was on a grim and bleak basis that I undertook my present task, and on that basis I have been given loyalty and support such as no Prime Minister has ever received. I cannot express my feeling of gratitude to the nation for their kindness to me and for the trust and confidence they have placed in me during long, dark, and disappointing periods. I am absolutely determined not to falsify or mock that confidence by making promises without regard to whether they can be performed or not. At my time of life I have no personal ambitions, no future to provide for. And I feel I can truthfully say that I only wish to do my duty by the whole mass of the nation and of the British Empire as long as I am thought to be of any use for that.

Therefore I tell you round your firesides to-night that I am resolved not to give or to make all kinds of promises and tell all kinds of fairy tales to you who have trusted me and gone with me so far, and marched through the valley of the shadow, till we have reached the upland regions on which we now stand with firmly planted feet.

However, it is our duty to peer through the mists of the future to the end of the war, and to try our utmost to be prepared by ceaseless effort and forethought for the kind of situations which are likely to occur. Speaking under every reserve and not attempting to prophesy, I can imagine that some time next year — but it may well be the year after — we might beat Hitler, by which I mean beat him and his powers of evil into death, dust, and ashes.

Then we shall immediately proceed to transport all the necessary additional forces and apparatus to the other side of the world to punish the greedy, cruel Empire of Japan, to rescue China from her long torment, to free our territory and that of our Dutch Allies, and to drive the Japanese menace forever from Australian, New Zealand, and Indian shores.

That will be our first and supreme task, and nothing must lure us from it. Nevertheless, in my opinion the moment when Hitler is beaten and Germany and Italy are prostrate will mark the grand climax of the war, and that will be the time to make a new declaration upon the task before us. We and our Allies shall have accomplished one great task. Nazi tyranny and Prussian militarism, which threatened to engulf the whole world, and against which we stood alone for a fateful year — these curses will have been swept from the face of the earth.

If I should be spared to see that day, and should be needed at the helm at that time, I shall then, with the assent of the Cabinet, propose a new task to the British nation. The war against Japan will demand a very different arrangement of our forces from what exists at present.

There will certainly be large numbers of British, and also no doubt United States, soldiers whom it will not be physically possible to employ across the vast distances and poor communications of the Japanese war. There will certainly be large numbers of men, not only abroad but at home, who will have to be brought back to their families and to their jobs or to other equally good jobs. For all these, after full provision has been made for the garrisoning of the guilty countries, return to something like home and freedom will be their hearts' desire. However vigorously the war against Japan is prosecuted, there will certainly be a partial demobilisation following on the defeat of Hitler, and this will raise most difficult and intricate problems, and we are taking care in our arrangements to avoid the mistakes which were so freely committed last time.

Of course these ideas may be completely falsified by events. It may be that Japan will collapse before Hitler, in which case quite another lay-out will be necessary. As, however, many people wish ardently to discuss the future, I adopt for this purpose to-night what seems to me the most likely supposition.

On this assumption it would be our hope that the United Nations, headed by the three great victorious Powers, the British Commonwealth of Nations, the United States, and Soviet Russia, should immediately begin to confer upon the future world organisation which is to be our safeguard against further wars by effectually disarming and keeping disarmed the guilty States, by bringing to justice the grand criminals and their accomplices, and by securing the return to the devastated and subjugated countries of the mechanical resources and artistic treasures of which they have been pillaged.

We shall also have a heavy task in trying to avert widespread famine in some at least of the ruined regions. We must hope and pray that the unity of the three leading victorious Powers will be worthy of their supreme responsibility, and that they will think not only of their own welfare but of the welfare and future of all.

One can imagine that under a world institution embodying or representing the United Nations, and some day all nations, there should come into being a Council of Europe and a Council of Asia. As, according to the forecast I am outlining, the war against Japan will still be raging, it is upon the creation of the Council of Europe and the settlement of Europe that the first practical task will be centred. Now this is a stupendous business. In Europe lie most of the causes which have led to these two world wars. In Europe dwell the historic parent races from whom our western civilisation has been so largely derived. I believe myself to be what is called a good European, and deem it a noble task to take part in reviving the fertile genius and in restoring the true greatness of Europe.

I hope we shall not lightly cast aside all the immense work which was accomplished by the creation of the League of Nations. Certainly we must take as our foundation the lofty conception of freedom, law and morality which was the spirit of the League.

A Four Years' Plan, March 21, 1943

We must try — I am speaking of course only for ourselves — to make the Council of Europe, or whatever it may be called, into a really effective League, with all the strongest forces concerned woven into its texture, with a High Court to adjust disputes, and with forces, armed forces, national or international or both, held ready to impose these decisions and prevent renewed aggression and the preparation of future wars.

Anyone can see that this Council when created must eventually embrace the whole of Europe, and that all the main branches of the European family must some day be partners in it. What is to happen to the large number of small nations whose rights and interests must be safeguarded? Here let me ask what would be thought of an army that consisted only of battalions and brigades, and which never formed any of the larger and higher organisations like army corps. It would soon get mopped up. It would therefore seem, to me at any rate, worthy of patient study that side by side with the Great Powers there should be a number of groupings of States or Confederations which would express themselves through their own chosen representatives, the whole making a Council of great States and groups of States.

It is my earnest hope, though I can hardly expect to see it fulfilled in my lifetime, that we shall achieve the largest common measure of the integrated life of Europe that is possible without destroying the individual characteristics and traditions of its many ancient and historic races. All this will I believe be found to harmonise with the high permanent interests of Britain, the United States, and Russia. It certainly cannot be accomplished without their cordial and concerted agreement and participation. Thus and thus only will the glory of Europe rise again.

I only mention these matters to you to show you the magnitude of the task that will lie before us in Europe alone. Nothing could be more foolish at this stage than to plunge into details and try to prescribe the exact groupings of States or lay down precise machinery for their co-operation, or still more to argue about frontiers now while the war even in the West has not yet reached its full height, while the struggle with the U-boats is raging, and when the war in the Far East is only in its first phase. This does not mean that many tentative discussions are not taking place between the great nations concerned, or that the whole vast problem of European destiny — for that is what I am speaking of now — is not the subject of ceaseless heart-searchings.

We must remember, however, that we in Britain and the British Commonwealth of Nations, although almost a world in ourselves, shall have to reach agreements with great and friendly equals, and also to respect and have a care for the rights of weaker and smaller States, and that it will not be given to any one nation to achieve the full satisfaction of its individual wishes. I have said enough, however, I am sure, to show you, at least in outline, the mystery, the peril, and, I will add, the splendour of this vast sphere of practical action into which we shall have to leap once the hideous spell of Nazi tyranny has been broken.

Coming nearer home, we shall have to consider at the same time how the inhabitants of this island are going to get their living at this stage in the world story, and how they are going to maintain and progressively improve their previous standards of life and labour. I am very much attracted to the idea that we should make and proclaim what might be called a Four Years' Plan. Four years seems to me to be the right length for the period of transition and reconstruction which will follow the downfall of Hitler. We have five-year Parliaments, and a Four Years' Plan would give time for the preparation of a second plan. This Four Years' Plan would cover five or six large measures of a practical character which must all have been the subject of prolonged, careful, energetic preparation beforehand, and which fit together into a general scheme.

When this plan has been shaped, it will have to be presented to the country, either by a National Government formally representative, as this one is, of the three parties in the State, or by a National Government comprising the best men in all parties who are willing to serve. I cannot tell how these matters will settle themselves. But in 1944 our present Parliament will have lived nine years, and by 1945 ten years, and as soon as the defeat of Germany has removed the danger now at our throats, and the register can be compiled and other necessary arrangements made, a new House of Commons must be freely chosen by the whole electorate, including, of course, the armed forces wherever they may be. Thus whoever is burdened with the responsibility of conducting affairs will have a clear policy, and will be able to speak and act at least in the name of an effective and resolute majority.

From what I have said already you will realise how very difficult and anxious this period will be, and how much will depend not only on our own action but on the action of other very powerful countries. This applies not only to the carrying to a conclusion of the war against Japan, but also to the disarming of the guilty and to the settlement of Europe; not only to the arrangements for the prevention of further wars, but also to the whole economic process and relationship of nations, in order that the ruin of our wealth may be rapidly repaired, in order that employment and production may be at a high level, and that goods and services may be interchanged between man and man, and between one nation and another, under the best conditions and on the largest scale.

The difficulties which will confront us will take all our highest qualities to overcome. Let me, however, say straight away that my faith in the vigour, ingenuity, and resilience of the British race is invincible. Difficulties mastered are opportunities won. The day of Hitler's downfall will be a bright one for our country and for all mankind. The bells will clash their peals of victory and hope, and we shall march forward together encouraged, invigorated, and still, I trust, generally united upon our further journey.

I personally am very keen that a scheme for the amalgamation and extension of our present incomparable insurance system should have a leading place in our Four Years' Plan. I have been prominently connected with all these schemes of national compulsory organised thrift from the time when I brought my friend Sir William Beveridge into the public service 35 years ago, when I was creating the labour exchanges, on which he was a great authority, and when, with Sir Hubert Llewellyn Smith, I framed the first unemployment insurance scheme. The prime parent of all national insurance schemes is Mr. Lloyd George. I was his lieutenant in those distant days, and afterwards it fell to me, as Chancellor of the Exchequer 18 years ago, to lower the pensions age to 65 and to bring in the widows and orphans.

The time is now ripe for another great advance, and anyone can see what large savings there will be in the administration once the whole process of insurance has become unified, compulsory, and national. Here is a real opportunity for what I once called "bringing the magic of averages to the rescue of the millions." Therefore, you must rank me and my colleagues as strong partisans of national compulsory insurance for all classes for all purposes from the cradle to the grave. Every preparation, including, if necessary, preliminary legislative preparation, will be made with the utmost energy, and the necessary negotiations to deal with worthy existing interests are being actively pursued, so that when the moment comes everything will be ready.

Here let me remark that the best way to insure against unemployment is to have no unemployment. There is another point. Unemployables, rich or poor, will have to be toned up. We cannot afford to have idle people. Idlers at the top make idlers at the bottom. No one must stand aside in his working prime to pursue a life of selfish pleasure. There are wasters in all classes. Happily they are only a small minority in every class. But anyhow we cannot have a band of drones in our midst, whether they come from the ancient aristocracy or the modern plutocracy or the ordinary type of pub-crawler.

There are other large matters which will also have to be dealt with in our Four Years' Plan, upon which thought, study, and discussion are advancing rapidly. Let me take first of all the question of British agriculture. We have, of course, to purchase a large proportion of our food and vital raw materials oversea. Our foreign investments have been expended in the common cause. The British nation that has now once again saved the freedom of the world has grown great on cheap and abundant food. Had it not been for the free trade policy of Victorian days, our population would never have risen to the level of a Great Power, and we might have gone down the drain with many other minor States, to the disaster of the whole world.

Abundant food has brought our 47,000,000 Britons into the world. Here they are, and they must find their living. It is absolutely certain we shall have to grow a larger proportion of our food at home. During the war immense advances have been made by the agricultural industry. The position of the farmers has been improved, the position of the labourers immeasurably improved. The efficient agricultural landlord has an important part to play.

I hope to see a vigorous revival of healthy village life on the basis of these higher wages and of improved housing, and, what with the modern methods of locomotion and the modern amusements of the cinemas and the wireless, to which will soon be added television, life in the country and on the land ought to compete in attractiveness with life in the great cities.

But all this would cost money. When the various handicaps of war conditions are at an end, I expect that better national house-keeping will be possible, and that, as the result of technical improvements in British agriculture, the strain upon the State will be relieved. At the same time the fact remains that if the expansion and improvement of British agriculture is to be maintained, as it must be maintained, and a reasonable level of prices is to be maintained, as it must be maintained, there are likely to be substantial charges which the State must be prepared to shoulder. That has to be borne in mind.

Next there is the spacious domain of public health. I was brought up on the maxim of Lord Beaconsfield which my father was always repeating: — "Health and the laws of health." We must establish on broad and solid foundations a National Health Service. Here let me say that there is no finer investment for any community than putting milk into babies. Healthy citizens are the greatest asset any country can have.

One of the most sombre anxieties which beset those who look 30 or 40 or 50 years ahead, and in this field one can see ahead only too clearly, is the dwindling birth-rate. In 30 years, unless present trends alter, a smaller working and fighting population will have to support and protect nearly twice as many old people: in 50 years the position will be worse still. If this country is to keep its high place in the leadership of the world, and to survive as a great Power that can hold its own against external pressures, our people must be encouraged by every means to have larger families.

For this reason, well-thought-out plans for helping parents to contribute this life-spring to the community are of prime importance. The care of the young and the establishment of sound hygienic conditions of motherhood have a bearing upon the whole future of the race which is absolutely vital. Side by side with that is the war upon disease, which, let me remind you, so

55

far as it is successful, will directly aid the national insurance scheme. Upon all this, planning is vigorously proceeding.

Following upon health and welfare is the question of education. The future of the world is to the highly-educated races who alone can handle the scientific apparatus necessary for pre-eminence in peace or survival in war. I hope our education will become broader and more liberal. All wisdom is not new wisdom, and the past should be studied if the future is to be successfully encountered. To quote Disraeli again in one of his most pregnant sayings: "Nations are governed by force or by tradition." In moving steadily and steadfastly from a class to a national foundation in the politics and economics of our society and civilisation, we must not forget the glories of the past, nor how many battles we have fought for the rights of the individual and for human freedom.

We must beware of trying to build a society in which nobody counts for anything except a politician or an official, a society where enterprise gains no reward and thrift no privileges. I say "trying to build," because of all races in the world our people would be the last to consent to be governed by a bureaucracy. Freedom is their life-blood. These two great wars, scourging and harrowing men's souls, have made the British nation master in its own house. The people have been rendered conscious that they are coming into their inheritance. The treasures of the past, the toil of the centuries, the long-built-up conceptions of decent government and fair play, the tolerance which comes from the free working of Parliamentary and electoral institutions, and the great Colonial possessions for which we are trustees in every part of the globe — all these constitute parts of this inheritance, and the nation must be fitted for its responsibilities and high duty.

Human beings are endowed with infinitely varying qualities and dispositions, and each one is different from the others. We cannot make them all the same. It would be a pretty dull world if we did. It is in our power, however, to secure equal opportunities for all. The facilities for advanced education must be evened out and multiplied. No one who can take advantage of a higher education should be denied this chance. You cannot conduct a modern community except with an adequate supply of persons upon whose education, whether humane, technical, or scientific, much time and money have been spent.

There is another element which should never be banished from our system of education. Here we have freedom of thought as well as freedom of conscience. Here we have been the pioneers of religious toleration. But side by side with all this has been the fact that religion has been a rock in the life and character of the British people upon which they have built their hopes and cast their cares. This fundamental element must never be taken from our schools, and I rejoice to learn of the enormous progress that is being made among all religious bodies in freeing themselves from sectarian jealousies and feuds, while preserving fervently the tenets of their own faith.

The secular schooling of the great mass of our scholars must be progressively prolonged, and for this we must both improve our schools and train our teachers in good time. After school-time ends, we must not throw our youth uncared-for and unsupervised on to the labour market, with its "blind alley" occupations which start so fair and often end so foul. We must make plans for part-time release from industry, so that our young people may have the chance to carry on their general education, and also to obtain a specialised education which will fit them better for their work.

Under our ancient monarchy, that bulwark of British liberties, that barrier against dictatorships of all kinds, we intend to move forward in a great family, preserving the comradeships of the war, free for ever from the class prejudice and other forms of snobbery from which in modern times we have suffered less than most other nations, and from which we are now shaking ourselves entirely free. Britain is a fertile mother, and natural genius springs from the whole people.

We have made great progress, but we must make far greater progress. We must make sure that the path to the higher functions throughout our society and Empire is really open to the children of every family. Whether they can tread that path will depend upon their qualities tested by fair competition. All cannot reach the same level, but all must have their chance. I look forward to a Britain so big that she will need to draw her leaders from every type of school and wearing every kind of tie. Tradition may play its part, but broader systems must now rule.

We have one large immediate task in the replanning and re-building of our cities and towns. This will make a very great call on all our resources in material and labour, but it is also an immense opportunity, not only for the improvement of our housing, but for the employment of our people in the years immediately after the war.

In the far-reaching scheme for reorganising the building industry, prepared by the Minister of Labour and the Minister of Works, will be found another means of protecting our insurance fund from the drain of unemployment relief. Mr. Bevin is attacked from time to time, now from one side, now from another. When I think of the tremendous changes which have been effected under the strain of war in the lives of the whole people, of both sexes and of every class, with so little friction, and when I consider the practical absence of strikes in this war compared to what happened in the last, I think he will be able to take it all right.

You will see from what I have said that there is no lack of material for a Four Years' Plan for the transition period from war to peace, and for another plan after that. For the present during the war our rule should be, no promises but every preparation, including where required preliminary legislative preparation.

Before I conclude I have to strike two notes, one of sober caution and the other of confidence. You shall have the caution first. All our improvements and expansion must be related to a sound and modernised finance.

A friend of mine said the other day in the House of Commons that "pounds, shillings, and pence were meaningless symbols." This made me open my eyes. What then are we to say about the savings of the people? We have just begun a "Wings for Victory" War Savings campaign, to which all classes have subscribed. Vast numbers of people have been encouraged to purchase war savings certificates. Income-tax is collected from the wage-earners of a certain level and carried to a nest-egg for them at the end of the war, the Government having the use of the money meanwhile. A nest-egg similar in character will be given to the armed forces. Those whose houses have been destroyed by air raid damage and who have in many cases paid insurance are entitled to compensation. All these obligations were contracted in pounds, shillings, and pence.

At the end of this war there will be seven or eight million people in the country with £200 or £300 apiece, a thing unknown in our history. These savings of the nation, arising from the thrift, skill, or devotion of individuals, are sacred. The State is built around them, and it is the duty of the State to redeem its faith in an equal degree of value. I am not one of those who are wedded to undue rigidity in the management of the currency system, but this I say: That over a period of 10 or 15 years there ought to be a fair, steady continuity of values if there is to be any faith between man and man or between the individual and the State. We have successfully stabilised prices during the war. We intend to continue this policy after the war to the utmost of our ability.

This brings me to the subject of the burden and incidence of taxation. Direct taxation on all classes stands at unprecedented and sterilising levels. Besides this there is indirect taxation raised to a remarkable height.

In war-time our people are willing and even proud to pay all these taxes. But such conditions could not continue in peace. We must expect taxation after the war to be heavier than it was before the war, but we do not intend to shape our plans or levy taxation in a way which, by removing personal incentive, would destroy initiative and enterprise.

If you take any single year of peace and take a slice through the industry and enterprise of the nation — see how important is the spirit of enterprise and ingenuity — you will find work which is being done at the moment, work that is being planned for the next year, and projects for the third, fourth, and even the fifth year ahead which are all maturing. War cuts down all this forward planning, and everything is subordinated to the struggle for national existence. Thus, when peace came suddenly, as it did last time, there were no long carefully prepared plans for the future. That was one of the main reasons why at the end of the last war, after a momentary recovery, we fell into a dreadful trough of unemployment. We must not be caught again that way.

It is therefore necessary to make sure that we have projects for the future employment of the people and the forward movement of our industries carefully foreseen, and, secondly, that private enterprise and State enterprise are both able to play their parts to the utmost.

A number of measures are being and will be prepared which will enable the Government to exercise a balancing influence upon development which can be turned on or off as circumstances require. There is a broadening field for State ownership and enterprise, especially in relation to monopolies of all kinds. The modern State will increasingly concern itself with the economic well-being of the nation, but it is all the more vital to revive at the earliest moment a widespread healthy and vigorous private enterprise without which we shall never be able to provide, in the years when it is needed, the employment for our soldiers, sailors, and airmen to which they are entitled after their duty has been done.

In this brief survey I have tried to set before you both hopes and fears: I have given both caution and encouragement. But if I have to strike a balance, as I must do before the end, let me proclaim myself a faithful follower of the larger hope. I will proceed to back this hope with some solid facts. Anyone can see the difficulties of placing our exports profitably in a world so filled with ruined countries. Foreign trade to be of value must be fertile. There is no use in doing business at a loss. Nevertheless I am advised that in view of the general state of the world after the defeat of Hitler, there will be considerable opportunities for re-establishing our exports. Immediately after the war there will be an intense demand, both for home and export, for what are called consumable goods, such as clothes, furniture, and textiles.

I have spoken of the immense building programme, and we all know the stimulus which that is to a large number of trades, including the electrical and metal industries. We have learnt much about production under the stress of war. Our methods have vastly improved. The lay-out of our factories presents an entirely new and novel picture to the eye. Mass production has been forced upon us. The electrification of industry has been increased 50 per cent. There are some significant new industries offering scope for the inventiveness and vigour which made this country great. When the fetters of wartime are struck off and we turn free hands to the industrial tasks of peace, we may be astonished at the progress in efficiency we shall suddenly find displayed. I can only mention a few instances of fields of activity. The ceaseless improvements in wireless and the wonders of radio-location, applied to the arts of peace, will employ the radio industry. Striking advances are open for both gas and electricity as the servants of industry, agriculture, and the cottage home. There is civil aviation. There is forestry. There is transportation in all its forms. We were the earliest in the world with railways; we must bring them up to date in every respect. Here, in these few examples, are gigantic opportunities which, if used, will in turn increase our power to serve other countries with the goods they want.

Our own effort must be supported by international arrangements and agreements more neighbourlike and more sensible than before. We must strive to secure our fair share of an augmented world trade. Our fortunes will be greatly influenced by the policies of the United States and the British Dominions, and we are doing our utmost to keep in ever closer contact with them. We have lately put before them and our other friends and allies some tentative suggestions for the future management of the exchanges and of international currency, which will shortly be published. But this is a first instalment only.

I have heard a great deal on both sides of these questions during the forty years I have served in the House of Commons and the twenty years or more I have served in Cabinets. I have tried to learn from events, and also from my own mistakes, and I tell you my solemn belief, which is that if we act with comradeship and loyalty to our country and to one another, and if we can make State enterprise and free enterprise both serve national interests and pull the national wagon side by side, then there is no need for us to run into that horrible, devastating slump or into that squalid epoch of bickering and confusion which mocked and squandered the hard-won victory we gained a quarter of a century ago.

I end where I began. Let us get back to our job. I must warn every one who hears me of a certain, shall I say, unseemliness and also of a danger of its appearing to the world that we here in Britain are diverting our attention to peace, which is still remote, and to the fruits of victory, which have yet to be won, while our Russian allies are fighting for dear life and dearer honour in the dire, deadly, daily struggle against all the might of the German military machine, and while our thoughts should be with our armies and with our American and French comrades now engaged in decisive battle in Tunisia. I have just received a message from General Montgomery that the Eighth Army are on the move and that he is satisfied with their progress.

Let us wish them Godspeed in their struggle, and let us bend all our efforts to the war and to the ever more vigorous prosecution of our supreme task.

The Tunisia Campaign

DURING THE LAST STAGES OF THE WAR IN NORTH AFRICA
THE PRIME MINISTER MADE THREE SHORT STATEMENTS TO
THE HOUSE OF COMMONS GIVING NEWS OF THE PROGRESS
OF THE CAMPAIGN

March 23.   The Eighth Army pierced the Mareth Line on the coastal flank and took 3,000 prisoners. A British flanking force approached El Hamma and struck towards Gabes and the sea.

March 24.   Enemy counter-attacks regained much of the ground which had been taken by the Eighth Army in the Mareth Line, and some of the fiercest fighting of the whole North African campaign ensued.

March 27.   The R.A.F. dropped 900 tons of bombs on Berlin — double the tonnage of the worst raid on London, and the heaviest raid made so far on the German capital.

March 28.   The enemy was forced to withdraw from the Mareth Line with heavy losses in men and material following a brilliant outflanking movement of the Eighth Army towards Gabes.

March 29.   The R.A.F. made a heavy raid on Berlin for the second time in 48 hours.

March 30.   The Eighth Army and the R.A.F. were in full pursuit of the Axis forces retreating to the North of Tunisia from the Mareth Line, while the British First Army struck in the North and took Sejenane.

March 31.   British submarines, co-operating in the continuous sea and air attack on Axis supply lines to Tunisia, sank six more supply ships.

April 1.   Allied forces in Tunisia closed in on all sectors.
One hundred U.S. Flying Fortresses made a
devastating raid on Sardinia.

April 2.   It was announced in Berlin that Rommel's
Afrika Corps had joined up with Von Arnim's
forces.

April 3.   Officially announced that more than 8,000 tons
of bombs were dropped on Germany during
March.

General Eisenhower, Commander-in-Chief in
Africa, stated: "The campaign in Tunisia is developing to its climax."

April 4.   U.S. heavy bombers made a daylight attack on
the Renault works in Paris, and at night the
R.A.F. gave Kiel, German naval base, its heaviest raid of the war.

April 6.   Colonel Knox, U.S. Secretary of the Navy, revealed that Allied losses from U-boats in March
were "considerably worse than in February."

April 7.   Following Mr. Churchill's announcement that
the Eighth Army had gained a great victory in
the Akarit position, the Eighth Army made contact with the Second U.S. Army Corps advancing from Gafsa.

[March 24, 1943

I T is my duty to let the House and the country know that this
great battle now proceeding in Tunisia has by no means reached
its climax, and that very much hard fighting now lies before the
British and the United States Forces. The latest information from
the Mareth Front — later, that is, than that published in this
morning's newspapers — shows that the Germans, by counter-
attacks, have regained the greater part of the bridgehead which
had been stormed, and that their main line of defence in that
quarter is largely restored. I take occasion to make that state-

ment, as I do not wish hopes of an easy decision to be encouraged. On the other hand, I have good confidence in the final result.

[March 30, 1943]

SINCE I informed the House last week of the check sustained on the Mareth front, the situation has turned very much in our favour. General Montgomery's decision to throw his weight on to the turning movement instead of persisting in the frontal attack has been crowned with success. Another severe defeat has been inflicted by the Desert Army upon the Axis forces they have so long pursued. According to my latest information, we occupied El Hamma last night, and our vanguards passed through Gabes this morning. The decisive break-through of General Freyberg's turning force was aided to an extraordinary degree by novel forms of intense air attack, in which many hundreds of British aircraft were simultaneously employed.

The enemy losses in men and material have of course been very serious to him, and the panzer divisions in particular are remarkably mauled and enfeebled. It is, however, too soon to say what proportion of the Italian 20th and 21st Army Corps has been left behind. The operations are being prosecuted with the utmost energy.

It must be remembered that this new exploit of the Desert Army must be viewed in its relation to the general scheme of action on the whole Tunisian front. The very fine unceasing advance of the United States Forces, and the increasing activities in the French sector and on the front of the British First Army, all play their part in the combinations of General Eisenhower, the Supreme Commander, and his Deputy, General Alexander.

I should not close, however, without uttering a warning against any underrating of the task which lies before the whole group of Allied Armies and Air Forces in Tunisia. The country is very difficult and abounds in defensive positions, but we have every reason to be satisfied with the progress already made by our superior forces and superior equipment under their skilful resolute commanders.

Onwards to Victory

Replying to a member who asked whether General Mont-gomery's Army included both French and New Zealand troops, the Prime Minister added to his March 30 statement: —

Yes, Sir. New Zealand troops have actually passed through Gabes this morning. That I am entitled to say, as they are actually in contact with the enemy.

[April 7, 1943

I HAVE received reports from the High Command in Tunisia that a new victory has been gained by the Desert Army. At half-past four yesterday morning, in the darkness of a moonless night, General Montgomery ordered his main forces to the assault of the Akarit position North of Gabes. The advance of the British and Indian infantry divisions was preceded and covered by a barrage of about 500 guns, which is practically the Alamein scale. The enemy appeared to be taken by surprise by this attack out of pitch darkness. His fortified positions were overwhelmed, and by noon all the dominant key-points were in our hands. A hole had been blasted in the centre of the enemy's 12-mile defensive line, through which our armoured and mobile forces were immediately ordered to advance. The enemy now fought with savage vigour to restore the situation, but all his counter-attacks were repulsed. The advance of the British armour continued, and by nightfall the open country had been reached. Over 6,000 prisoners have been taken so far. Rommel's army is now retreating Northward, and is being hotly pursued. This successful battle and frontal attack should enable the Desert Army to join hands with the United States Forces who have been pressing the enemy unceasingly from the West. The whole of the operations of the group of Armies on the Tunisian front are being concerted by General Alexander under the supreme command of the Allied Commander-in-Chief, General Eisenhower.

In reply to a question the Prime Minister added: —

The enemy retreat did not begin until after the assault was successful.

The Tunisia Campaign, April 7, 1943

[NOTE: *The North African campaign ended on May 12, when all organised resistance by Axis troops ceased, and General von Arnim, German Commander-in-Chief, was taken prisoner. Mr. Churchill was in Washington at the time, and his first public statement on the great Allied victory was made in his speech to the United States Congress on May 19.*]

The Tunisian Campaign, April 7, 1943

[Note: *The North African campaign ended on May 12, when all organised resistance by Axis troops ceased, and General von Arnim, German Commander-in-Chief, was taken prisoner. Mr. Churchill was in Washington at the time, and his first public statement on the great Allied victory was made in his speech to the United States Congress on May 19.*

The Voting Register

IN THE HOUSE OF COMMONS ON MARCH 30, 1943, SIR
RICHARD ACLAND (INDEPENDENT) OPPOSED THE MOTION
FOR A WRIT FOR A BY-ELECTION AT DAVENTRY (FOLLOWING
THE DEATH OF MR. SPEAKER FITZROY) IN ORDER TO HAVE
THE OPPORTUNITY OF ASKING THE PRIME MINISTER TO
MAKE A STATEMENT REGARDING THE BETTERING OF THE
ELECTORAL REGISTER

Mr. Churchill replied:—

THE Report of the Departmental Committee on Electoral
Machinery did not deal with by-elections. That Report is under
consideration by the Government; it involves complicated and
important issues, and no statement can yet be made. When the
Government has come to its conclusions on the Report, it will
consider whether any inferences can be drawn as to modifications in by-election arrangements in war-time. While it is the
wish of His Majesty's Government that all possible qualified persons should have the right to record their votes, I think it proper
to warn the House that the technical and practical difficulties
may be formidable. It is in any case not possible for the Government to reach any conclusion as to by-elections at present. In
the meantime constituencies without the services of a Member
will naturally expect us to take the usual steps to enable the
vacancies to be filled.

*Later the same day other members raised the matter again, and
in a further statement the Prime Minister said:* —

It is not correct to say that the Government are ignoring this
question. I gave an answer in exactly the opposite sense, and
said that we were considering it actively with a view to seeing
whether the difficulties can be solved. Our desire is that qualified
persons should be able to vote at by-elections. At the same time,

with that candour and frankness which the hon. Gentleman urged me to display — a request which I thought I had anticipated — I also stated that from what I had heard the difficulties appeared very considerable, and it might well be that on a survey of the advantages on the one hand and the difficulties and complications on the other, especially when it comes to the Army under the prevailing conditions of war, the Government might think it better, and the House might endorse their view, that we should not make the changes that would be required.

I agree with the view that some further statement will be needed from the Government when our survey of this matter has been completed, and I hope that something may be said by the Home Secretary even before we rise for the Easter Recess. I say that to show that the Government's position is not at all one of ignoring the matter or of dull resistance, but that it will be a position of giving the House the best advice and putting the pros and cons fairly before it.

On the whole, I think that honesty must make me say that the prognosis looks somewhat adverse at the present time. It is a very odd remedy for those who wish to see more people vote that they should disfranchise all the others. That is certainly illogical and inconsistent, and this attempt to disfranchise the people of Daventry, of whom we have heard so much to-day, shows a tendency which should certainly be resisted by the House.

Messages

TO GENERAL MacARTHUR

[A MESSAGE OF CONGRATULATION TO THE COM-
MANDER-IN-CHIEF, S. W. PACIFIC, FOLLOWING
THE CAPTURE OF BUNA, NEW GUINEA,
MARCH 1, 1943]

THE rapid movements I have been making and the pressure upon me made me delay till my return sending you my most cordial congratulations upon the capture of Buna by American and Australian forces, and the important and resolute operations under your distinguished command which have resulted in the destruction of the Japanese invaders in Papua. I have watched with particular admiration your masterly employment of transport aircraft to solve the most complicated and diverse logistical problems. I should like to let you know how grateful we all feel throughout the British Empire that you stand on guard over all these vital interests. Pray also accept my own personal good wishes. I look forward indeed to the day when we may meet.

[NOTE: *In his reply to the above message, General MacArthur said he hoped that the Prime Minister would visit the S.W. Pacific area, adding:* "*The effect would be almost magical. Personally, I would rather have you come than to receive a fresh Army corps.*"]

THE GROWING AIR OFFENSIVE

[*March 1, 1943*

[A MESSAGE TO AIR CHIEF MARSHAL SIR ARTHUR
HARRIS, BOMBER COMMAND]

I CONGRATULATE you and all ranks of the Metropolitan
Bomber Command upon the fine rate of discharge upon Germany
and Italy and other enemy targets achieved during the month
of February. In total volume you exceeded by half as much again
any previous month of the war. February thus marks a quite
definite advance, on which further improvements will be made.

SPITFIRES IN THE PACIFIC

[*March 4, 1943*

[MR. JOHN CURTIN, PRIME MINISTER OF AUSTRALIA,
SENT A MESSAGE OF THANKS TO MR. CHURCHILL
FOR SENDING SQUADRONS OF SPITFIRES TO
HELP IN THE WAR IN THE PACIFIC. THIS
WAS MR. CHURCHILL'S REPLY ON
MARCH 4, 1943]

I FEEL I must let you know at once how deeply I am touched
by the terms of your announcement about the Spitfire fighter
squadrons. It is a great satisfaction to me to learn of the ascend-
ancy they have immediately established over the enemy, and it is
my earnest wish that these squadrons, which are manned by airmen from Australia and Britain, will long continue to give you
powerful aid in your magnificent fight against the Japanese. I
am sure that their only desire will be to live up to the high tradi-

tions of the armed forces of Australia, and their only aim to hasten the certain victory over Japan.

"THE DAYS ARE BRIGHTER"

[*March 6, 1943*

[A MESSAGE TO MR. MACKENZIE KING, PRIME MINIS-
TER OF CANADA, WHO HAD CONGRATULATED
MR. CHURCHILL ON HIS RECOVERY FROM
ILLNESS]

I AM deeply touched by your very generous message, and I send to you and to all members of the Parliament of Canada my heartfelt thanks. I recall with gratitude the warmth of the reception which you all gave me when I visited Canada in December, 1941. In the darkest days Canada, under your leadership, remained confident and true. Now the days are brighter; and when victory is won you will be able to look back with just pride upon a record surpassed by none.

TRIBUTE TO CARDINAL HINSLEY

[*March 20, 1943*

[A MESSAGE TO THE PROVOST OF WESTMINSTER
CATHEDRAL

IT IS with profound and personal regret that I hear of the death of Cardinal Hinsley, whom I held in high regard. I desire to assure you, and through you the Roman Catholic community of this country, of my deep sympathy with them in the loss of a leader of character and courage, a great patriot, and a true love of justice and freedom.

72

U.S. AIRMEN PRAISED

[March 21, 1943

[A MESSAGE TO LT.-GEN. ANDREWS, U.S. COMMAND-
ING GENERAL, EUROPEAN THEATRE OF OPERA-
TIONS, AND MAJ.-GEN. EAKER, COMMANDING
GENERAL UNITED STATES ARMY EIGHTH
AIR FORCE, UPON THE SUCCESSFUL
ATTACK BY AMERICAN BOMBERS
ON THE U-BOAT BASE AT
VEGESACK]

ALL my compliments to you and your officers and men on
your brilliant exploit, the effectiveness of which the photographs
already reveal.

THE SPIRIT OF GREECE

[March 23, 1943

[A MESSAGE TO M. TSOUDEROS, THE PRIME MINISTER
OF GREECE, ON GREEK INDEPENDENCE DAY]

WHILE Greece is groaning under tyranny, her people are
more conscious than ever of their historic greatness, and remember the glories of their war of independence.

To-day the people of Britain salute the heroes of the new war
of liberation now being fought in the mountains, cities, and
villages of Greece.

The British people grieve for the cruel sufferings which the
Greeks are enduring with fortitude. But they know, too, how
the Greeks strike back at the invader; how neither torture nor
firing squads can break their spirit. Greece fights on, unyielding

73

in her indomitable resistance to the conqueror and in the courage of her Army, Air Force, Navy, and Merchant Marine now serving side by side with the British forces.

The night of slavery will pass. To-day, the King of the Hellenes and his Government are in Cairo in order to make ready for the day which will restore to Greece the liberty for which she has always fought. When the hour strikes — and you will be given warning when it is time to act as one man — Greece will drive the barbarous usurpers from her soil.

Then, united in victory as in suffering, Greece will take her place among the free peoples of the world. Victory is sure.

LEADERSHIP FOR GREAT TASKS

[March 31, 1943

[A MESSAGE TO THE FIRST WAR-TIME CONFERENCE
OF THE FEDERATION OF UNIVERSITY
CONSERVATIVE AND UNIONIST
ASSOCIATIONS IN LONDON]

WE are waging a bitter and inexorable war to ensure that the spirit of liberty and human dignity shall triumph over the Satanic forces that have set at nought all the laws of God and man. Until victory is made secure there can be no slackening or respite from our labours, but when the power of the tyrant and slave-driver has been utterly broken great tasks of reconstruction and regeneration will be before us, calling for enlightened and enthusiastic leadership.

Our universities have for generations been the training-ground of statesmen. They are zealous guardians of spiritual values. They encourage the quest of truth for truth's sake. They provide a stimulus to thought and opportunity for disputation, and an access to the knowledge which is essential to them. Out of these things, wedded to experience, is born a capacity for leadership in thought and action. I rejoice at the evidence that this conference affords of a revival of faith among the young in heart in Conservative principles. Conservatism has played a significant part in the progressive history of the British nation, and must exert a potent influence on the shaping of her future.

Answers in the House of Commons

DURING MARCH, 1943, MR. CHURCHILL ANSWERED IN THE HOUSE OF COMMONS QUESTIONS ADDRESSED TO THE SECRETARY OF STATE FOR FOREIGN AFFAIRS (MR. ANTHONY EDEN, WHO WAS ABSENT ON A VISIT TO THE UNITED STATES) IN ADDITION TO THOSE PUT TO HIM AS PRIME MINISTER. A SELECTION OF THE MORE IMPORTANT OF THESE ANSWERS IS GIVEN HERE.

[March 16, 1943

[MINISTERIAL OFFICES]

Replying to a member who suggested that the Ministry of War Transport should be given additional representation in the House of Commons, Mr. Churchill said:—

I CANNOT feel that the appointment of an additional Under-Secretary to the Ministry of War Transport would be justified. I understand that the Parliamentary Secretary has been absent from the House for a short time through illness, but he is now fully restored. Every effort should be made to keep Ministerial offices at a minimum, especially in times like these when the ordinary checks are not fully operative.

[SERVICE COMMANDS]

In reply to a member who suggested that "in view of the successful cohesion that has been achieved in the Middle East since the appointment of a Commander-in-Chief" the Prime Minister should now consider appointing a Commander-in-Chief in Britain and in other theatres of war, Mr. Churchill said:—

My hon. and gallant Friend is evidently under a misapprehension when he refers to the appointment of a Supreme Commander-in-Chief in the Middle East, since no such appointment has been made. I entirely agree that successful inter-Service cohesion has been achieved in that theatre, but I would point out that this is the result of intimate co-operation between all three Commanders-in-Chief (Navy, Army and Air). So far as the co-operation between the Army and the Air is concerned, the Commanders-in-Chief have worked in accordance with my ruling of 7th October, 1941, which I quoted to the House on 7th July, 1942. From this ruling has sprung a most successful co-operation between the Army and the Air in the Middle East. This relationship will be taken as a model for operations under British command elsewhere, and it is not proposed to make any changes at present in the system of command prevailing in the United Kingdom, India or the Persia-Iraq area.

[NOTE: *The ruling referred to was as follows: "Upon the Military Commander-in-Chief in the Middle East announcing that a battle is in prospect, the Air Officer Commanding-in-Chief will give him all possible aid irrespective of other targets, however attractive. The Army Commander-in-Chief will specify to the Air Officer Commanding-in-Chief the targets and tasks which he requires to be performed, both in the preparatory attack on the rearward installations of the enemy and for air action during the progress of the battle. It will be for the Air Officer Commanding-in-Chief to use his maximum force for these objects in the manner most effective. This applies not only to any squadrons assigned to Army co-operation permanently, but also to the whole air force available in the theatre."*]

[STATE FACTORIES]

Asked whether a statement by the President of the Board of Trade that State factories should be used for peace-time production represented the policy of the Government, Mr. Churchill said: —

I understand that my right hon. Friend, as reported in the Press, said that State factories should be retained wherever possible and adapted to suitable peace-time production; and that it was particularly necessary to consider those factories now es-

tablished in the former distressed areas. As the House will remember, my right hon. Friend developed this subject in some
detail, when replying for the Government in the debate on
Economic Policy on 3rd February last. He was speaking on that
occasion for the Government.

*When Mr. Shinwell asked whether it would not be useful if
the Prime Minister dissociated himself from the majority in his
party, Mr. Churchill replied: —*

I think it is very mischievous to try to cause disunity about this
matter.

[*March 17, 1943*

[BOMBS ON FRANCE]

*Asked whether the sufferings of French civilians had been
considered in the planning of air attacks on Lorient, Mr.
Churchill said: —*

AS I stated in this House on 11th February, the task of overcoming the U-boats has been given first priority in all the British
and American plans. The destruction of U-boat bases is an
essential part of this strategy. Very heavy blows have already been
delivered by the R.A.F. and the United States Army Air Corps
against the U-boat bases, both in Germany and in occupied
France. We have repeatedly urged the French population to
leave coastal areas. A large part of the civil population of Brest
and Lorient have in fact been evacuated, and the Germans have
attempted to conceal the severity of the raids from the German
crews expected to use Lorient. The qualities of resistance displayed by the French people day by day are well known, and I
have no doubt that they will understand that operations such
as the bombing of Lorient will bring victory nearer and thus
hasten the day of France's deliverance.

Answers in the House of Commons, March, 1943

[THE INTERNATIONAL BRIGADE]

Replying to a member who raised the question of the continued internment in French North Africa of members of the International Brigade and other anti-Fascists, Mr. Churchill said: —

His Majesty's Government are endeavouring to obtain the release of all political prisoners interned in North Africa, including, of course, members of the International Brigade.

[ANTI-U-BOAT WARFARE]

Asked to which department questions should be addressed concerning the work of Anti-U-Boat Committee, of which the Prime Minister was Chairman and the Minister of Aircraft Production, Vice-chairman, Mr. Churchill said: —

The Anti-U-Boat Warfare Committee in no way supersedes or replaces the regular and systematic control of anti-U-boat warfare by the Admiralty. Questions on this subject should therefore be addressed to the First Lord of the Admiralty, unless they raise wide strategic issues which would more appropriately be addressed to me as Minister of Defence.

The relations of the House are with Ministers of the Crown and not with the chairmen or heads of committees, Cabinet or otherwise, in their capacity as chairmen or heads of committees.

[RESPONSIBILITY FOR THE COLONIES]

Asked whether the views upon the future development of the British Colonial Empire expressed by the Colonial Secretary in a recent speech represented the Government policy, Mr. Churchill said: —

Yes, Sir. His Majesty's Government are convinced that the administration of the British Colonies must continue to be the sole responsibility of Great Britain. The policy of His Majesty's Government is to plan for the fullest possible political, economic, and social development of the Colonies within the British Empire, in close co-operation with neighbouring and friendly nations.

When the member then suggested that the Colonial Secretary's speech had been "of a somewhat truculent nature," Mr. Churchill commented: —

We must equally beware of truculence and grovelling.

When another member asked whether the Prime Minister still adhered to the principles of the Atlantic Charter, Mr. Churchill answered: —

Yes, of course.

Asked whether his answer precluded the Government's future consideration of international mandates, Mr. Churchill replied: —

We should be opposed to the idea of condominiums, which have always been found to bring about very bad results to the regions affected, but we naturally shall be in the closest touch and intercourse with our great Allies, whose interests are closely connected with our own in some parts of the world.

Asked whether the Dominions would also have a voice in the future of the Colonies, Mr. Churchill replied: —

They already have a considerable voice in the future of certain Colonies which come in their regions.

And to a member who asked whether the declaration meant that this country would not give up its occupied territories at the end of the war as Germany would have to do, Mr. Churchill replied: —

I think that would be a very insulting parallel to draw.

[NOTE: *In the speech which formed the subject of these questions, the Secretary of State for the Colonies, Colonel Oliver Stanley, told the Oxford Conservative Association that the administration of the British Colonies must continue to be the sole responsibility of Britain. His speech was a reply to what he described as "the great volume of friendly criticism and disinterested advice" from America.*]

[GENERAL GIRAUD'S SPEECH]

[NOTE: *General Giraud, leader of the French in North Africa, made a broadcast from Algiers on March 14, in which he pledged that the rights of the French people to choose their Provisional Government themselves, as soon as France was liberated, would be fully safeguarded. He promised that the Municipal Assemblies should resume their traditional role, with their members elected by the people, and announced that all racial distinctions in North Africa would be abrogated. He appealed for a union of all Frenchmen, and said he was ready to co-operate with all those who accepted the fundamental principles of which he had spoken. Asked to make a statement on this speech, Mr. Churchill said:* —

His Majesty's Government warmly welcome General Giraud's speech, in particular his repudiation of the armistice and his abolition of French legislation subsequent to 22nd June, 1940, as well as his decision that the municipal assemblies and the *Conseils Généraux* will resume their traditional role, with their members elected by the people, and his abrogation of all racial distinction between native, Moslem, and Jewish inhabitants.

In order to achieve the liberation of France through victory, Frenchmen everywhere must be united, and above all, all Frenchmen outside the Nazi power should act loyally against the common enemy without a day's needless delay. In view of General Giraud's speech and the National Committee's memorandum, it now appears that no questions of principle divide these two bodies of Frenchmen.

I have informed the United States Government that I was proposing to make this statement, and I have reason to believe that they are in entire agreement with it.

Asked whether General de Gaulle would accept General Giraud's invitation to visit him, Mr. Churchill said: —

I do not know at the present time, because I understand the invitation has gone through General Catroux, as head of the Mission, and General Catroux is at present moving about, but I trust that a meeting between the two Generals will be arranged in due course.

[GOVERNMENT DEPARTMENT HISTORIES]

*Asked to make a statement regarding the practice of Govern-
ment Departments employing historians to write up the war
histories of the Departments, Mr. Churchill said: —*

EXPERIENCE has shown the need for having available a
record of the development of war-time administration of Government Departments, and that such a record cannot be ade-
quately compiled if it is left entirely until the end of hostilities.
With this object in view, a number of appointments have been
made, under arrangements concerted generally by the Historical
Section of the War Cabinet Office, formerly of the Committee
of Imperial Defence. I am circulating in the OFFICIAL REPORT
a list of the Departments covered by these arrangements, which
may be extended as thought necessary to other Departments
whose war-time activities could with advantage be recorded in
this way.

*When a member asked whether in the histories of these Gov-
ernment Departments a few interpolations from outside sources
would be allowed, Mr. Churchill said: —*

There is no reason why persons in unofficial positions should
not compile histories of their own activities during the war, and
I trust I may be given the opportunity of making some interpolations of my own.

*Asked whether the Prime Minister himself was compiling notes
"for the great benefit of us all in the future," Mr. Churchill
replied: —*

My time is wholly given to the State.

[NOTE: *The list of Government Departments subsequently
circulated by the Prime Minister was as follows: —*

Ministry of Agriculture and Fisheries.
Ministry of Aircraft Production.

Colonial Office.
Ministry of Economic Warfare.
Board of Education.
Ministry of Food.
Foreign Office.
Ministry of Health.
Home Office.
Ministry of Home Security.
Ministry of Labour.
Ministry of Supply.
Board of Trade.
Treasury.
Ministry of War Transport.]

[THE SPEAKER'S SEAT]

Capt. E. A. Fitzroy, the Speaker of the House of Commons, died on March 3, 1943, and on March 18, a member asked whether the opportunity would be taken to review the question of the Speaker's constituency. Mr. Churchill replied: —

His Majesty's Government have no intention to review this matter at the present time. A Select Committee of this House reported on the question of Mr. Speaker's seat as recently as April, 1939. I refer my hon. and gallant Friend to the Report of that Committee. (House of Commons Paper 98 of 4th April, 1939.)

The matter was very carefully considered at the time of the last difficulty on this subject before the Report of the Committee which examined the problem, and it touches very deep-seated principles in the constitution of the House of Commons.

[NOTE: *The Select Committee, which reported in 1939, was appointed to consider whether any steps should be taken to en-sure that the Speaker of the House of Commons should not, while in office, be required to take part in a contested Parliamentary election in his constituency. The Committee decided that no such action was necessary, as such a change would be an infringe-ment of democratic principles and repugnant to the tradition of Parliament. The Committee rejected any proposal which would*

*reduce the Speaker to the status of an official, and also the scheme
for a special constituency for the Speaker.*]

[FARM WORKERS' COTTAGES]

*Replying to a member who drew attention to the fact that four
or more Ministries were dealing with the proposals for the erection of 3,000 cottages for farm workers, and asked whether effective co-ordination was being maintained, Mr. Churchill said:—*

Yes, Sir. I am assured that proper arrangements have been
made for effective co-ordination at the departmental, the regional, and the local government level, and that preparations
for the erection of these cottages are in fact proceeding as fast
as possible.

I am well aware of the need for building cottages, but that
need has to be fitted in with a great many other claims.

[*March 23, 1943*

[AXIS PEACE PROPOSALS]

*Asked to give an undertaking that no answer to any Axis
peace proposals should be made until the House of Commons
had had an opportunity of expressing its opinion of them, Mr.
Churchill said:—*

AN assurance of this kind would be contrary to constitutional usage, by which such issues are reserved to the Crown,
acting on the advice of Ministers, who are themselves responsible
to Parliament for their conduct.

[A POLITICAL PAMPHLET]

*Replying to a member who drew attention to a pamphlet
entitled "Square Meals and Square Deals" which, the questioner
stated, was by the Minister of Labour (Mr. Ernest Bevin), Mr.
Churchill said:—*

This is a Labour Party publication of a highly polemical character, with which His Majesty's Government are in no way concerned. It is open to any person or organisation to publish an extract from Hansard with what comments they please. As to the accuracy of any quotation made from our Debates, that is a matter to which attention can always be drawn in the course of political controversy. As to the insinuation made against the Minister of Labour that he was connected with this publication, I can give the most complete denial.

The member then drew attention to the wording of the pamphlet — "Square Meals and Square Deals, by the right hon. Ernest Bevin, M.P." — and Mr. Churchill commented: —

That is a most misleading and, in my opinion, most improper description, because it suggests that the Minister of Labour had written the offensive comments at the beginning and the end, whereas, of course, it refers literally to the quotations from the Minister's speech in Parliament.

Asked whether, in view of the bitterness aroused by this particular measure (the Catering Bill), the Prime Minister would consider not proceeding with it, Mr. Churchill replied: —

We shall certainly not be deterred from measures which are necessary because they arouse heat or bitterness.

Asked whether the Opposition was to understand that there had been "a little friction in the ranks of the Government," Mr. Churchill replied: —

Friction is healthy, and is widely and almost universally dispersed.

[March 25, 1943

[EUROPEAN RECONSTRUCTION]

Asked who was responsible for the selection and training of personnel for assistance in the reconstruction of Europe after the War, Mr. Churchill said: —

THE personnel to assist individual European Governments in the reconstruction of their countries will be recruited internationally. Until the number of British subjects required by such international agencies can be more accurately assessed, His Majesty's Government consider it inadvisable to initiate training schemes which would interfere with the war-time occupation of the candidates.

[SHIPPING LOSSES]

Replying to a member who urged that figures of shipping losses should be made known to the public, Mr. Churchill said: —

All sorts of claims are made by the German radio, and they would very much like to know how far adrift they are from the truth. But nothing would induce me, while I am responsible, to do anything to clarify enemy knowledge on this matter. I may however state for general reassurance that the United Nations have afloat to-day a substantially larger fleet than they had at the worst moment in the U-boat war, and that this improvement is continuous.

I think the public have pretty good confidence in the Government, and that it would be undesirable to add to the information which has been given. I feel that very strongly. I see the enemy making all sorts of absurd claims, and I much prefer to leave him in his delusions than to give him the accurate information to enable him to find out what success he has had with which attacks, and which submarine commanders were telling the truth, and so on.

If there is a general desire, I could say things in Secret Session that I should not be able to say outside, and I could, in particular, give an idea to the House of the difficulties we are encountering and are surmounting. On the other hand, I should not like, even in Secret Session, to give the facts.

[THE FOUR YEARS' PLAN]

Asked whether his broadcast statement that there would be a Four Years' Plan after the war based on a Coalition Govern-

ment represented the policy of the Government, Mr. Churchill replied: —

The answer about a Four Years' Plan is in the affirmative, but whether it will be put forward by a Coalition Government or not depends on what the various Parties decide to do.

[*March 30, 1943*]

[DEPUTATIONS TO MINISTERS]

Asked whether he had completed his inquiry into the refusal of the Minister of Labour to receive Members of Parliament in deputation unless accompanied by a trade union official, Mr. Churchill said: —

I HAVE now looked into this matter as I promised, and have discussed it fully with the Minister of Labour. The position is as follows. On 25th May, 1940, in the deadly crisis of the war, the Minister of Labour met the executives of all the trade unions at a conference at the Central Hall, and appealed to them to join with the Government in increasing production, preventing strikes or lock-outs, and facilitating and speeding up procedure so as to avoid difficulties arising. The Minister then, with the authority of the Government, gave a pledge, not in any way subsequently challenged in the House of Commons, that so far as His Majesty's Government were concerned they would deal with these problems through the executives of the respective organisations. This was followed by a conference of both the parties, the Trades Union Congress and the British Employers' Confederation. As a result of these negotiations, which must be taken as a whole, the parties agreed to accept compulsory arbitration, and this was embodied in an Order, No. 1305, made under Defence Regulations.

It would, in my opinion, be a breach of this understanding, from which we have derived and are deriving enormous benefit, if the Minister of Labour were to allow the official representatives of the trade unions to be by-passed, and were to discuss or negotiate with unofficial bodies, behind the backs of the responsible representatives of the unions, in respect of any of the matters covered directly or indirectly by Defence Regulation No. 1305.

I must make it clear that His Majesty's Government is working hand in hand with the Trades Union Congress in this task of beating down Hitler and Nazism, and that both sides intend to stand strictly to their engagements until this great quarrel is brought to a satisfactory conclusion.

On the other hand, the Minister of Labour assures me that he is always ready to see any Member of Parliament on any subject, as is the usual practice, and he has, in fact, seen Members repeatedly on these very subjects.

There is no constitutional obligation upon Ministers to receive any particular deputations, whether headed by Members of Parliament or not; I believe, however, that the practice of Ministers in making themselves as accessible as possible to Members of this House works smoothly, and that there are no serious reasons for departing from our usual methods. If any hon. Members have grounds for dissatisfaction at any time there are Parliamentary opportunities for raising such matters. I must make it clear, however, that so far as His Majesty's present advisers are concerned, we consider ourselves pledged by the negotiations of May, 1940, and we shall ask the House to support us in this view, which we regard as essential to the war effort.

[THE WAR FRONTS]

Asked to state on how many fronts His Majesty's Land, Sea and Air Forces are engaged or in position, Mr. Churchill said: —

His Majesty's Land Forces are at the moment actively engaged on three fronts — in North Africa, in Burma, and in the South-West Pacific. It would not be in the public interest to state on what other fronts they are in position. So far as His Majesty's Sea and Air Forces are concerned, the term "front" is hardly appropriate. His Majesty's ships have to operate continuously on all the oceans of the globe. The areas in which our Air Forces are engaged may be defined as follows: —

Western Europe.
The Atlantic.
The Mediterranean.
India and Burma.
The Pacific.

Replying to another member who asked that the use of "that very misleading phrase 'Second Front'" should be discontinued, the Prime Minister said: —

No, Sir, I do not want to discourage the use of it, because our good friends, fighting so hard, know very well what they mean by it.

[*March 31, 1943*

[ROAD REGULATION]

Replying to a member who asked whether his attention had been drawn to the fact that Statutory Rule and Order No. 2533 of 1942 was made under the Defence Regulations when precisely similar powers had been provided for such an Order under the Road Traffic Act, 1930, and whether he would give an assurance that Orders made under the Defence Regulations would not in future be used for the purpose of indirectly increasing penalties in cases where the law was not otherwise changed, Mr. Churchill said: —

WHILE it is possible that a Regulation in similar terms might have been made under Section 30 of the Road Traffic Act, 1930, that provision was designed for the regulation of traffic in peace-time in the interests of public safety and the prevention of damage to road surfaces, and it would have been inappropriate to use it to meet a war-time need for which it was never intended. The sole purpose of the Order to which my hon. Friend refers is to conserve rubber as a measure of war economy, and as such it is appropriate that it should be made under the Defence Regulations. The suggestion in the second part of the Question does not therefore arise.

Honorary R.A.F. Wings

IN MARCH, 1943, THE AIR COUNCIL, WITH THE KING'S AP-
PROVAL, AWARDED HONORARY WINGS, THE FLYING BADGE
OF THE ROYAL AIR FORCE, TO THE PRIME MINISTER.
MR. CHURCHILL ACKNOWLEDGED THIS HONOUR IN THE
FOLLOWING LETTER TO AIR MARSHAL SIR BERTINE SUTTON,
AIR MEMBER FOR PERSONNEL

[April 1, 1943

DEAR Air Marshal Sutton,

I take it as a high compliment that the Air Council should wish to give one of their honorary commodores his honorary wings. I value this distinction the more because it comes to me on the twenty-fifth anniversary of the formation of the Royal Air Force. My memories go back six years earlier, when in 1912, as First Lord of the Admiralty, I began to cherish the Royal Naval Air Service.

I consider that Marshal of the Royal Air Force Lord Trenchard is the founder of the Royal Air Force. He it was who proposed to me, when I was Air Minister in 1919, that Mesopotamia should be held by air power, thus releasing a number of army divisions, which cost us £40,000,000 a year to maintain in that country. This proved, in a manner patent to all intelligent minds, the immense part which the air would play not only in war but in peace.

Since those now distant days, we have had the epic of the Battle of Britain, upon which, under Providence, the freedom of the world, perhaps for several generations, was staked. The name of Sir Hugh Dowding is linked with this historic episode.

At this moment we may say without vanity that the Royal Air Force — taken for all in all — is "Second to None." At this moment it is the spearpoint of the British offensive against the proud and cruel enemy who boasted that he would "erase" the cities of our native land, and hoped to lay all the lands under his toll and thrall. As the world conflict deepens, the war future of the Royal Air Force glows with a still brighter and fiercer light.

I am honoured to be accorded a place, albeit out of kindness, in that comradeship of the air which guards the life of our island and carries doom to tyrants, whether they flaunt themselves or burrow deep.

WINSTON S. CHURCHILL.

Help for Refugees

A WRITTEN ANSWER TO A MEMBER OF PARLIAMENT WHO ASKED WHAT HELP THE BRITISH EMPIRE HAD GIVEN TO REFUGEES, APRIL 7, 1943

[April 7, 1943

AT the outbreak of war the number of adult refugees from Germany and Austria in this country was approximately 55,000. A large number of these had children, and, further, there were more than 13,000 child refugees who had been admitted without their parents. In addition, nearly 10,000 Czecho-slovak nationals had found a refuge in this country during the 12 months preceding the war. Since the outbreak of war there have been, it is estimated, the following admissions of aliens who came as refugees from enemy and enemy-occupied countries, namely: In 1940, about 35,000; in 1941, more than 13,000; and in 1942, over 15,000. The total number of these refugees in the three years 1940–42 thus amounted to more than 63,000. This total includes about 20,000 seamen, but is exclusive of the very large numbers who have come as members of Allied Forces. If all the children who came with their parents are allowed for, the total of refugees who were here at the beginning of the war or who have come here since is approximately 150,000.

The sum spent on refugees out of Government grants from the National Exchequer between 1st October, 1939, and 31st December, 1942, amounted to £1,210,000. This does not include the expenditure incurred by the Ministry of Health, as no separate record is kept of the cost falling on this Department in respect of the accommodation and support of alien, as distinct from British, refugees. From 1933 to the present date the contributions in money and kind from private sources are estimated at not less than £9,500,000. Large numbers of British subjects, for example those from the Channel Islands and Gibraltar, have had to be given refuge and be maintained in the United Kingdom.

Colonial and United Kingdom Mandated Territories

The latest figures for those principally concerned may be summarised as follows: —

1. *Jamaica.* — Additional population maintained is 3,058; this includes 558 refugees, 1,500 evacuees from Gibraltar and a number of prisoners of war and civilian internees.

2. *Cyprus.* — Additional population maintained is 4,830 (including 4,650 refugees from Greece).

3. *East African Colonies.* — Additional population, including Italian prisoners of war and Polish refugees, 90,964, nearly three times the normal white population. Polish refugees, moved or in the process of being moved from Persia, amount to 21,000, and are distributed between Uganda, Tanganyika, Northern Rhodesia and Nyasaland. Camps in Kenya and Tanganyika have accommodated 3,000 Greek refugees in transit from the Greek mainland via Turkey and Egypt to the Belgian Congo.

Palestine

Over 18,000 legal immigrants reached Palestine between 1st April, 1939, and 30th September, 1942. The total number of Jewish immigrants who entered the country during that period, including illegal immigrants, was about 38,000 and the great majority of these came from countries in Central and Eastern Europe. The quota for the period ended 30th September, 1942, provided for the grant of 1,000 certificates, 800 of them being allocated to Polish-Jewish refugee children in Persia. Actually 858 children, accompanied by 369 adults, reached Palestine from Persia on the 18th February last. The immigration quota for the three months' period ending 31st December, 1942, provides for 3,000 Jewish immigrants, and this includes 1,000 orphan children and 200 adults from former Vichy France. In addition arrangements have been made to admit Jewish children from Roumania and Hungary, and it has now been decided to admit further children from these countries up to a total of 500.

The Government of Palestine have agreed to admit from Bulgaria 4,000 Jewish children and 500 adults, and the necessary negotiations for their release and transport are taking place through the Protecting Power. As the Secretary of State for the Colonies announced on 3rd February, His Majesty's Government are prepared, provided the necessary transport is available, to continue to admit into Palestine Jewish children with a proportion of accompanying adults, up to the limits of immigration permissible for the five-year period ending 31st March, 1944, that is up to approximately 29,000. In addition Palestine has provided a temporary refuge during the war for some 4,000 people from Central Europe and Greece.

India

India has provided accommodation, and where necessary, support for over 400,000 evacuees. The bulk of this number is of Indian origin, but she has also received large numbers of evacuees from the Balkans, Malta and other areas, covering many nationalities. She has already received 1,000 Polish refugee children, and has undertaken to provide for 5,000 Polish adults and 5,000 more Polish children.

Grand Total

The total number of refugees, evacuees, and additional population in the form of internees and prisoners of war maintained in British territory and Palestine (but exclusive of the Dominions and of the very large numbers who have come as members of the Allied forces) amounts to 682,700. It will be appreciated that a great part of the work on behalf of the refugees indicated in this statement has been carried through by Government and local authorities, and by private generosity, under exceptional conditions, with all the well-known difficulties of food supplies, accommodation and restrictions occasioned by enemy action or the demands of the war effort. The resources of Great Britain have been strained to the utmost in maintaining her traditions of asylum and hospitality, while subjected to intensive enemy attack and forming not only a base for offensive operations, but an armed camp to an extent far beyond anything in her previous history.

General de Gaulle's Visit to Africa

A STATEMENT ISSUED BY THE PRIME MINISTER FROM NO. 10, DOWNING STREET, FOLLOWING THE POSTPONEMENT OF THE MEETING BETWEEN GENERAL DE GAULLE, LEADER OF THE FIGHTING FRENCH, AND GENERAL GIRAUD, FRENCH HIGH COMMISSIONER FOR NORTH AFRICA

APRIL 7, 1943

[April 7, 1943

WITH regard to the statement issued by the French National Committee on Monday last about the delay imposed on General de Gaulle's visit to North Africa, the Prime Minister wishes it to be known that he has been throughout in the fullest agreement with General Eisenhower in deprecating a visit by General de Gaulle during the battle crisis in Tunisia, which requires the undivided attention of the Allied High Command.

Messages

DEATH OF GENERAL WELVERT

[*April 15, 1943*

[A MESSAGE TO GENERAL GIRAUD]

I SHARE your sorrow at the death of General Welvert during a victorious action at the head of a French division. Please convey this message of respect from the British Army to the French soldiers whom he was leading to the liberation of France.

EXECUTION OF U.S. AIRMEN

[*April 23, 1943*

[A MESSAGE TO GENERAL ARNOLD, CHIEF OF THE UNITED STATES ARMY AIR FORCES, FOLLOWING THE EXECUTION BY THE JAPANESE OF AMERICAN AIRMEN WHO RAIDED TOKIO]

I HAVE read with indignation of the cold-blooded execution of your airmen by the Japanese. This barbarous and unusual action reveals in a peculiarly significant manner the fear the Japanese have of having the munition factories and other military objectives in their homeland bombed. I cannot resist sending you this message to assure you that the Royal Air Force earnestly look forward to the day when they will be able to fly side by side with their American comrades to attack Tokyo and other cities of Japan, and strip this cruel and greedy nation of their power to molest the civilised world. We shall certainly claim for our airmen a full share in this task, which, however long it takes, must be thoroughly done by the combined forces of both our peoples.

"YOU GAVE US THE TOOLS"

[April 30, 1943

[A MESSAGE TO THE UNITED STATES CHAMBER OF COMMERCE AT ITS ANNUAL DINNER IN NEW YORK]

PLEASE allow me to extend to American management and labour my warmest and deepest appreciation of what it has accomplished since your last meeting in supplying the materials of war to the men on the Allied fighting fronts.

We asked for the tools. You gave them to us. Without the constant flow from your factories to supplement our own output, the Allied armies could not have gained the remarkable victories of the last six months. Without the ships that you have built and are building on a prodigious scale, the life-lines of civilisation across the oceans of the world would have worn thin, if indeed they had not snapped. All our future efforts to accomplish the purposes of this righteous war against aggression, and to bring it to a final decision at the earliest moment, depend upon the faithful exertions of the munition plants and kindred industries of every description. These will assuredly be forthcoming in generous measure from all true friends of freedom, and with them we may move forward together in comradeship, and indeed in brotherhood, through the overthrow of our embattled enemies in Europe and Asia, to that brighter age which is our hearts' desire.

[*April 1, 1943*

[U–BOAT WARFARE DEBATE]

Replying to a member who urged that the conduct of the anti-U-boat war should be debated at an early date, Mr. Churchill said: —

I SHOULD deprecate a discussion upon this subject. Certainly it would be quite impossible in public, and even in Secret Session I should feel very much hampered in stating the full case. I must ask for a measure of confidence.

[*April 6, 1943*

[POST–WAR AIRCRAFT]

Replying to a member who asked whether the manufacture of civil aircraft would be nationalised after the war, and urged that Parliament should be consulted before any final decision was taken, Mr. Churchill said: —

HIS Majesty's Government have taken no decision about the nationalisation after the war of the manufacture of aircraft, whether for civilian or military purposes. I cannot conceive that the Government would embark upon such a policy with all its implications without consulting not only the House but the country. There is no intention to use the war-time powers to prejudice unjustly any existing firm or their shareholders. Decisions as to the future policy of the State in time of peace must be taken on general grounds and by regular constitutional means, and not as a result of the application of war-time measures in particular instances.

Our policy is everything for the war and, after the war is won fair, free review under normal political conditions.

[SCOTTISH BUSINESS]

Replying to a member who asked that the House of Commons should devote more time to the discussion of Scottish business or that the Scottish Grand Committee should be re-established for the discussion of purely Scottish business, Mr. Churchill said: —

I am not aware of any grounds for reconsidering at present the time allotted to the discussion of purely Scottish business, which does not appear to have suffered restriction in comparison with other Business of the House as a result of war-time conditions. In the present abnormal circumstances the Government feel it impracticable to refer Bills to Standing Committees, for reasons which will be readily understood in all quarters of the House.

When another member said: "All that we are after is justice for Scotland," Mr. Churchill replied: —

It is the most earnest desire of the Government that justice in the fullest measure should be given to that gallant nation.

[LORD REITH]

Asked in what way the services of Lord Reith (who had formerly held posts as Director General of the British Overseas Airways Corporation, Minister of Information, Minister of Transport and Minister of Works and Buildings) were now being utilised, Mr. Churchill wrote: —

As a Peer of the Realm the whole field of Parliamentary duties and activities is open to Lord Reith. I understand also that he has undertaken work under the Admiralty with the rank of temporary lieutenant-commander. I should be very glad if opportunity arose of making use of his services in a wider sphere, but these are not matters which can suitably be ventilated at Question time.

[U–BOAT WARFARE]

Replying to a member who drew attention to the U.S. Secretary of the Navy's statement that shipping losses in March exceeded those in February, and who added that there was "considerable disquiet" about the statement, Mr. Churchill said: —

My attention has been drawn to this statement. I agree with Colonel Knox that the results of U-boat warfare are serious, as they always must be. His statement, however, refers to a limited period following one in which sinkings were comparatively small. Viewing the battle against the U-boats as a whole, I can repeat my previous assurance that we are more than holding our own.

I do not want to give exact information, which would be of great advantage to the enemy; but a great deal of information of a general character has been given upon the subject. I do not believe that the disquiet is more serious than it naturally would be at a time when this form of warfare is being levied upon us, and certainly, if it were, there is no ground for it.

When the member then drew attention to a statement by the Minister of Aircraft Production that "we have not mastered the U-boat," Mr. Churchill added: —

The actual significance of the word "master" is, of course, open to discussion. I should prefer my phrase "more than holding our own."

[EMPIRE ECONOMIC POLICY]

Replying to a member who suggested the formation of a Council of the British Empire, composed of representatives of Great Britain, the Dominions, India and the Colonial Empire, which would direct the economic policy of the British Empire as a whole, Mr. Churchill said: —

It is, of course, the established policy to maintain the closest co-operation and contact with the Governments of the Empire on all economic questions of common concern. Having regard, however, to the responsibility which must rest with the respective Governments and Parliaments, a centralised executive body such as that suggested would not be practicable.

[WINNING THE PEACE]

When a member said: "Is the Prime Minister aware that while he is using up his genius and undoubted energy in winning the war, the big industrialists and big financiers are taking care that they win the peace?" and asked "What is the Prime Minister going to do to prevent terrible disaster such as happened after the last war?" Mr. Churchill replied: —

A firm reliance on representative government and Parliamentary institutions, based on the operation of practically universal suffrage.

[DR. EVATT'S VISIT]

Asked whether Dr. Evatt, Australian Minister for External Affairs, would be invited to attend meetings of the War Cabinet during his visit to this country, Mr. Churchill said: —

Yes, Sir. At the request of the Prime Minister of the Commonwealth of Australia, Dr. Evatt will attend meetings of the War Cabinet as accredited representative of the Commonwealth Government during his stay in this country.

[April 15, 1943

[WAR PENSIONS]

Urged to set up a Select Committee of the House to consider War Pensions, Mr. Churchill said: —

I SHOULD not be justified in placing upon this House and on the Minister of Pensions the very heavy burden which would inevitably result from the appointment of a Select Committee, unless the main principles of the war pensions system were the subject of serious controversy. Such questions as have been raised in Debate or otherwise do not affect essential principles, but are rather concerned with matters which fall properly within the scope of existing machinery. I understand that my right hon. Friend has already brought a number of these questions before his Central Advisory Committee, on which the various parties in this House are well represented, and that others are being put down for discussion at future meetings. This procedure is likely to be much more expeditious than the deliberations of a Select Committee.

Replying to another member who said the recent debate on pensions had produced nothing but criticisms, Mr. Churchill said: —

During the whole of my service in this House I have never known any occasion when a Debate on pensions has not given universal dissatisfaction.

[NORTHERN IRELAND CONSCRIPTION]

Replying to a member who said that conscription should be extended to Northern Ireland, where between 20,000 and 25,000 men and women of military age were unemployed, Mr. Churchill said: —

I understand that, according to the latest information, the number of men and women of all ages registered as unemployed in Northern Ireland was 19,778.

When this matter was last raised, about 18 months or two years ago, I think, I came to the conclusion that it would be more trouble than it was worth, and I have not seen any reason up to the present moment for making a pronouncement on the subject.

Certainly, it is a very unsatisfactory situation when large numbers of Americans are taken by compulsion from their homes and made to stand on guard while large numbers of local inhabitants are under no such obligation.

[BOMBING OF U-BOAT BASES]

Asked what damage had been done to submarine shelters at Lorient and St. Nazaire by the recent intensive bombing, Mr. Churchill said: —

Some damage has been done to the shelters, but serious damage was not expected. The object of the attacks was to cause dislocation to the repair, transport and power facilities afforded by these bases to U-boats. In this respect a considerable measure of success has been achieved.

[POLITICAL TRUCE]

Replying to a member who asked him to advise that the political truce at by-elections should be terminated, Mr. Churchill said: —

The truce at by-elections was decided upon by the main political parties in the time of my precedessor. It followed therefore that when a national coalition was formed, in which all three parties officially participated with full representation in Ministerial office, the foundations and authority of the truce should be even more firmly established. The only advice I have to offer is that all those who are resolute to see the war through to a victorious conclusion should avail themselves of every occasion to mark their disapproval of truce-breakers.

I conceive that a Government must stand together as long as it is constituted on a regular constitutional basis.

When the member pointed out that the truce was creating a number of small political groups, Mr. Churchill replied: —

I cannot think these small political groups will live very long after the great parties divide and set about each other. I think that will at any rate exercise a salutary effect in clearing no-man's-land.

[MINISTERS' SPEECHES]

When a member stated that public relations officers in Government Departments prepared speeches made by their Ministers in the country and asked whether public funds should be ex-pended for such purposes, Mr. Churchill replied: —

I have no official knowledge of the methods used by Ministers or indeed by Members in the preparation of their speeches, and I am certainly not going to inquire into the matter.

[NORTHERN IRELAND AT WAR]

Asked whether Northern Ireland was a belligerent or non-belligerent state, Mr. Churchill wrote: ·

Northern Ireland is not a separate state but an integral part of the United Kingdom, and no separate declaration of war in respect of Northern Ireland was necessary. War with Germany was declared on 3rd September, 1939.

[April 20, 1943

[CHURCH BELLS BAN REMOVED]

Replying to a member who asked for a statement on the re-sumption of ringing of church bells, Mr. Churchill said: —

THE War Cabinet, after receiving the advice of the Chiefs of Staff, have reviewed this question in the light of changing cir-cumstances. We have reached the conclusion that the existing orders on the subject can now be relaxed, and that the church bells should be rung on Sundays and other special days in the ordinary manner to summon worshippers to church. This new arrangement will be brought into effect in time for the Easter celebrations this year.

[CHANCELLOR OF THE DUCHY OF LANCASTER]

Replying to a member who asked what were the present func-tions of the Chancellor of the Duchy of Lancaster (Mr. Duff Cooper), Mr. Churchill said: —

Besides attending to the affairs of the Duchy of Lancaster, which are the ordinary duties of the Chancellor, my right hon. Friend is Chairman of the Security Executive.

Asked if he would state what salary attached to the post, Mr. Churchill replied:—

Yes, certainly, but reference to any of the official publications would have supplied the answer. I thought it was well known that the Chancellor of the Duchy is not paid by the taxpayers. His salary of £2,000 a year comes out of the revenue of the Duchy, that is to say, out of the Privy Purse.

When another member asked whether the £2,000 was the total salary, Mr. Churchill replied:—

Yes, Sir, the total amount. No extra salary is paid to my right hon. Friend for his very arduous and laborious work at the head of the Security Executive. This has been a matter of concern.

[DISCHARGED SERVICEMEN (NEUROSIS)]

Replying to a member who asked whether Service Departments when discharging men on grounds of neurosis or mental instability informed civil authorities of the facts of each case, and whether the civil authorities took steps to protect such men from the consequences of actions for which they may not be responsible, Mr. Churchill said:—

A scheme is at present being developed by which any man or woman discharged from any of the three Services on grounds of neurosis or temporary instability who appears likely to need social service care can receive it. This may imply medical treatment, the finding of suitable work, or other help. The discharged man will at his own request be put in touch with a suitable civilian social agency. Work of this type has already been done informally, but it is hoped in future to make it much more widely available. The Ministry of Pensions is fully informed of the facts relating to all discharges, and arranges continuance of hospital treatment where necessary. It is neither desirable nor legally correct to notify medical facts about individuals who are discharged to civil authorities in any automatic way.

[TRADE DISPUTES ACT]

Asked for a report on the consultations over the Trade Unions and the Trade Disputes Act, Mr. Churchill said: —

THE Government cannot make themselves responsible for reporting to the House upon discussions of this character.

Asked to state the Government's intentions, Mr. Churchill said: —

I certainly could not make a statement on Government policy in reply to a supplementary on a matter which raises many large, far-reaching, and even delicate issues.

When the member then asked for an assurance that "consideration will be given to the matter," the Prime Minister replied: —

Consideration is always given by the Government to every matter, especially to those which seem to have a bearing on the general march of national cohesion and unity.

And added, after an interruption by another member: —

Consideration in no way implies conclusion.

[QUESTIONS ABOUT THE B.B.C.]

Asked whether arrangements would be made to enable Governors of the British Broadcasting Corporation to answer Questions in the House of Commons for that part of the B.B.C.'s activities over which the Minister of Information has no control in the same way that the Forestry and Charity Commissioners reply for their respective departments, Mr. Churchill said: —

No, Sir. The present arrangements enable Parliament to be informed as to any matters of general policy affecting the British Broadcasting Corporation; but it has never been contemplated that matters affecting the day-to-day administration of the Corporation should be the subject of Question and Answer in the

House. There is no analogy with the Forestry Commission and the Charity Commission, which are Government Departments.

Replying to another member who pointed out that the B.B.C. drew its finances through Government Departments and that therefore the House was responsible for its expenditure, Mr. Churchill replied: —

There are a great many public bodies and corporations which are directly or indirectly supplied by moneys under the control of Parliament which do not have Ministerial representatives.

Asked for an assurance that close Government control of the B.B.C. would go after the war, Mr. Churchill said: —

Let us get there first.

[April 22, 1943

[SALUTING IN LONDON]

Asked if he would abolish saluting in London and other large cities because of its embarrassing frequency, Mr. Churchill said: —

No, Sir. A salute is an acknowledgment of the King's Commission and a courtesy to Allied officers, and I do not consider it desirable to differentiate between one city or town and another in this matter.

[CHURCH BELLS]

Replying to questions regarding the Government's decision not to use church bells as warning of an invasion, Mr. Churchill said: —

We have come to the conclusion that this particular method of warning was redundant, and not in itself well adapted to the present conditions of the war.

Replacement does not arise. For myself, I cannot help feeling that anything like a serious invasion would be bound to leak out.

The improbability of invasion depends on the high degree of preparation maintained in this country.

[REGIMENTATION AND COMPULSION]

Asked for an assurance that the existing methods of regimentation and compulsion would be relaxed at the earliest possible date after the war, Mr. Churchill said: —

The transition from war to peace will no doubt bring many changes in its train; but I do not desire at present to expatiate unduly on these topics.

Victory in North Africa

April 8. *All Allied forces advanced in Tunisia, the British
First Army reaching to within 27 miles of Tunis.*

April 10. *The Tunisia advance continued and the Eighth
Army swept on past Sfax.*

April 11. *It was revealed that Hitler and Mussolini had
conferred from April 7 to 10.*

April 12. *Kairouan and Sousse were occupied by the Eighth
Army, while a great Allied air offensive was maintained on the Axis troops in Tunisia and the sea
and air routes from Sicily. It was also announced
that British submarines had sunk eight Axis ships.*

 *Budget changes included 100 per cent. purchase
tax on luxuries and increased duties on tobacco,
beer, spirits and wines.*

April 13. *General Blamey, commanding Allied land forces
in the South-West Pacific, said the Japanese were
massing nearly 200,000 men North of Australia.*

April 15. *Total of Axis prisoners taken since the first attack
on the Mareth Line reached 30,000.*

April 16. *Mussolini announced that Sicily and Sardinia
were "Operational areas."*

 *Russians resumed their offensive against the
last German positions in the Kuban, and crossed
the river.*

April 19. *Seventy-four German aircraft, including 58 huge
transports, were destroyed by Allied fighters near
Cape Bon, Tunisia, while other heavy air attacks
were made on Sicily and Sardinia.*

April 21. The Eighth Army, in a new push, captured En-fidaville and all initial objectives.

It was officially announced in Washington that some of the American airmen captured after the raid on Tokio a year ago were executed by the Japanese.

April 24. Documents captured in Tunisia showed that Rommel had left Africa and that Von Arnim was in command.

April 25. All Allied gains in Tunisia were consolidated, and patrol activity showed that new attacks were imminent.

April 26. U.S.S.R. broke off diplomatic relations with the Polish Government on the ground that they had upheld German allegations of Russian atrocities against Polish officers.

One of the heaviest raids of the war was made when the R.A.F. attacked Duisburg and dropped bombs at the rate of 30 tons a minute.

April 27. General Sikorski conferred with Mr. Churchill and Mr. Eden on the Russo-Polish situation.

April 30. Agreements with Admiral Robert, French commander in Martinique, were repudiated by the U.S. Government and the U.S. Consul-General was recalled.

May 1. British submarines and Allied aircraft operating against Axis supply lines to Tunisia sank 15 more ships.

R.A.F.'s bombs on Essen reached total of 10,000 tons.

May 3. Mateur, important centre of enemy communications in Tunisia, was captured by the Americans.

May 4. R.A.F. dropped 1,500 tons of bombs on Dortmund, Ruhr industrial and transport centre.

May 5. Stalin declared that Russia wanted to see a strong, independent Poland after the war, and would favour a Russo-Polish alliance of mutual assistance.

May 6.   *The Allied armies launched their great decisive offensive in Tunisia.*

May 7.   *Tunis and Bizerta were captured by the Allies, many thousands of prisoners being taken.*

May 8.   *R.A.F. Spitfires smashed an attempt to make a daylight raid on London.*

May 9.   *Great Tunisia advance continued, Axis prisoners taken in three days totalling 50,000.*

Japanese thrust in Western Burma forced British troops to withdraw from Buthidaung.

May 10.   *Navy blockaded Cape Bon peninsula to prevent enemy troops escaping from Tunisia by sea. On land the Allied armies continued to advance.*

May 11.   *It was revealed that Mr. Churchill, accompanied by Service chiefs, including Sir A. Wavell, had arrived in Washington to confer with President Roosevelt.*

May 12.   *End of the war in North Africa. All organised resistance by Axis troops ceased. General Von Arnim, German commander-in-chief, was among the huge number of prisoners.*

R.A.F. carried out the war's heaviest air raid, dropping nearly 2,000 tons of bombs on Germany, mainly on Duisburg.

[*May 11, 1943*

[TO GENERAL EISENHOWER, COMMANDER–IN–CHIEF OF THE ALLIED FORCES IN NORTH AFRICA]

LET me add my heartfelt congratulations to those which have been sent to you by His Majesty and the War Cabinet on the brilliant result of the North African campaign by the army under your supreme direction. The comradeship and conduct with which you have sustained troops engaged in the fierce and prolonged battle in Tunisia and the perfect understanding and harmony preserved amidst the shock of war between British and United States forces and with our French Allies have prove solid foundation of victory. The simultaneous advance of Britis and United States armies side by side into Tunis and Bizerta an augury full of hope for the future of the world. Long ma they march together, striking down the tyrants and oppressors mankind.

[TO GENERAL ALEXANDER, DEPUTY COMMANDE IN-CHIEF OF THE ALLIED FORCES IN NORTH AFRIC

It has fallen to you to conduct a series of battles which ha ended in the destruction of the German and Italian power i Africa. All the way from Alamein to Tunis, in the ceasele fighting and marching of the last six months, you and you brilliant lieutenant, Montgomery, have added a glorious chapt to the annals of the British Commonwealth and Empire. You combinations in the final great battle will be judged by histor as a model of the military art. But more than this, you hav known how to inspire your soldiers with confidence and ardou which overcame all obstacles and outlasted all fatigue and har ship. They and their trusty United States and French Allie soldiers and airmen together can now be told of the admiratio and the gratitude with which the entire British nation and th Empire regard them and their famous deeds. The generou rivalry in arms of the First and Eighth British Armies ha achieved victory, with full honour for each and for all.

[TO AIR CHIEF MARSHAL TEDDER, AIR COMMANDER-IN-CHIEF, MEDITERRANEAN]

It is certain the victories in Tunisia would never have bee gained without the splendid exertions of the Allied Air Forc under your skilful and comprehending direction. Will you te Spaatz, Coningham, Doolittle, and Broadhurst how much thei work is admired. The united, efficient, and individual devotio to duty which enables so amazing a number of sorties to be mad each day is beyond all praise.

Victory in North Africa, May 11, 1943

[TO GENERAL GIRAUD, COMMANDER-IN-CHIEF FRENCH FORCES IN NORTH AFRICA]

It cheers all our hearts to see a line of French divisions advancing triumphantly against the common foe, and leading German prisoners by the thousand to the rear. Accept my most hearty congratulations on the fighting spirit of the French Army under your command, and the tenacity in defence and aggression in assault which it has displayed in spite of being at a disadvantage in equipment. Every good wish.

The Home Guard

A BROADCAST FROM THE UNITED STATES OF AMERICA
ON THE THIRD ANNIVERSARY OF THE FORMATION
OF BRITAIN'S HOME GUARD
MAY 14, 1943

[May 14, 1943

I HAVE felt for some time a great desire that a tribute should be paid throughout Great Britain and in Ulster to the faithful, unwearying, and absolutely indispensable work done by the Home Guard month after month, and year after year. Accordingly, next Sunday, military parades and religious services will be held throughout the land, to associate the nation and the Home Guard in the celebration of its first three years of life.

As we move through these tremendous times, with their swift succession of formidable, or glittering, events, we must not overlook, or consider as matters of mere routine, those unceasing daily and nightly efforts of millions of men and women which constitute the foundation of our capacity to wage this righteous war wherever it may carry us, all over the world.

All British war energies depend upon the unfailing defence and adequate nourishment of our small island home, which lies only 21 miles from the German batteries, and only a few minutes' flight from their airfields. Great Britain is the advanced fighting base of the United Nations, and is still under constant siege and assault by air and sea.

It is in a very large measure the power-house and directing centre of the whole of the British Commonwealth and Empire; it is the source of a vast output of war equipment; it is the home and cradle of the Navy; from its ports sail the convoys which carry forth the expeditionary armies, and to them come the food and supplies by which our tense, organised, vibrant life is sustained. In this home there burns the light of freedom — guard it well, Home Guard!

The Home Guard, May 14, 1943

Our eyes are fixed upon the future, but we may spare a moment to glance back to those past days of 1940, which are so strangely imprinted upon our memories that we can hardly tell whether they are near or far away. In those days of May and June, and July, in that terrible summer, when we stood alone, and as the world thought, forlorn, against the all-powerful aggressor with his vast armies and masses of equipment, Mr. Anthony Eden, as Secretary of State for War, called upon the Local Defence Volunteers to rally round the searchlight positions. Shot-guns, sporting rifles, and staves, were all they could find for weapons; it was not until July that we ferried safely across the Atlantic the 1,000,000 rifles and 1,000 field guns, with ammunition proportionable, which were given to us by the Government and people of the United States by an act of precious and timely succour.

You will remember how we had special trains waiting to carry the rifles to all the Home Guard areas, and how you worked night and day to clean them from the grease in which they had been stored for a generation; you will remember how we hardly dared to fire a round for practice, so dire was the stringency; but this was the great turning-point in your story, and I asked that your name should be changed and that you should assume the proud title of Home Guard.

Thenceforward, at any rate, you had military weapons in your hands; thenceforward, when imagining the horrors of a Hun invasion, there rose that last consoling thought which rises naturally in unconquerable races and in unenslavable men resolved to go down fighting — "you can always take one with you."

Very different is our condition to-day; we are an armed people. The strength of the Home Guard has risen steadily, clothing and equipment are complete. Instead of the shot-guns and home-made bombs, most now have rifles or Sten guns or machine-guns, or serve in the anti-tank or anti-aircraft teams. Ammunition, long so scarce, is now sufficient to allow each man to practice with his own weapons. We have just authorised a substantial increase for firing practice.

Since 1940 many of the Home Guard have joined the Regular forces; some older men have retired, having done their duty in the hour of need. Younger men owe to them the experience and leadership they have inherited.

Nearly a year ago compulsory enrolment was introduced, and the "directed" men, as they are called, have proved as good and as willing as the original volunteers. With them came the lads of 17, many already trained in the Army Cadet forces. New units have been formed for special duties, many hundreds of ack-ack guns are manned by the Home Guard, scores of batteries have been in action and have acquitted themselves worthily. Women have played an ever larger part at the guns. The coast defence and motor transport units which have been formed will grow in efficiency throughout the year.

Credit is due not only to the Home Guardsmen themselves but to all who have helped them — to the employers and managements who make it easy to fit in Home Guard duties with men's employment, to the wives and mothers who have made Home Guard service easier in so many ways, and to the voluntary women helpers to whom we have now given in official recognition a badge of service.

We have now nearly 2,000,000 resolute, trained and equipped men, all of whom do their daily work in field or factory, and add to it free, gratis, and for nothing but honour, the last and proudest duty of a citizen of the Empire and a soldier of the King.

People who note and mark our growing mastery of the air, not only over our islands but penetrating into ever-widening zones on the Continent, ask whether the danger of invasion has not passed away. Let me assure you of this: That until Hitler and Hitlerism are beaten into unconditional surrender, the danger of invasion will never pass away.

The degree of the invasion danger depends entirely upon the strength or weakness of the forces and preparations gathered to meet it. The larger the army that must be brought across the seas to attack and subjugate us, the greater the difficulties of the operation, and the better the targets which would be open to the Royal Navy and to the British and American air forces on the spot.

You Home Guardsmen are a vital part of those forces; you are specially adapted to meet that most modern form of oversea attack — the mass descent of parachute troops; the Home Guard might well share the motto of the Royal Artillery — "Ubique" — for they are everywhere.

And if the Nazi villains drop down upon us from the skies, any night, in raid or heavy attack upon key production centres, you will make it clear to them that they have not alighted in the poultry-run, or in the rabbit-farm, or even in the sheep-fold, but in the lion's den at the Zoo! Here is the reality of your work; here is that sense of imminent emergency which cheers and inspires the long routine of drills and musters after the hard day's work is done.

But I have more to say to you than this. I am speaking to you now from the White House in Washington, where I am staying with my honoured friend the President of the United States. These are great days; they are like the days in Lord Chatham's time, of which it was said you had to get up early in the morning not to miss some news of victory. Ah!—but victory is no conclusion; even final victory will only open a new and happier field of valiant endeavour; the victories gained by the way must be a spur.

We are gathered here now with the highest professional authorities in all the fighting services of the two great English-speaking nations to plan well ahead of the armies who are moving swiftly; it is no good having only one march ahead laid out; march after march must be planned as far as human eye can see.

Design and foresight must be our guides and heralds; we owe it to the fighting troops; we owe it to the vast communities we are leading out of the dark places; we owe it to heroic Russia, to long-tormented China; we owe it to the captive and enslaved nations who beckon us on through their prison bars.

At present we have strong armies in Great Britain, and it is the assembly base for the United States armies of liberation coming across the broad Atlantic. But this is not the end. We must prepare for the time which is approaching, and will surely come, when the bulk of these armies will have advanced across the seas into deadly grapple on the Continent.

Just in the same way as the Home Guard render the Regular forces mobile against an invader, so the Home Guard must become capable of taking a great deal of the burden of home defence on to themselves, and thus set free the bulk of our trained troops for the assault on the strongholds of the enemy's power.

It is this reason which, above all others, has prompted me to make you and all Britain realise afresh by this Home Guard celebration and demonstration the magnitude and lively importance of your duties, and of the part you have to play in the supreme cause now gathering momentum as it rolls forward to its goal.

The Speech to the U.S. Congress

DELIVERED IN THE CAPITOL, WASHINGTON, D.C., AND
BROADCAST TO THE WORLD
MAY 19, 1943

May 13. *Officially announced that in the final offensive in Tunisia seventeen Axis generals had been captured. Booty included 1,000 guns and 250 tanks.*

R.A.F. broke the record it had established only 24 hours earlier with still heavier attacks on objectives in the Ruhr, Czechoslovakia and Berlin.

May 14. *The King sent a message to Mr. Churchill on the "glorious conclusion" of the African campaign.*

May 16. *R.A.F. struck the most devastating blow of the war at Germany by smashing the walls of the Möhne and Eder dams, causing huge floods to sweep through the Ruhr valley.*

General Giraud deposed the Bey of Tunis.

May 17. *American troops landed on Attu Island in the Aleutians and attacked Japanese stationed there.*

May 19. *Mr. Churchill addressed both Houses of Congress in Washington, his speech being broadcast to the world.*

R.A.F. Mosquitoes made a night attack on Berlin without loss.

[*May 19, 1943*

MR. PRESIDENT, Mr. Speaker, members of the Senate and the House of Representatives. Seventeen months have passed since I last had the honour to address the Congress of the United States. For more than 500 days, every day a day, we have toiled and suffered and dared shoulder to shoulder against the cruel and mighty enemy. We have acted in close combination or concert in many parts of the world, on land, on sea, and in the air. The fact that you have invited me to come to Congress again a second time, now that we have settled down to the job, and that you should welcome me in so generous a fashion, is certainly a high mark in my life, and it also shows that our partnership has not done so badly.

I am proud that you should have found us good allies, striving forward in comradeship to the accomplishment of our task without grudging or stinting either life or treasure, or, indeed, anything that we have to give. Last time I came at a moment when the United States was aflame with wrath at the treacherous attack upon Pearl Harbour by Japan, and at the subsequent declarations of war upon the United States made by Germany and Italy. For my part I say quite frankly that in those days, after our long — and for a whole year lonely — struggle, I could not repress in my heart a sense of relief and comfort that we were all bound together by common peril, by solemn faith and high purpose, to see this fearful quarrel through, at all costs, to the end.

That was the hour of passionate emotion, an hour most memorable in human records, an hour, I believe, full of hope and glory for the future. The experiences of a long life and the promptings of my blood have wrought in me the conviction that there is nothing more important for the future of the world than the fraternal association of our two peoples in righteous work both in war and peace.

So in January, 1942, I had that feeling of comfort, and I therefore prepared myself in a confident and steadfast spirit to bear the terrible blows which were evidently about to fall on British interests in the Far East, which were bound to fall upon us, from the military strength of Japan during a period when the American and British fleets had lost, for the time being, the naval command of the Pacific and Indian Oceans.

One after another, in swift succession, very heavy misfortunes fell upon us, and upon our Allies, the Dutch, in the Pacific theatre. The Japanese have seized the lands and islands they so greedily coveted. The Philippines are enslaved; the lustrous, luxuriant regions of the Dutch East Indies have been overrun. In the Malay Peninsula and at Singapore we ourselves suffered the greatest military disaster, or at any rate the largest military disaster, in British history.

Mr. President, Mr. Speaker, all this has to be retrieved, and all this and much else has to be repaid. And here let me say this: let no one suggest that we British have not at least as great an interest as the United States in the unflinching and relentless waging of war against Japan. And I am here to tell you that we will wage that war, side by side with you, in accordance with the best strategic employment of our forces, while there is breath in our bodies and while blood flows in our veins.

A notable part in the war against Japan must, of course, be played by the large armies and by the air and naval forces now marshalled by Great Britain on the eastern frontiers of India. In this quarter there lies one of the means of bringing aid to hard-pressed and long-tormented China. I regard the bringing of effective and immediate aid to China as one of the most urgent of our common tasks.

It may not have escaped your attention that I have brought with me to this country and to this conference Field-Marshal Wavell and the other two Commanders-in-Chief from India. Now, they have not travelled all this way simply to concern themselves about improving the health and happiness of the Mikado of Japan. I thought it would be good that all concerned in this theatre should meet together and thrash out in friendly candour, heart to heart, all the points that arise; and there are many.

You may be sure that if all that was necessary was for an order to be given to the great armies standing ready in India to march towards the Rising Sun and open the Burma Road, that order would be given this afternoon. The matter is, however, more complicated, and all movement or infiltration of troops into the mountains and jungles to the North-East of India is very strictly governed by what your American military men call the science of logistics.

But, Mr. President, I repudiate, and I am sure with your sympathy, the slightest suspicion that we should hold anything back that could be usefully employed, or that I and the Government I represent are not as resolute to employ every man, gun and airplane that can be used in this business, as we have proved ourselves ready to do in other theatres of the war.

In our conferences in January, 1942, between the President and myself, and between our high expert advisers, it was evident that, while the defeat of Japan would not mean the defeat of Germany, the defeat of Germany would infallibly mean the ruin of Japan. The realisation of this simple truth does not mean that both sides should not proceed together, and indeed the major part of the United States forces is now deployed on the Pacific fronts. In the broad division which we then made of our labours, in January, 1942, the United States undertook the main responsibility for prosecuting the war against Japan, and for helping Australia and New Zealand to defend themselves against a Japanese invasion, which then seemed far more threatening than it does now.

On the other hand, we took the main burden on the Atlantic. This was only natural. Unless the ocean life-line which joins our two peoples could be kept unbroken, the British Isles and all the very considerable forces which radiate therefrom would be paralysed and doomed. We have willingly done our full share of the sea work in the dangerous waters of the Mediterranean and in the Arctic convoys to Russia, and we have sustained, since our alliance began, more than double the losses in merchant tonnage that have fallen upon the United States.

On the other hand, again, the prodigious output of new ships from the United States building-yards has, for six months past, overtaken, and now far surpasses, the losses of both Allies, and if no effort is relaxed there is every reason to count upon the ceaseless progressive expansion of Allied shipping available for the prosecution of the war.

Our killings of the U-boat, as the Secretary of the Navy will readily confirm, have this year greatly exceeded all previous experience, and the last three months, and particularly the last three weeks, have yielded record results. This of course is to some extent due to the larger number of U-boats operating, but it is also due to the marked improvement in the severity and power of our measures against them, and of the new devices continually employed.

While I rate the U-boat danger as still the greatest we have to face, I have a good and sober confidence that it will not only be met and contained but overcome. The increase of shipping tonnage over sinkings provides, after the movement of vital supplies of food and munitions has been arranged, that margin which is the main measure of our joint war effort.

We are also conducting from the British Isles the principal air offensive against Germany, and in this we are powerfully aided by the United States Air Force in the United Kingdom, whose action is chiefly by day as ours is chiefly by night. In this war numbers count more and more, both in night and day attacks. The saturation of the enemy's *flak*, through the multiplicity of attacking planes and the division and diversion of his fighter protection by the launching of several simultaneous attacks, are rewards which will immediately be paid from the substantial increases in British and American numbers which are now taking place.

There is no doubt that the Allies already vastly outnumber the hostile air forces of Germany, Italy, and Japan, and still more does the output of new aeroplanes surpass the output of the enemy. In this air war, in which both Germany and Japan fondly imagined that they would strike decisive and final blows, and terrorise nations great and small into submission to their will — in this air war it is that these guilty nations have already begun to show their first real mortal weakness. The more continuous and severe the air fighting becomes, the better for us, because we can already replace casualties and machines far more rapidly than the enemy, and we can replace them on a scale which increases month by month.

Progress in this sphere is swift and sure, but it must be remembered that the preparation and development of airfields, and the movement of the great masses of ground personnel on whom the efficiency of modern air squadrons depends, however earnestly pressed forward, are bound to take time.

Opinion, Mr. President, is divided as to whether the use of air power could by itself bring about a collapse in Germany or Italy. The experiment is well worth trying, so long as other measures are not excluded. Well, there is certainly no harm in finding out. But however that may be, we are all agreed that the damage done to the enemy's war potential is enormous.

The condition to which the great centres of German war industry, and particularly the Ruhr, are being reduced, is one of unparalleled devastation. You have just read of the destruction of the great dams which feed the canals, and provide the power to the enemy's munition works. That was a gallant operation, costing eight out of the nineteen Lancaster bombers employed, but it will play a very far-reaching part in reducing the German munitions output.

It is the settled policy of our two Staffs and war-making authorities to make it impossible for Germany to carry on any form of war industry on a large or concentrated scale, either in Germany, in Italy, or in the enemy-occupied countries. Wherever these centres exist or are developed, they will be destroyed, and the munitions populations will be dispersed. If they do not like what is coming to them, let them disperse beforehand on their own. This process will continue ceaselessly with ever-increasing weight and intensity until the German and Italian peoples abandon or destroy the monstrous tyrannies which they have incubated and reared in their midst.

Meanwhile, our air offensive is forcing Germany to withdraw an ever larger proportion of its war-making capacity from the fighting fronts in order to provide protection against air attack. Hundreds of fighter aircraft, thousands of anti-aircraft cannon, and many hundreds of thousands of men, together with a vast share of the output of the war factories, have already been assigned to this purely defensive function. All this is at the expense of the enemy's power of new aggression, and of his power to resume the initiative.

Surveying the whole aspect of the air war, we cannot doubt that it is a major factor in the process of victory. That I think is established as a solid fact. It is agreed between us all that we should, at the earliest moment, similarly bring our joint air power to bear upon the military targets in the home lands of Japan. The cold-blooded execution of the United States airmen by the Japanese Government is a proof, not only of their barbarism, but of the dread with which they regard this possibility.

It is the duty of those who are charged with the direction of the war to overcome at the earliest moment the military, geographical, and political difficulties, and begin the process, so necessary and desirable, of laying the cities and other munitions centres of Japan in ashes, for in ashes they must surely lie before peace comes back to the world.

That this objective holds a high place in the present conference is obvious to thinking men, but no public discussion would be useful upon the method or sequence of events which should be pursued in order to achieve it. Let me make it plain, however, that the British will participate in this air attack on Japan in harmonious accord with the major strategy of the war. That is our desire. And the cruelties of the Japanese enemy make our airmen all the more ready to share the perils and sufferings of their American comrades.

At the present time, speaking more generally, the prime problem which is before the United States, and to a lesser extent before Great Britain, is not so much the creation of armies or the vast output of munitions and aircraft. These are already in full swing, and immense progress, and prodigious results, have been achieved. The problem is rather the application of those forces to the enemy in the teeth of U-boat resistance across the great ocean spaces, across the narrow seas, or on land through swamps, mountains, and jungles in various quarters of the globe. That is our problem. All our war plans must, therefore, be inspired, pervaded, and even dominated by the supreme object of coming to grips with the enemy under favourable conditions, or at any rate tolerable conditions — we cannot pick and choose too much — on the largest scale, at the earliest possible moment, and of engaging that enemy wherever it is profitable, and indeed I might say wherever it is possible, to do so. Thus, in this way, shall we make our enemies in Europe and in Asia burn and consume their strength on land, on sea, and in the air with the maximum rapidity.

Now you will readily understand that the complex task of finding the maximum openings for the employment of our vast forces, the selection of the points at which to strike with the greatest advantage to those forces, and the emphasis and priority to be assigned to all the various enterprises which are desirable, is a task requiring constant supervision and adjustment by our combined Staffs and Heads of Governments.

This is a vast, complicated process, especially when two countries are directly in council together, and when the interests of so many other countries have to be considered, and the utmost good will and readiness to think for the common cause, the cause of all the United Nations, are required from everyone participating in our discussions. The intricate adjustments and arrangements can only be made by discussion between men who know all the facts, and who are and can alone be held accountable for success or failure. Lots of people can make good plans for winning the war if they have not got to carry them out. I dare say if I had not been in a responsible position I should have made a lot of excellent plans, and very likely should have brought them in one way or another to the notice of the executive authorities.

But it is not possible to have full and open argument about these matters. It is an additional hardship to those in charge that such questions cannot be argued out and debated in public except with enormous reticence, and even then with very great danger that the watching and listening enemy may derive some profit from what he overhears. In these circumstances, in my opinion, the American and British Press and public have treated their executive authorities with a wise and indulgent consideration, and recent events have vindicated their self-restraint. Mr. President, it is thus that we are able to meet here to-day in all faithfulness, sincerity, and friendship.

Geography imposes insuperable obstacles to the continuous session of the combined Staff and Executive chiefs, but as the scene is constantly changing, and lately I think I may say constantly changing for the better, repeated conferences are indispensable if the sacrifices of the fighting troops are to be rendered fruitful, and if the curse of war which lies so heavily upon almost the whole world is to be broken and swept away within the shortest possible time.

I therefore thought it my duty, with the full authority of His Majesty's Government, to come here again with our highest officers in order that the combined Staffs may work in the closest contact with the chief executive power which the President derives from his office, and in respect of which I am the accredited representative of Cabinet and Parliament.

The wisdom of the founders of the American Constitution led them to associate the office of Commander-in-Chief with that of the Presidency of the United States. In this they were following the precedents which were successful in the days of George Washington. It is remarkable that after more than 150 years this combination of political and military authority has been found necessary, not only in the United States, but in the case of Marshal Stalin in Russia and of Generalissimo Chiang Kai-shek in China. Even I, as Majority Leader in the House of Commons — one branch of the Legislature — have been drawn from time to time, not perhaps wholly against my will, into some participation in military affairs.

Modern war is total, and it is necessary for its conduct that the technical and professional authorities should be sustained and if necessary directed by the Heads of Government, who have the knowledge which enables them to comprehend not only the military but the political and economic forces at work, and who have the power to focus them all upon the goal.

These are the reasons which compelled the President to make his long journey to Casablanca, and these are the reasons which bring me here. We both earnestly hope that at no distant date we may be able to achieve what we have so long sought — namely, a meeting with Marshal Stalin and if possible with Generalissimo Chiang Kai-shek. But how and when and where this is to be accomplished is not a matter upon which I am able to shed any clear ray of light at the present time, and if I were I should certainly not shed it.

In the meanwhile we do our best to keep the closest association at every level between all the authorities of all the Allied countries engaged in the active direction of the war. It is my special duty to promote and preserve this intimacy and concert between all parts of the British Commonwealth and Empire, and especially with the great self-governing Dominions, like Canada, whose Prime Minister is with us at this moment, whose contribution is so massive and invaluable. There could be no better or more encouraging example of the fruits of our consultations than the campaign in North-West Africa, which has just ended so well.

One morning in June last, when I was here, the President handed me a slip of paper which bore the utterly unexpected news of the fall of Tobruk, and the surrender, in unexplained circumstances, of its garrison of 25,000 men. That indeed was a dark and bitter hour for me, and I shall never forget the kindness and the wealth of comradeship which our American friends showed me and those with me in such adversity. Their only thought was to find the means of helping to restore the situation, and never for a moment did they question the resolution or fighting quality of our troops. Hundreds of Sherman tanks were taken from the hands of American divisions and sent at the utmost speed round the Cape of Good Hope to Egypt. When one ship carrying fifty tanks was sunk by torpedo, the United States Government replaced it and its precious vehicles before we could even think of asking them to do so. The Sherman was the best tank in the desert in the year 1942, and the presence of these weapons played an appreciable part in the ruin of Rommel's army at the battle of Alamein and in the long pursuit which chased him back to Tunisia.

And at this time, June of last year, when I was here last, there lighted up those trains of thought and study which produced the memorable American and British descent upon French North-West Africa, the results of which are a cause of general rejoicing. We have certainly a most encouraging example here of what can be achieved by British and Americans working together heart and hand. In fact one might almost feel that if they could keep it up there is hardly anything that they could not do, either in the field of war or in the not less tangled problems of peace.

History will acclaim this great enterprise as a classic example of the way to make war. We used the weapon of sea power, the weapon in which we were strongest, to attack the enemy at our chosen moment and at our chosen point. In spite of the immense elaboration of the plan, and of the many hundreds, thousands even, who had to be informed of its main outlines, we maintained secrecy and effected surprise.

We confronted the enemy with a situation in which he had either to lose invaluable strategical territories, or to fight under conditions most costly and wasteful to him. We recovered the initiative, which we still retain. We rallied to our side French forces which are already a brave and will presently become a powerful army under the gallant General Giraud. We secured bases from which violent attacks can and will be delivered by our Air power on the whole of Italy, with results no one can measure, but which must certainly be highly beneficial to our affairs.

We have made an economy in our strained and straitened shipping position worth several hundreds of great ships, and one which will give us the advantage of far swifter passage through the Mediterranean to the East, to the Middle East, and to the Far East. We have struck the enemy a blow which is the equal of Stalingrad, and most stimulating to our heroic and heavily-engaged Russian allies. All this gives the lie to the Nazi and Fascist taunt that Parliamentary democracies are incapable of waging effective war. Presently we shall furnish them with further examples.

Still, I am free to admit that in North Africa we builded better than we knew. The unexpected came to the aid of the design and multiplied the results. For this we have to thank the military intuition of Corporal Hitler. We may notice, as I predicted in the House of Commons three months ago, the touch of the master-hand. The same insensate obstinacy which condemned Field-Marshal von Paulus and his army to destruction at Stalingrad has brought this new catastrophe upon our enemies in Tunisia.

We have destroyed or captured considerably more than a quarter of a million of the enemy's best troops, together with vast masses of material, all of which had been ferried across to Africa after paying a heavy toll to British submarines and British and United States aircraft. No one could count on such follies. They gave us, if I may use the language of finance, a handsome bonus after the full dividend had been earned and paid.

At the time when we planned this great joint African operation, we hoped to be masters of Tunisia even before the end of last year; but the injury we have now inflicted upon the enemy, physical and psychological, and the training our troops have obtained in the hard school of war, and the welding together of the Anglo-American Staff machine — these are advantages which far exceed anything which it was in our power to plan. The German lie factory is volubly explaining how valuable is the time which they bought by the loss of their great armies. Let them not delude themselves. Other operations which will unfold in due course, depending as they do upon the special instruction of large numbers of troops and upon the provision of a vast mass of technical apparatus, these other operations have not been in any way delayed by the obstinate fighting in Northern Tunisia.

Onwards to Victory

Mr. President, the African war is over. Mussolini's African Empire and Corporal Hitler's strategy are alike exploded. It is interesting to compute what these performances have cost these two wicked men and those who have been their tools or their dupes. The Emperor of Abyssinia sits again upon the throne from which he was driven by Mussolini's poison gas. All the vast territories from Madagascar to Morocco, from Cairo to Casablanca, from Aden to Dakar, are under British, American, or French control. One continent at least has been cleansed and purged for ever from Fascist or Nazi tyranny.

The African excursions of the two Dictators have cost their countries in killed and captured 950,000 soldiers. In addition nearly 2,400,000 gross tons of shipping have been sunk and nearly 8,000 aircraft destroyed, both of these figures being exclusive of large numbers of ships and aircraft damaged. There have also been lost to the enemy 6,200 guns, 2,550 tanks and 70,000 trucks, which is the American name for lorries, and which, I understand, has been adopted by the combined staffs in North-West Africa in exchange for the use of the word petrol in place of gasolene.

These are the losses of the enemy in the three years of war, and at the end of it all what is it that they have to show? The proud German Army has by its sudden collapse, sudden crumbling and breaking up, unexpected to all of us, the proud German Army has once again proved the truth of the saying, "The Hun is always either at your throat or at your feet;" and that is a point which may have its bearing upon the future. But for us, arrived at this milestone in the war: we can say "One Continent redeemed."

The North-West African campaign, and particularly its Tunisian climax, is the finest example of the co-operation of the troops of three different countries and of the combination under one supreme commander of the sea, land, and air forces which has yet been seen: in particular the British and American Staff work, as I have said, has matched the comradeship of the soldiers of our two countries striding forward side by side under the fire of the enemy.

It was a marvel of efficient organisation which enabled the Second American Corps, or rather Army, for that was its size, to be moved 300 miles from the Southern sector, which had become obsolete through the retreat of the enemy, to the Northern coast, from which, beating down all opposition, they advanced and took the fortress and harbour of Bizerta. In order to accomplish this march of 300 miles, which was covered in twelve days, it was necessary for this very considerable Army, with its immense modern equipment, to traverse at right angles all the communications of the British First Army, which was already engaged or about to be engaged in heavy battle; and this was achieved without in any way disturbing the hour-to-hour supply upon which that Army depended. I am told that these British and American officers worked together without the slightest question of what country they belonged to, each doing his part in the military organisation which must henceforward be regarded as a most powerful and efficient instrument of war.

There is honour, Mr. President, for all; and I shall at the proper time and place pay my tribute to the British and American commanders by land and sea who conducted or who were engaged in the battle. This only will I say now: I do not think you could have chosen any man more capable than General Eisenhower of keeping his very large, heterogeneous force together, through bad times as well as good, and of creating the conditions of harmony and energy which were the indispensable elements of victory.

I have dwelt in some detail, but I trust not at undue length, upon these famous events; and I shall now return for a few minutes to the general war, in which they have their setting and proportion. It is a poor heart that never rejoices; but our thanksgiving, however fervent, must be brief.

Heavier work lies ahead, not only in the European, but, as I have indicated, in the Pacific and Indian spheres; and the President and I, and the combined Staffs, are gathered here in order that this work may be, so far as lies within us, well conceived, and thrust forward without losing a day.

Not for one moment must we forget that the main burden of the war on land is still being borne by the Russian armies. They are holding at the present time no fewer than 190 German divisions and 28 satellite divisions on their front. It is always wise, while doing justice to one's own achievements, to preserve a proper sense of proportion; and I therefore mention that the figures of the German forces opposite Russia compare with the equivalent of about 15 divisions which we have destroyed in Tunisia, after a campaign which has cost us about 50,000 casualties. That gives some measure of the Russian effort, and of the debt which we owe to her.

It may well be that a further trial of strength between the German and Russian armies is impending. Russia has already inflicted injuries upon the German military organism which will, I believe, prove ultimately mortal; but there is little doubt that Hitler is reserving his supreme gambler's throw for a third attempt to break the heart and spirit and destroy the armed forces of the mighty nation which he has already twice assaulted in vain. He will not succeed. But we must do everything in our power that is sensible and practicable to take more of the weight off Russia in 1943. I do not intend to be responsible for any suggestion that the war is won, or that it will soon be over. That it will be won by us I am sure. But how and when cannot be foreseen, still less foretold.

I was driving the other day not far from the field of Gettysburg, which I know well, like most of your battlefields. It was the decisive battle of the American Civil War. No one after Gettysburg doubted which way the dread balance of war would incline, yet far more blood was shed after the Union victory at Gettysburg than in all the fighting which went before. It behoves us, therefore, to search our hearts and brace our sinews and take the most earnest counsel, one with another, in order that the favourable position which has already been reached both against Japan and against Hitler and Mussolini in Europe shall not be let slip. If we wish to abridge the slaughter and ruin which this war is spreading to so many lands and to which we must ourselves contribute so grievous a measure of suffering and sacrifice, we cannot afford to relax a single fibre of our being or to tolerate the slightest abatement of our efforts. The enemy is still proud and powerful. He is hard to get at. He still possesses enormous armies, vast resources, and invaluable strategic territories. War is full of mysteries and surprises. A false step, a wrong direction, an error in strategy, discord or lassitude among the Allies, might soon give the common enemy power to confront us with new and hideous facts. We have surmounted many serious dangers, but there is one grave danger which will go along with us till the end; that danger is the undue prolongation of the war. No one can tell what new complications and perils might arise in four or five more years of war. And it is in the dragging-out of the war at enormous expense, until the democracies are tired or bored or split, that the main hopes of Germany and Japan must now reside. We must destroy this hope, as we have destroyed so many others, and for that purpose we must beware of every topic however attractive and every tendency however natural which turns our minds and energies from this supreme objective of the general victory of the United Nations. By singleness of purpose, by stead-fastness of conduct, by tenacity and endurance such as we have so far displayed — by these, and only by these, can we discharge our duty to the future of the world and to the destiny of man.

A Talk to the American Press

May 20. *Officially announced that a force of British and Indian troops, led by Brigadier Wingate, had emerged from the Burma jungle after three months of wrecking operations in enemy territory.*

    R.A.F. Mosquitoes again bombed Berlin without loss.

May 21. *Estimated that 113 Axis aircraft were destroyed in one day by Allied attacks on Italy's airfields.*

May 22. *The disbanding of the Communist International was officially announced by Moscow.*

May 23. *The ever-increasing air bombardment of Germany reached a new high record, the R.A.F. dropping more than 2,000 tons of bombs in an hour on Dortmund.*

May 24. *Pantellaria, Italy's island fortress in the Mediterranean, was subjected to day and night attack.*

May 25. *More than 300 aircraft were used in air attacks on ports and airfields in Sardinia, Sicily and Pantellaria.*

May 26. *Russian leaders, in messages on the occasion of the anniversary of the Anglo-Soviet Treaty, emphasized the need for continued co-operation after the war.*

    The King conferred the G.C.B. on the American Generals Eisenhower and MacArthur.

May 27. *Conferences in Washington between Mr. Churchill, President Roosevelt and the service chiefs ended in complete agreement on future operations on every front.*

    Wing Commander Gibson, leader of the great raid on the German dams, was awarded the V.C.

A Talk to the American Press, May 25, 1943

During his visit to Washington, Mr. Churchill attended President Roosevelt's press conference on May 25, 1943, and answered many questions from a gathering of 150 American newspaper representatives. He said:—

THE Allies' future plans are to wage this war to the unconditional surrender of all who have molested us — that applies to Asia as well as to Europe.

The situation is very much more satisfactory than when I was last here. It was in this house that I got the news of the fall of Tobruk. I don't think any Englishman in the United States has ever been so unhappy as I was that day; certainly no Englishman since General Burgoyne surrendered at Saratoga.

Since the attack on Alamein and the descent on North Africa we have had a great measure of success and a decisive victory.

A year ago Russia was subjected to such a heavy attack that it seemed she might lose the Caucasus; but she, too, recovered and gained another series of successes.

Hitler has been struck two tremendous, shattering blows — Stalingrad and Tunisia. In eleven months the Allies have given some examples of highly successful war-making, and have indisputably turned the balance.

I quote the words of your great general, Nathan Bedford Forrest, the eminently successful Confederate leader. Asked the secret of his victories, Forrest said, "I git thar fustest with the mostest men." The Allies can see a changed situation. Instead of, as hitherto, getting somewhere very late with very little, we are arriving first with most.

There is danger in wishful thinking that victory will come by internal collapse of the Axis. Victory depends on force of arms. I stand pat on a knock-out, but any windfalls in the way of internal collapses will be gratefully accepted.

*　　*　　*　　*

Italy is a softer proposition than Germany, and the Allies might be aided by a change of heart or a weakening of morale.

No one wishes to take the native soil of Italy from the Italians, who will have their place in Europe after the war. The trouble is that they allow themselves to be held in bondage by intriguers, with the result that they are now in a terrible plight. I think they would be well advised to throw themselves upon the justice of those whom they have so grossly attacked. We shall not stain our name for posterity by any cruel, inhuman acts. It is a matter for the Italians to settle among themselves. All we can do is to apply the physical stimuli which we have at our disposal to bring about a change of mind in these recalcitrant persons. Of this you may be sure: we shall continue to operate on the Italian donkey at both ends, with a carrot and with a stick.

* * * * *

I am only too anxious to increase the war effort in the Far East. It will be prosecuted with the utmost vigour. We have talked about that, and reached some sound and good decisions. Both the Asiatic and European wars will now be waged with equal force — they will be concurrent, not consecutive. The forces we have at our disposal now make this possible.

It is a matter of the application of our munitions of war, which is a question of shipping. Our principle is that all soldiers and all ships must be engaged all the time on the widest front possible. We are the big animal now, shaking the life out of the smaller animal, and he must be given no rest, no chance to recover.

I quote the words of your great general, Nathan Bedford For-

* * * *

It is a matter of poetic justice that the Allies have attained air superiority, the weapon with which the enemy chose to attempt to subjugate the world. The greater Allied superiority in manufactures will, so far as the air war is concerned, be decisive.

Two thousand tons of bombs were dropped on Dortmund, with, I believe, a highly satisfactory impression.

The recent heavy air blows against the Axis will be continued without cessation, but not to the exclusion of other methods.

To draw the conclusion from my speech before Congress that the United Nations are concentrating on bombing alone as a means of beating Germany would be distorting it. The ultimate results of the incessant Allied aerial offensive against the Axis have yet to be seen. There is nothing like a 24-hours service.

* * * *

The shipping situation is improving, thanks to the prodigious American production. The surplus over sinkings is substantial, and the killings of U-boats are more than at any previous time.

New inventions and combat efforts have greatly added to the destruction of U-boats, particularly last month. Wonderful things have been thought of, and these discoveries are being freely exchanged between the American and British navies. Supplies are crossing the ocean on an increasing scale.

* * * *

Hitler

I know of no reason to suppose that Hitler is not in full control of his faculties and the resources of his country.

I think he probably repents that he brought appetite unbridled and ambition unmeasured to his dealings with other nations.

I have very little doubt that if Hitler could have the past back he would play his hand a little differently. He probably regrets having turned down repeated efforts to avoid war, efforts which almost brought the British Government into disrepute. I should think he now repents that he did not curb his passions before he brought the world to misery.

* * * *

Referring to the possibility of an early meeting between General Giraud, High Commissioner for French North Africa, and General de Gaulle, leader of the Fighting French, Mr. Churchill said: —

It will be very satisfactory when this back-chat comes to an end and Frenchmen get together and look to the future and the duty they owe to France rather than to sectional interests.

* * * *

Replying to a question regarding the prospects of Russia fighting Japan, Mr. Churchill said: —

The matter has not been overlooked, but I am not giving directions to the Russians. Russia must know that the Japs have watched her with a purely opportunist eye.

I do not feel I should ask the Government to ask any more from

Russia. The Russians have held the weight of 190 German divisions and 28 divisions of satellite Axis nations. They have done what no one else could do — torn part of the guts out of the German war machine. They have been grand allies in the heroic fashion.

Russia is in a better position than a year ago. I have the utmost confidence in Russia's ability to hold out this year and hurl back any attack.

Messages

POLAND'S STRUGGLE

[*May 2, 1943*

[A MESSAGE TO A LONDON MEETING HELD TO COM-
MEMORATE POLISH NATIONAL DAY]

O<small>N</small> the occasion of the Polish National Day, I send you the
greetings of His Majesty's Government and the British people.
We celebrate this anniversary to-day in renewed confidence that
Poland's liberation has been brought nearer by the joint efforts
of the United Nations during the past year. Poles both at home
and abroad are at one in their determination to continue the
struggle against the German oppressors of their country. The
valuable contribution which they have made to the common
cause of the United Nations has not been achieved without heavy
sacrifices. But these sacrifices will be crowned by the restoration,
to which we all look forward, of a great and independent Poland.

ULSTER'S HELP

[*May 6, 1943*

[A LETTER TO MR. J. M. ANDREWS ON HIS RELIN-
QUISHING THE OFFICE OF PRIME MINISTER
OF NORTHERN IRELAND]

M<small>Y</small> dear Mr. Andrews,
  I am indeed sorry that the ties which have been so warmly
established between us in our public work should have to be

broken. After your long services to Northern Ireland as Minister of Labour and as Minister of Finance, you became Prime Minister in December, 1940. That was a dark and dangerous hour. We were alone, and had to face singlehanded the full fury of the German attack, raining down death and destruction on our cities and, still more deadly, seeking to strangle our life by cutting off the entry to our ports of the ships which brought us our food and the weapons we so sorely needed.

Only one great channel of entry remained open. That channel remained open because loyal Ulster gave us the full use of the Northern Irish ports and waters, and thus ensured the free working of the Clyde and the Mersey. But for the loyalty of Northern Ireland and its devotion to what has now become the cause of thirty Governments or nations, we should have been confronted with slavery and death, and the light which now shines so strongly throughout the world would have been quenched.

To you fell the honour of being at the head of the Government of Northern Ireland, not only during the supreme crisis, but throughout the two and a half years which have led us steadily forward to safety and final deliverance. I have always found in you a faithful and helpful colleague and comrade, and a man who had no thought but to do his duty. During your Premiership the bonds of affection between Great Britain and the people of Northern Ireland have been tempered by fire, and are now, I firmly believe, unbreakable.

You carry with you in your retirement the regard and respect of all who have worked with you, including, in a grateful spirit,

Yours very sincerely,

WINSTON S. CHURCHILL.

PLEDGE TO CHINA

[A REPLY TO GENERAL CHIANG KAI-SHEK'S CONGRATULATIONS ON THE ALLIED VICTORY IN NORTH AFRICA]

THE day will come when we shall rejoice at the feats of arms of the United Nations, which will surely drive the Japanese invader from the soil of China.

AID AND COMFORT FROM THE KING

[May 16, 1943

[A REPLY TO A MESSAGE FROM THE KING, WHO HAD CONGRATULATED THE PRIME MINISTER ON HIS CONCEPTION AND SUCCESSFUL PROSECUTION OF THE CAMPAIGN IN NORTH AFRICA]

I AM deeply grateful for the most gracious message with which Your Majesty has honoured me. No Minister of the Crown has ever received more kindness and confidence from his Sovereign than I have done during the three fateful years which have passed since I received Your Majesty's commission to form a national administration. This has been a precious aid and comfort to me, especially in the dark time through which we have passed.

My father and my grandfather both served in Cabinets of Queen Victoria's design, and I myself have been a Minister under Your Majesty's grandfather, your father, and yourself for many years. The signal compliment which Your Majesty has paid me on this occasion goes far beyond my deserts, but it will remain as a source of lively pleasure to me as long as I live.

TO THE CONSERVATIVES

[May 24, 1943

[A MESSAGE FROM WASHINGTON TO THE CON-
SERVATIVE PARTY'S ANNUAL CONFERENCE
IN LONDON]

I HAD much looked forward to being present at the annual meeting of the Conservative and Unionist Conference, whose loyal support has meant so much to me; but duty made it necessary for me to be in Washington, where your generous and heartening message has reached me. Much has been accomplished, but even more remains to be done; and if you carry on your work as resolutely and as well in the future as you have in the past, we can look forward with confidence to the utter defeat of the enemy and the establishment of justice and lasting peace.

"CUT MORE COAL"

[May 24, 1943

[AN APPEAL TO EVERY MINEWORKER IN
GREAT BRITAIN]

SIX months ago Field-Marshal Smuts and I spoke to your leaders and delegates at a great secret meeting in London. We told them how grave the position was; how, if the gap between coal production and consumption was not closed, the war would go against us. That gap was closed. You raised more coal, consumers burnt less, and we have come safely through the winter. Our ships, our armies, our air fleets have been increased and sustained, and at this hour we are thrusting swiftly and deeply at the enemy.

But now — just as we are massing our strength in this year of vigorous assault — the news comes to me from the Minister of Fuel and Power that coal production is slipping back again, that again has come the ugly danger that our strokes at the enemy may be weakened and hampered. I thought it might be of interest to you if a copy of the speeches, made in secret six months ago to your leaders and delegates, were placed in the hands of every miner in the country — that each one of you may see plainly his own responsibility and our country's need.

Again I call upon you, in this testing time, for greater output. I appeal to you personally, fighting with your tools in the mines, to think of your countrymen-in-arms, to stand solidly behind them, and to cut more coal.

TO GENERAL SMUTS

[*May 24, 1943*

[BIRTHDAY GREETINGS]

IT is the earnest prayer of all that you may be spared to continue your notable work in the cause of the British Commonwealth and Empire, and indeed of the whole world.

TO THE JEROMES

[A MESSAGE TO THE JEROME FAMILY ASSOCIATION IN REPLY TO AN INVITATION TO ATTEND A REUNION]

[NOTE: Mr. Churchill's mother was a Miss Jerome.]

WILL you please convey to members of the Jerome Family Association my deep gratitude for their kind and inspiring message, and offer to those assembled at the reunion my best wishes for the health and happiness of my Jerome cousins.

[May 4, 1943

[SERVICE PAY]

Replying to a member who asked what machinery existed for co-ordinating rates of pay and allowances between the three Services, and added that senior officers in the Navy had received no advance in pay since 1938, Mr. Churchill said: —

CO-ORDINATION in this sphere of Government, as in others, rests ultimately on the existence of a united Government collectively responsible for its acts. It is maintained in practice by the normal machinery of constant Ministerial and inter-departmental consultation, and I cannot accept my hon. and gallant Friend's suggestion that the Services or the Ministers responsible for them fail to co-operate to the fullest extent in matters of common concern. As regards the pay of senior naval officers, no general advances have been made since 1938 in the pay of senior members of any Crown Service, and none is at present contemplated.

[REHABILITATION OF EX–SERVICEMEN]

Asked for a statement on the scheme for the rehabilitation of men discharged from the Services on grounds of neurosis or temporary instability, Mr. Churchill said: —

All cases of personnel who are being discharged from the Services on the grounds stated in the Question are considered by the Ministry of Pensions and, where appropriate, medical treatment, including rehabilitation treatment, is provided for them either at Ministry of Pensions hospitals or at neurosis centres under the Emergency Hospital Scheme. These centres, eleven in number in England and Wales, and two in Scotland, are residential, and are under the supervision of the Ministry of Health or the Department of Health for Scotland. For those not requiring, or no longer requiring, in-patient treatment, out-patient facilities and social help are available at clinics and through other mental health agencies conducted by local authorities or voluntary bodies. These latter services are not at present complete or fully co-ordinated, but are being developed under the auspices of the Board of Control as far as war conditions allow.

[GAS WARFARE]

Replying to members who asked that before we embarked on gas warfare a neutral observer should certify beyond doubt that the enemy had used gas, Mr. Churchill said: —

Retaliatory action will not be taken until His Majesty's Government are convinced that gas has been used by the enemy, but we have no intention of inviting neutrals to assist us in this matter.

I have very good confidence that we shall receive true information from our Russian Allies.

"Brighter and Solid Prospects"

THE PRIME MINISTER'S SPEECH TO THE HOUSE OF COMMONS
ON HIS RETURN FROM HIS VISITS TO THE UNITED
STATES AND NORTH AFRICA.
JUNE 8, 1943

May 28. President Roosevelt announced the creation of the Office of War Mobilisation.

Hitler was reported to have ordered a purge of "lukewarm and untrustworthy" members of the Nazi party.

May 30. Japanese resistance in Attu Island ceased, the Americans being left in complete control.

June 2. May officially stated to have been R.A.F.'s heaviest and most successful bombing month of the war. In one week, 7,500 tons of bombs were dropped on Germany. It was officially announced that May was also the best month for U-boat "kills."

A British civil aircraft was shot down by German planes between Lisbon and England, Mr. Leslie Howard, the film actor, being among the passengers to lose their lives.

June 3. A French Committee for National Liberation, presided over by General Giraud and General de Gaulle, was formed in Algiers.

June 4. Mr. Churchill met Generals Giraud and de Gaulle in Algiers.

Revolution broke out in Argentina and President Castillo fled the country.

June 5. Mr. Churchill arrived back in England, having visited North Africa on his way home from Washington. He was accompanied by Mr. Anthony Eden (Foreign Secretary) who had joined him in Algiers.

June 6.   Pantellaria was bombarded night and day by sea
          and air.
              General Rawson became President of a Provi-
          sional Government in Argentina.
June 7.   General Rawson resigned Presidency of Argentina
          Government and was succeeded by General Ra-
          mirez.
June 8.   President Roosevelt gave warning that any use of
          poison gas by the enemy would bring swift and full
          retaliation.
              Mr. Churchill made a statement on the war situ-
          ation to the House of Commons.

[June 8, 1943

As the Allied war effort passes into the offensive phase and
its scale and pace grow continually, more frequent consultations
between the Staffs and those concerned with the high control become necessary. In January, 1942, broad agreements on principle
and on our joint or respective tasks were reached by our conferences in Washington. In the June meeting these took a sharper
point, and, among other things, the operations in North Africa
began to shape themselves. In October and November, action
occurred. At Casablanca, in January of this year, the President
and I, with the combined British and United States Staffs, were
able to survey new scenes and wider prospects. Plans and pro-
grammes were approved which have by no means yet been accomplished. Nevertheless the progress of events became more rapid,
and the Armies marched faster, than had been foreseen. It became
necessary to explore new fields. To have the initiative is an immense advantage; at the same time, it is a heavy and exacting
responsibility. Left to itself, opportunity may easily lead to diver-
gency. Therefore, having consulted the President, I thought it
necessary at the beginning of May to go with our Chiefs of Staff
and a very large body of officers and secretaries — nearly 100 —
for a third time to Washington, in order that the success then
impending in Tunisia might be examined and comprehended

from a common viewpoint, and then turned to the best possible account.

At Washington the entire expanse of the world war, on which the mellow light of victory now begins to play, was laid open to the British and American leaders. We have shown that we can work together. We have shown that we can face disaster. We have still to show that we can keep ourselves at the height and level of successful events and be worthy of good fortune. Perhaps that may be the hardest task of all.

It would not be right, of course, for me to attempt to give, even in outline, an account of the decisions which were reached. All I can say is that we have done our best. A complete agreement about forward steps has been reached between the two Governments. There has been no trace of differences, such as occurred in the last war, inevitably on account of the forces at work, between the politicians and the military men. I shall make no predictions as to what will happen in the future, and still less in the near future. All I can say is that Anglo-American policy, strategy, and economy were brought into full focus and punch in these fifteen days' talks at Washington. The elaboration of modern war renders these prolonged discussions necessary. A conference lasting a day or two, such as sufficed in previous wars, is no longer sufficient to cover the ground and test the different propositions. As I said, very large numbers of officers, expert in their particular branches, are required at the various levels to be in close consultation. This gives the best chance to the troops, the sailors, and the airmen, wherever they may be, from Gibraltar to New Guinea, and from the Aleutian Islands to the Burma Road. In so vast and diverse a scene many questions of emphasis and priority arise, even where principles are agreed, and beneath them lie all those problems of transportation, of munitions industry, of the food of nations, of the distribution and application of resources, most of which can best be settled, and many of which can only be settled, at the summit of war direction, and which at that summit present themselves in fairly simple and yet at the same time in somewhat awe-inspiring forms.

After we had completed our task at Washington, I thought it well to go to North Africa, and I was very glad that the President decided to send along with me General Marshall, the Chief of the

United States Army and Air Force, a man of singular eminence of mind and character. We flew together across the Atlantic to Gibraltar and Algiers, in order to deal more particularly and precisely on the spot with the problems of the Mediterranean theatre. There, for another week, we had the advantage of full discussions with General Eisenhower, the Supreme Commander, with General Alexander, Admiral Cunningham, Air Chief Marshal Tedder, Air Marshal Coningham, General Montgomery, General Spaatz, and General Bedell Smith, and other high British and United States officers directly concerned with the execution of plans which I can best describe as directed to the application upon the enemy of force in its most intense and violent forms. I can assure the House that the most complete concord and confidence prevailed at General Eisenhower's headquarters, and that the Forces of the two great nations of the English-speaking world are working together literally as if they were one single Army. I was told by officers of both countries that in the movement of troops or in the distribution of supplies no questions of national origin arise between the Staff officers who are interleaved at every stage and tier of the vast organisation. It is just a question of what is the best thing to do — that and no more. The commanders are men in the full tide of successful experiment. They are proud of the troops they lead, and they are resolute in the plans they have made. In travelling about these Armies, seeing perhaps 20,000 troops and airmen in a day, I sustained the impression of their extraordinary ardour and zeal to engage the enemy again at the earliest moment. Very fine Armies have come into being in this African war, and to be conscious of their spirit is an ennobling experience for a visitor. Cheered by remarkable victory after many bafflings and disappointments, the British and American Armies, and now the French Army, have become a most powerful and finely-tempered weapon. They have full confidence in themselves, and also in the High Command and in the general war direction. This is also true of the more numerous and powerful forces, British Canadian, and American, which have been formed and are forming in the United Kingdom.

It is evident that amphibious operations of peculiar complexity and hazard, on a large scale, are approaching. I can give no guarantee, any more than I have done in the past, of what will happen. I am sorry that a few days ago, in the press of travel and affairs, I let slip the expression, "Brilliant prospects lie before us." I would prefer to substitute the words, "Brighter and solid prospects lie before us." That, I think, would be more appropriate and becoming in such anxious days. Yet, all the same, I have good hopes that neither Parliament nor the Congress of the United States will find themselves ill-served by the Forces, whether in the British Isles or on the African shore. At any rate, I can assure the House that on neither side, British or American, have any narrow or selfish motives entered into the common task. The rest, I must leave to action and to the march of events.

When I visited Tripoli in January, I had the pleasure of seeing the troops of the Eighth Army whom I had already met in the now far-off Alamein position, before their victory and their marvellous advance across the desert. I was particularly glad on this last occasion to meet men of the First Army, who after a very hard time in the rainy winter have come into their own, and had the honour, with their comrades of the Second United States Army Corps, of striking the final blow.

The British losses in Tunisia have been severe. The Eighth Army, since they crossed the frontier from Tripolitania, have sustained about 11,500 casualties, and the First Army about 23,500 casualties, in all 35,000 killed, missing and wounded during the campaign in the two British Armies.

The total number of prisoners taken who have passed through the cages of all the Allies, now amounts to over 248,000 men, an increase of 24,000 on the previously published total, and there must certainly have been 50,000 of the enemy killed, making a total loss of about 300,000 men to the enemy in Tunisia alone. More than half of these men are Germans. In fact, of the 37,000 prisoners taken by the United States 2nd Corps — actually it was more the size of an army than a corps — 33,000 were Germans. The French 19th Corps also led tens of thousands of German and Italian captives to the rear, and must have felt that after all their country had gone through, they were once again reliving the great days of Foch and Clemenceau. All this takes no account of the very heavy toll levied on the German and Italian forces as they crossed over the seas, or passed through the air. This toll was taken by the Allied Air Forces and by the British submarines, cruisers, destroyers and motor torpedo boats. These British naval forces at the same time cast an impassable barrier between the enemy in Tunisia and all prospects of escape. During the later phases, a continuous patrol was maintained in strength which would have prevented any attempt at escape except by individuals. In fact, I believe only 638 persons have escaped, and these for the most part by air, from this scene of surrender.

We cannot doubt that Stalingrad and Tunisia are the greatest military disasters that have ever befallen Germany in all the wars she has made, and they are many. There is no doubt from the statements of captured generals that Hitler expected his Tunisian army to hold out at least until August, and that this was the view and intention of the German High Command. The suddenness of the collapse of these great numbers of brave and skilful fighting men, with every form of excellent equipment, must be regarded as significant and in a sense characteristic of the German psychology which was shown after Jena and also at the very end of the last war. Though this fact should certainly be noted and weighed, no undue expectations should be based upon it. We are prepared to win this war by hard fighting, and if necessary by hard fighting alone.

In years of peace, the peoples of the British Commonwealth and those of the United States are easy-going folk, wishing to lead a free life, with active politics and plentiful opportunities of innocent diversion and of national self-improvement. They do not covet anything from others, perhaps because they have enough themselves; and they have often failed to keep a good look-out upon their own safety. They have many martial qualities, but they certainly do not like drill. Nevertheless, when they are attacked and assailed and forced in defence of life and liberty to make war, and to subject all their habits of life to war conditions and to war discipline, they are not incapable, if time is granted to them — and time was granted to them — of making the necessary transformation. Indeed, a great many of them are taking to it with increasing zest and zeal. Such nations do not become exhausted by war. On the contrary, they get stronger as it goes on. It is an error on the part of certain neutrals to suppose that the previously unprepared and ill-armed Anglo-Saxon democracies will emerge from this war weakened and prostrate even though victorious. On the contrary, we shall be stronger than ever before in force, and I trust also in faith. It may well be that those guilty races who trumpeted the glories of war at the beginning will be extolling the virtues of peace before the end. It would certainly seem right, however, that those who fix, on their own terms, the moment for beginning wars should not be the same men who fix, on their own terms, the moment for ending them. These observations are of a general character, but not without their particular application.

I must not neglect to make it clear that the operations now impending in the European theatre have been fitted into their proper place in relation to the general war. I am very sorry that we have not yet been able to bring into council Marshal Stalin, and/or other representatives of our great Ally Russia, which is bearing the heaviest burden and paying by far the highest price in blood and life. But I can assure the House that taking some of the weight off Russia, giving more speedy and effective aid to China, and giving a stronger measure of security to our beloved Australia and New Zealand — these objects were never absent for one moment from our thoughts and aims.

This war is so universal, so world-wide, that it would take several hours to make an exposition of what is happening in the various theatres. Each of the Allies naturally sees these theatres from a different angle and in a somewhat different relation. We British must continue to place the anti-U-boat war first, because it is only by conquering the U-boat that we can live and act. The might of America is deployed far over the Pacific, laying an ever stronger grip on the outlying defences of Japan, and offering at every moment to the Japanese fleet the supreme challenge of sea-power. The Russian Armies, as I mentioned to Congress the other day, are in deadly grapple with what we estimate to be 190 German and 28 satellite divisions along their 2,000 miles front. It is here that the greatest battles seem to impend.

Then there is the war in the air. The steady wearing-down of the German and Japanese Air Forces is proceeding remorselessly. The enemy, who thought that the air would be their weapon of victory, are now finding in it instead the first cause of their ruin. It is necessary for me to make it plain that, so far as the British Government and the Governments of the Dominions, and also the Governments of the United States and of the Russian Soviet Republic, are concerned, nothing will turn us from our endeavour and intention to accomplish the complete destruction of our foes by bombs from the air in addition to all other methods. Loud and lamentable outcries are being made by the enemy now that this form of warfare, by which they thought to obtain the mastery of the world, has turned markedly to their disadvantage. This outcry will only be regarded by us as a very satisfactory proof of the growing efficiency of our attack. Compared with this time last year, we British alone can now drop more than double the weight of bombs at 1,500 miles range there and back.

In the summer of last year, as Minister of Defence, I set on foot a policy of increasing our bomber effort, which, of course, entailed certain sacrifices in other directions. All this is now coming to hand. At the same time we took the measures which have thrown the long-range aircraft — the very long-range aircraft — the V.L.R., as they are called — effectively into the anti-U-boat struggle. All this is now being brought to bear. The month of May is, from every point of view, the best month we have ever had in the anti-U-boat war since the United States was attacked by Japan, Germany and Italy. At that time we gained much greater combined resources, but we exposed much larger targets. We made at that time a budget of sinkings and buildings on which we knew we could survive indefinitely. The sinkings have been a good deal less than we apprehended, and the buildings have more than made good the prodigious programme undertaken by the American nation. This month of May has been one of the very best for the imports carried safely into this Island since the end of 1941. Our combined new building has exceeded our losses by more than 3 to 1. This first week in June could not possibly be taken as a criterion, but, as a matter of fact, it is the best for many, many months past.

During the last few months the enemy has made very heavy attacks on our convoys. These have given us the opportunity of hitting him hard in open battle. There are so many U-boats employed now that it is impossible not to run into one or other of these great screens of them which are spread out, and therefore you have to fight your way through. But there is no reason why we should regret that. On the contrary, it is around the convoys that the U-boats can best be destroyed. New weapons and new methods, and the close co-ordination of effort between surface and air escort, have enabled us to inflict casualties which have surpassed all previous records. My right hon. Friend the First Lord of the Admiralty made a statement of a very reassuring character upon this subject the other day, and I can only repeat that in May, for the first time, our killings of U-boats substantially outnumbered the U-boat output. That may be a fateful milestone. The Germans seem to be staking their hopes upon the U-boat war, as we may judge by the appeals made to them. They are encouraged to bear the evils — "terrors," they call them, perhaps not an ill-chosen word — of the air bombardment by the hope that on the sea the U-boats are taking their revenge. If it should be made clear that this hope has failed them, they may be seriously disappointed; and they are people who, when seriously disappointed, do not always find the resources to confront approaching disaster, once their reason tells them that it is inevitable. Again I say, I make the observation in passing, but do not let us build on such deductions. It would be foolish to assume that the good results of a single month are a guarantee of a continuing process. We may have set-backs, though I have always looked forward to this summer as being a period which would be favourable to us. Moreover, of course, the enemy may decline battle, or he may look only for the most tempting opportunities. In this case we shall have fewer killings but more imports, and freer movement of troops and munitions will be possible to all the various theatres. I must say I feel confident that the U-boat war will not stand between the United Nations and their final victory, while all the time the air war will grow in weight and severity. I might well speak with more emphasis upon this point, but it is prudent to forbear.

It happened at the time when I was in Algiers that General de Gaulle and his friends arrived, and I thought it would be well if my right hon. Friend the Foreign Secretary were on the spot in case it should prove in our power to help. We did not in fact intervene at all in these tense discussions between Frenchmen. But, like General Eisenhower, the Supreme Commander, we watched them closely and vigilantly in the light of British and United States interests and of the well-being of our Armies in North

Africa. We all rejoiced that agreement was made, and that the French National Committee of Liberation was set up and constituted as the single and sole authority over all Frenchmen seeking to free France from the German yoke. When we met these seven men by and around whom the new French Cabinet has been formed, we could not but be struck by the many different aspects of French energy and capacity to resist which they represented, and also by their high personal qualities. The gravest responsibility lies upon these men, and opportunity shines brightly before them. They have only to act together in good faith and loyalty to one another, to set aside sectional or personal interests, and keep all their hatreds for the enemy — they have only to do this to help regain for France her inheritance, and in so doing to become themselves the inheritors of the gratitude of future generations of Frenchmen. The formation of this Committee, with its collective responsibility, supersedes the situation created by the correspondence between General de Gaulle and myself in 1940. Our dealings, financial and otherwise, will henceforward be with the Committee as a whole. There is a further and larger question, namely, the degree of recognition of this Committee as representative of France. This question requires consideration from the British and United States Governments, but if things go well, I should hope that a solution satisfactory to all parties may shortly be reached.

Let me now sum up the two predominant impressions I have sustained from this journey. The first is the spirit, quality and organisation of the British and Allied Armies in North Africa. The second is the intimacy and strength of the ties now uniting the British and United States Governments and the British and American peoples. All sorts of divergences, all sorts of differences of outlook and all sorts of awkward little jars, necessarily occur as we roll ponderously forward together along the rough and broken road of war. But none of these makes the slightest difference to our ever-growing concert and unity, there are none of them that cannot be settled face to face by heart-to-heart talks and patient argument. My own relations with the illustrious President of the United States have become in these years of war those of personal friendship and regard, and nothing will ever happen to separate us in comradeship and partnership of thought and action while we remain responsible for the conduct of affairs.

The reason why I have not had to make a longer speech to-day is that I have already given to the joint Session of the Congress of the United States the statement which I should have made to this House on the victory in Tunisia had I been in this country. That, I think, is a valid explanation. Certainly, when I found myself walking into that august Assembly, the free Congress of the most powerful community in the world, and when I gave them, exactly as I would do in this House, a businesslike, stock-taking survey of the war and of our joint interests, even touching upon controversial matters or matters of domestic controversy over there, and when I thought of all our common history and of the hopes that lie before us, I felt that this was an age of memorable importance to mankind. For there can be no doubt that whatever world organisation is brought into being after this war, that organisation must be the richer and the stronger if it is founded on the friendship and fraternal relations and the deep understanding prevailing and now growing between the British Commonwealth of Nations and the United States of America.

I have one thing more to say before I sit down. I must acknowledge with gratitude the extraordinary kindness with which I have been treated in the House and out of doors throughout the land. That is a very great help in these days of continuing crisis and storm. Let me, in return, record the fact that this House, a democratic institution, based upon universal suffrage, which has preserved its functions and authority intact and undiminished during the war, and has shown that it can change, correct and sustain Governments with equal constancy of purpose, has proved itself a foundation and an instrument for the waging of successful war and for the safety of the State never surpassed in modern or ancient times.

"Before the Autumn Leaves Fall"

A SPEECH AT THE GUILDHALL ON RECEIVING THE FREEDOM
OF THE CITY OF LONDON
JUNE 30, 1943

June 9. Lord Selborne, Minister of Economic Warfare, said industrial production in the Ruhr had been cut 35 per cent. in the past year, bombing being responsible for half of this reduction.

June 10. Major-General Eaker, Commander of the U.S. air forces in Britain, revealed that American air strength based on Britain, was doubling in hitting power every four months.

June 11. Pantellaria, Italy's fortress island, surrendered after days of ceaseless air and sea bombardment. The Italians declared 1,000 aircraft were used in the final raid.

President Roosevelt advised the Italian people to get out of the war.

June 12. The King arrived in Algiers on a visit to the British and American land and sea forces in the Mediterranean.

Lampedusa Islands surrendered after one day of naval and air bombardment.

June 15. The Germans said that troops had been withdrawn from Russia to strengthen the Western front.

June 17. Sir Archibald Sinclair, Air Minister, announced that enemy submarines sunk or seriously damaged last month were about equal to new ones sent out.

June 18. Field-Marshal Sir Archibald Wavell appointed Viceroy of India in succession to Lord Linlithgow. General Auchinleck appointed Commander-in-Chief, India.

June 19.   *Following repeated air-attacks, civilians were warned to leave Naples and the chief towns of Sicily.*

June 20.   *The King visited Malta.*

June 22.   *Second anniversary of Germany's attack on Russia.*

June 23.   *R.A.F. Lancaster planes which had flown to North Africa, after bombing a radiolocation factory at Friedrichshaven on June 20, raided Spezia, the Italian naval base, on the return flight.*

June 25.   *The King returned to England by air from his visit to North Africa and Malta. He announced that the Africa Star would be awarded to the victors in the North African campaign and the 1939–43 Star to those who had fought in other theatres.*

June 26.   *It was announced in Washington that the tonnage of bombs dropped on Germany would be immediately increased by 45 per cent.*

June 29.   *U.S. land, sea and air forces opened a new attack in the Solomons with a landing on Rendova Island in the New Georgia group, and officially announced the destruction of 65 out of 110 Japanese aircraft which attempted to prevent the landing.*

June 30.   *Mr. Churchill, receiving the Freedom of the City of London, warned the Axis that there would be heavy fighting in the Mediterranean and elsewhere "before the leaves of autumn fall."*

[*June 30, 1943*

I AM deeply grateful for the kindness with which I am treated, not only here to-day on this, to me, outstanding occasion, but in the whole discharge of my responsibilities.

The strain of protracted war is hard and severe upon the men at the executive summit of great countries, however lightly care may seem to sit upon them. They have need of all the help and comfort their fellow countrymen can give them. I feel myself buoyed up by your good will here to-day, and indeed I have felt uplifted through all these years by the consideration with which the British people have treated me, even when serious mistakes have been made. Always they have given a generous measure of trust and friendship, and I have never felt hustled or barracked or racketed in any of the decisions it is my duty to take in conjunction with my colleagues, or in regard to matters it is my task to submit to Parliament.

There is no doubt that this consideration shown to their leader by the British people, although far above his deserts, is a very real and practical help in the conduct of the war. It gives me confidence to act and to dare, that is a draught of life amid many toils and burdens. Of all the wars that we have ever waged in the long continuity of our history, there has never been one which more truly united the entire British nation and British race throughout the world than this present fearful struggle for the freedom and progress of mankind.

We entered it of our own free will, without being ourselves directly assaulted. We entered it upon a conviction of purpose which was clearly comprehended by all classes and parties and by the whole mass of the people, and we have persevered together through good and evil fortune without the slightest weakening of our will power or division of our strength. We entered it ill-prepared and almost unarmed. We entered it without counting the cost, and upon a single spontaneous impulse at the call of honour.

We strove long, too long, for peace, and suffered thereby; but from the moment when we gave our guarantee that we would not stand by idly and see Poland trampled down by Nazi violence, we have never looked back, never flagged, never doubted, never flinched. We were sure of our duty, and we have discharged it and will discharge it, without swerving or slackening, to the end.

We seek no profit, we covet no territory or aggrandisement. We expect no reward and we will accept no compromise. It is on that footing that we wish to be judged, first in our own consciences and afterwards by posterity.

It is even more remarkable that the unity which has existed and endured in this small, densely-populated island should have extended with equal alacrity and steadfastness to all parts of our world-wide Commonwealth and Empire. Some people like the word Commonwealth; others, and I am one of them, are not at all ashamed of the word Empire. But why should we not have both?

Therefore I think the expression British Commonwealth and Empire may well be found the most convenient means of describing this unique association of races and religions, which was built up partly by conquest, largely by consent, but mainly unconsciously and without design, within the all-embracing golden circle of the Crown.

Wars come with great suddenness, and many of the deep, slow courses which lead to the explosion are often hidden from or only dimly comprehended by the masses of the people, even in the region most directly affected. Time, distance, the decorum of diplomacy, and the legitimate desire to preserve peace — all impose their restraints upon public discussion and upon prior arrangements.

Alone in history, the British people, taught by the lessons they had learned in the past, have found the means to attach to the Motherland vast self-governing Dominions upon whom there rests no obligation, other than that of sentiment and tradition, to plunge into war at the side of the Motherland.

None of these Dominions, except Southern Ireland, which does not under its present dispensation fully accept Dominion status, has ever failed to respond, with all the vigour of democratic institutions, to the trumpet-call of a supreme crisis, to the overpowering influences and impulses that make Canada, that make Australia — and we have here in Dr. Evatt a distinguished Australian — that make New Zealand and South Africa send their manhood across the ocean to fight and die.

In each one of these countries, with their long and varied history behind them, this extraordinary spectacle is an outstanding example of the triumph of mind over matter, of the human heart over fear and short-sighted self-interest.

In the vast sub-continent of India, which we trust will presently find full satisfaction within the British Commonwealth of Nations, the martial races and many others have thronged to the Imperial standards. More than 2,000,000 have joined the armed forces, and have distinguished themselves in many cases during the fiercest conflicts with Germans, Italians, and Japanese.

All the great countries engaged in this war count their armies by millions, but the Indian Army has a peculiar characteristic not found in the armies of Britain or the United States or Russia or France or in the armies of our foes, in that it is entirely composed of volunteers. No one has been conscripted or compelled. The same thing is broadly true throughout our great Colonial Empire.

Many scores of thousands of troops have been drawn from the immense tropical spaces, or from lonely islands nursed by the waves of every sea. Many volunteers there were for whom we could not find arms. Many there are for whom even now we cannot find opportunities. But I say that the universal ardour of our Colonial Empire to join in this awful conflict, and to continue in that high temper through all its ups and downs, is the first answer that I would make to those ignorant and envious voices who call into question the greatness of the work we are doing throughout the world, and which we shall still continue to do.

The time came when this loosely and variously knit world-spread association, where so much was left unwritten and undefined, was confronted with the most searching test of all. The Mother Country, the home of the kingship, this famous island, seemed to enter the very jaws of death and destruction.

Three years ago, all over the world, friend and foe alike — everyone who had not the eye of faith — might well have deemed our speedy ruin was at hand. Against the triumphant might of Hitler, with the greedy Italians at his tail, we stood alone with resources so slender that one shudders to enumerate them even now.

Then, surely, was the moment for the Empire to break up, for each of its widely-dispersed communities to seek safety on the winning side, for those who thought themselves oppressed to throw off their yoke and make better terms betimes with the all-conquering Nazi and Fascist power. Then was the time. But what happened?

It was proved that the bonds which unite us, though supple as elastic, are stronger than the tensest steel. Then it was proved that they were the bonds of the spirit and not of the flesh, and thus could rise superior alike to the most tempting allurements of surrender and the harshest threats of doom. In that dark, terrific, but also glorious hour we received from all parts of His Majesty's Dominions, from the greatest and from the smallest, from the strongest and from the weakest, from the most modern to the most simple, the assurance that we would all go down or come through together. You will forgive me if on this occasion, to me so memorable, here in the heart of mighty London, I rejoice in the soundness of our institutions and proclaim my faith in our destiny.

But now I must speak of the great Republic of the United States, whose power arouses no fear and whose pre-eminence excites no jealousy in British bosoms. Upon the fraternal association and intimate alignment of policy of the United States and the British Commonwealth and Empire depends, more than on any other factor, the immediate future of the world. If they walk, or if need be march, together in harmony and in accordance with the moral and political conceptions to which the English-speaking peoples have given birth, and which are frequently referred to in the Atlantic Charter, all will be well. If they fall apart and wander astray from the commanding beacon-light of their destiny, there is no end or measure to the miseries and confusion which await modern civilisation.

This is no rhetorical extravagance, no genial sentiment for a festive occasion; it is the hard, cold, vindictive truth. Yet there are many light and wayward spirits in both our countries who show themselves by word and action unmindful of this fundamental fact. It is a fact in no way derogatory to other mighty nations now fighting by our side, or to any nation, great or small, making its way through the perils of the present age.

We seek no narrow or selfish combination. We trespass not at all upon the lawful interests and characteristics of any allied or friendly State. We nourish the warmest feelings of fellowship towards the valiant Russian people, with whom we have made a twenty years' treaty of friendship and mutual aid. We foresee an expanding future for the long-enduring Republic of China. We look forward to a revival of the unity and the true greatness of France. We offer loyal and faithful comradeship to all. Nevertheless, the tremendous and awe-inspiring fact stares the British and American democracies between the eyes, that acting together we can help all nations safely into harbour, and that if we are divided all will toss and drift for a long time on dark and stormy seas.

You have given me this casket, which contains my title as a Freeman of the City of London. I have not always been wrong about the future of events, and if you will permit me, I shall inscribe some of these words within it as my testament, because I should like to be held accountable for them in years which I shall not see.

It is fitting in a singular manner to speak upon this theme of the fraternal association of Britain and the United States here amid the proud monuments and prouder ruins of the City of London, because nothing ever made a warmer feeling between the British and American peoples than the unflinching resistance of London to the formidable, prolonged assault of the enemy. The phrase "London can take it," and the proof of it that was given, stirred every generous heart in the United States, and their illustrious Chief, watching the whole scene of the world with eyes of experience and conviction, sustained by the Congress of the United States, came to our aid with the famous Lend-Lease Act in a manner most serviceable to the great causes which were at stake.

There is no doubt that the sympathy of the United States for the cause of freedom, and their detestation of the Nazi creed and all the menace that it bears to American institutions, drew the United States so near the edge of the conflict that the foul Japanese saw his chance to make his bid for Asiatic domination by striking his traitor blow at Pearl Harbour. Since then we and the Americans have waged war in common, sharing all alike, taking the rough with the smooth, keeping no accounts of blood or treasure — I do not say as if we were one people, but certainly as though we were one army, one navy, and one air force. And so we shall continue like brothers, certainly until the unconditional surrender of all our foes has been achieved, and I trust thereafter until all due measures have been taken so as to secure over a long period of years our safety from future ill-usage.

Should Hitler's Germany and Mussolini's Italy collapse under the flail of Soviet Russia, and the not inconsiderable exertions of the British and American armies in the Mediterranean and elsewhere, should the war industries of Germany be blasted out of existence by the British and American air-power, should this prime and capital victory be achieved before Japan has been laid low — I stand here to tell you to-day, as I told the Congress of the United States in your name, that every man, every ship, and every aeroplane in the King's service that can be moved to the Pacific will be sent and will be there maintained in action by the peoples of the British Commonwealth and Empire in priority over all other interests for as many flaming years as are needed to make the Japanese in their turn submit or bite the dust.

I will turn for a moment on this occasion from the tide of world events to our domestic affairs. And here it may justly be said that our slowly-wrought British institutions have proved themselves even better adapted to this crisis than to any we have known in the past. His Majesty has at his disposal a National Government composed of the leading men of all parties, officially authorised by their parties to serve the State and only the State at the present juncture.

On the home front, I submit with diffidence, but with confidence underlying it, that in the four most important spheres of finance, of labour, of agriculture, and food — and several others which I could add — an efficient, vigorous, and successful administration has been provided, and that this will bear comparison not only with what happened in the last war — which we also won and from whose lessons we have profited much — but also is not outclassed by what is happening in any other country or under any other system of government, democratic or totalitarian.

Further I declare that our vast influential newspaper Press has known how to combine independence and liveliness with discretion and patriotism. I rejoice that both Houses of Parliament have preserved and asserted, even in our most perilous and bitter periods, their full authority and freedom. And as a very old House of Commons man I may add that, if I am here to-day to receive as Prime Minister the honours which you pay me, it is because, and only because, of the resolute, overwhelming, unwearying support which I have received from the oldest, the most famous and the most vital of all existing Parliamentary assemblies.

Finally, of all our institutions there is none which has served us better in the hour of need than our ancient Monarchy. We rely on this, for all that we have is centred upon and at the present time is embodied by the King and Queen, most dearly beloved and honoured by all their country. We all welcome back home our gracious and gallant King from his visit to his victorious army in Africa, and, may I say, none rejoices at his return with more fervour than his Ministers who took the responsibility of advising him not to restrain his royal pleasure in respect of a journey of this peculiar character.

The general progress of the war is satisfactory. In May two great battles were won by the allies. Every one has heard about the victory in Tunisia, with 350,000 Germans and Italians made captive or slain, and immense quantities of war material and shipping captured or destroyed. We have rejoiced soberly but all the more profoundly at this signal military episode, which ranks with the magnificent Russian victory at Stalingrad, and takes its place in British eyes and in British annals among our most famous victories of former times.

But there was another victory. A not less notable battle was fought in May in the Atlantic against the U-boats. For obvious reasons much less has been said about that. In May the German Admiralty made extreme exertions to prevent the movement to Great Britain of the enormous convoys of food and war materials which are continually received by us from the United States, and which we must bring in safely and punctually if our war-making capacity is to be maintained. Long lines of U-boats were spread to intercept these convoys, and packs of 15 or 20 U-boats were then concentrated upon the attempt. To meet this, British and American and Canadian forces of the sea and air hurled their strength upon the U-boats. The fighting took place mainly around the convoys, but also over wide expanses of the ocean. It ended in the total defeat of the U-boat attack.

More than 30 U-boats were certainly destroyed in the month of May, many of them foundering with their crews into the dark depths of the sea. Staggered by these deadly losses, the U-boats have recoiled to lick their wounds and mourn their dead. Our Atlantic convoys came safely through, and now, as the result of the May victory and the massacre of U-boats, we have had in

June the best month from every point of view we have ever known in the whole 46 months of the war. The prodigious ship-building exertions of the United States, and the considerable contribution of Britain and also of Canada, have produced an output of new ships which is somewhere between seven and ten times as great as our losses from enemy action in the month of June. Since the middle of May scarcely a single merchant ship has been sunk in the whole of the North Atlantic, and in June also, although the convoys are not being seriously attacked at the present time, the U-boat losses, which should certainly not be exaggerated, have been most solid and encouraging. I give these facts purposely in a form which conveys the truth without giving precise or detailed information to circles wider than those with which we are ourselves amply concerned.

There are two conclusions to be drawn from them. The first is that we must not assume that this great improvement will be maintained or that bad patches do not lie ahead. The second is that, encouraged by the growing success of our methods, we must redouble our own efforts and ingenuity. The disasters which have overtaken the U-boat campaign in May and also in June have their bearing upon another phase of our offensive war. These two months have seen the heaviest discharge of bombs upon munitions and war-time industrial centres of Germany. Nothing like the shattering effects of this upon the cities of the Ruhr and elsewhere has ever been achieved so far.

Three years ago Hitler boasted that he would "rub out" — that was the term — the cities of Britain, and certainly in the nine months before he abandoned his attack we suffered very heavy damage to our buildings and grievous hindrance to our life and work, and more than 40,000 of our people were killed and more than 120,000 wounded. But now those who sowed the wind are reaping the whirlwind. In the first half of this year, which ends to-day, the Royal Air Force alone has cast upon Germany alone 35 times the tonnage of bombs which in the same six months of this year has been discharged upon this island. Not only has the weight of our offensive bombing grown and its accuracy multiplied, but our measures of defence, tactical and scientific, have improved beyond all compare. In one single night, nay, mainly in one single hour, we cast upon Düsseldorf, to take an example, 2,000 tons of terrible explosive and incendiary bombs for a loss of 38 aircraft, while in the first half of this same year the enemy has discharged upon us no more than 1,500 tons of bombs at a cost to him of 245 aircraft.

In addition to this, the United States air fleet in this country, already so powerful and growing with extraordinary rapidity, has by its precision daylight bombing inflicted grave injuries upon the most sensitive nerve and key centres of the enemy's war production, and American crews and pilots are continually performing feats of arms of the highest skill with dauntless audacity and devotion. All these facts and tendencies, which, it must be admitted, however prosaically viewed, are by no means wholly unfavourable in their general character, must stimulate our joint exertions in the most intense degree and on an ever-larger scale.

I have never indulged in shallow or fugitive optimism, but I have thought it right to make these statements because I am sure they will not lead to the slightest complacency, or to any relaxation of that superb yet awful force which is now being brought into action. These forces will be remorselessly applied to the guilty nation and its wicked leaders, who imagined their superiority of air-power would enable them to terrorise and subjugate first all Europe and afterwards the world. They will be applied, and never was there such a case of the biter bitten.

During the summer our main attack is upon that mainspring of German war industry, the Ruhr; but as the nights become longer and as the United States Air Force becomes more numerous our strong arm will lengthen both by night and by day, and there is no industrial or military target in Germany that will not receive as we deem necessary the utmost application of exterminating force. The war industry of Germany has already to some extent been dispersed in the numerous smaller towns. When the cities are disposed of we shall follow it there. Presently the weight of the Russian air attack, now mainly absorbed by their long active fighting front, will contribute an additional quota to the total blitz.

This is, I can quite well believe, a sombre prospect for the German people, and one which Dr. Goebbels is certainly justified in painting in the darkest hues. But when we remind ourselves of the frightful tyrannies and cruelties with which the German armies, their gauleiters and subordinate tormentors, are now afflicting almost all Europe; when we read every week of the mass executions of Poles, Norwegians, Dutchmen, Czechoslovaks, Frenchmen, Yugoslavs, and Greeks; when we see these ancient and honoured countries of whose deeds and traditions Europe is the heir, writhing under this merciless alien yoke, and when we see their patriots striking back with every week a fiercer and more furious desperation, we may feel sure that we bear the sword of justice, and we resolve to use that sword with the utmost severity to the full and to the end.

It is at this point that the heavy defeats recently sustained by the U-boats play their part in the general attack upon German morale. Apart from his mysterious promises of revenge, the one hope which Dr. Goebbels holds out to the German people is that though they suffer the extreme tribulation of air bombing, the U-boat on the ocean is inflicting equal or even more deadly injuries upon the British and American power to wage war. When that hope dies, as die it well may, it would appear to the most dispassionate observer that a somewhat bleak and raw outlook is beginning to open itself before Hitler's accomplices and dupes. We must allow these corrective processes to take their course.

Meanwhile this is certainly no time for us to indulge in sanguine predictions. Rather should we remind ourselves of St. Paul's Epistle to the Corinthians: — "Wherefore let him that thinketh he standeth take heed lest he fall." I therefore say no more than that our affairs are in considerably better posture than they were some time ago, and that we intend to remain steadfast and unwearying in doing our duty and doing our best whatever may betide.

I have still to speak of the war in the Mediterranean, about which there is so much talk at the present time. Mussolini's Italian Fascists, who are, after all, only a small privileged portion of the real Italian nation, seem to be already suffering from that war of nerves of which they and their German masters made so much use in former times. So far they have only been subjected to preliminary and discursive bombardment, but they are already speculating feverishly where the blow will fall, against how many of the shores or islands from the Gulf of Lions to the

Levant, from the Riviera to the Dodecanese, it may be directed, when the blow will fall, and what will be its weight at each point. It is no part of our business to relieve their anxieties or their uncertainties.

They may remember how they themselves struck at the Turks in Tripoli in bygone years, at Abyssinia in recent times, still later at Albania, and how they fell upon Greece and set out to conquer Egypt. And they may look back regretfully to the days when they used to disturb a peaceful world, and when it rested with their pinchbeck Cæsar to settle which weaker community should be struck down first.

I can do nothing to help them to resolve their fears, which, communicated to their allies, may perhaps have led to the remarkably long delay in the opening of the promised German offensive against Russia. But I have some words of caution to say to our own people. First of all, all great military operations are dominated by risks and turns of fortune. I know of no certainty in war. This is particularly true of amphibious war. Therefore any mood of over-confidence should be austerely repressed.

There is another point which should be comprehended. All large amphibious operations, especially if they require the co-operation of two or more countries, require long months of organisation, with refinements and complexities hitherto unknown in war. Bold impulses, impatient desires, and sudden flashes of military instinct cannot hasten the course of events.

I cannot go farther to-day than to say that it is very probable there will be heavy fighting in the Mediterranean and elsewhere before the leaves of autumn fall.

For the rest, we must leave the unhappy Italians and their German tempters and task-masters to anxieties which will aggravate from week to week and from month to month.

This, however, I will add before I sit down. We, the United Nations, demand from the Nazi, Fascist, and Japanese tyrannies unconditional surrender. By this we mean that their will power to resist must be completely broken, and that they must yield themselves absolutely to our justice and mercy. It also means that we must take all those far-sighted measures which are necessary to prevent the world from being again convulsed, wrecked and blackened by their calculated plots and ferocious aggressions.

It does not mean, and it never can mean, that we are to stain our victorious arms by inhumanity or by mere lust of vengeance, or that we do not plan a world in which all branches of the human family may look forward to what the American Constitution finely calls "life, liberty, and the pursuit of happiness."

Mr. Churchill later made this short speech in the Mansion House at the luncheon which followed the Guildhall ceremony: —

This is indeed a joyous occasion for me, and one which gives me the most lively pleasure — to be received by the ancient City of London, which I have visited so often on political business in varying atmospheres during the last forty or fifty years. To be received with such entire cordiality and treated with so much honour is an immense satisfaction to me. It refreshes me, and will make me do my very best to give good service in the difficult times that lie ahead.

We must not think that the difficult times are over. Death and damnation are no longer at the nation's throat. Survival and victory are well within our grasp, but long may be the road and hard and painful the processes by which we shall arrive at a satisfactory conclusion. But we shall come, bringing other countries with us, out of the frightful welter into which we have been plunged and by which civilisation has been threatened.

I should like to tell you how kind I think it is of you to have asked so many of my friends and colleagues and fellow-workers and chiefs of staff, with whom I am in very close association, and who do the work, and run the war, and bring the victories about. No one can tell whether the struggle will be long or short, and nobody, however bold a prophet he may be, however luxuriant in imagination, can pretend to lift up the veil which lies before the period into which we are moving. All I can say is this — that Britain holds together and retains her old traditions and greatness. However events may go, we shall not only be able to stand firmly ourselves, but to be a guide and help to others who move forward on their path.

I thank the Lord Mayor for his hospitality and for the great honour that has been done to me. This event will always rank in my mind with the very highest days of rejoicing that I have passed in my journey through the world.

General Sikorski's Death

July 2.   *U.S. forces, continuing their S.W. Pacific offensive,
captured Rendova Island.*

July 4.   *At least 43 enemy fighters were destroyed in heavy
Allied attacks on Sicilian airfields.*

July 5.   *Lull on the Russian front ended with German offensive at Orel, Kursk and Byelgorod.*

*General Sikorski, Polish Prime Minister and
Commander-in-Chief, was killed in an air crash
near Gibraltar. Two British M.P.'s, Colonel Cazalet and Brigadier Whiteley, died in the same disaster.*

[July 6, 1943

WE learned yesterday that the cause of the United Nations
had suffered a most grievous loss. It is my duty to express the
feelings of this House, and to pay tribute to the memory of a
great Polish patriot and staunch ally, General Sikorski. His
death in the air crash at Gibraltar was one of the heaviest
strokes we have sustained. From the first dark days of the Polish
catastrophe and the brutal triumph of the German war machine
until the moment of his death on Sunday night, he was the
symbol and the embodiment of that spirit which has borne the
Polish nation through centuries of sorrow and is unquenchable
by agony.

When the organised resistance of the Polish Army in Poland
was beaten down, Sikorski's first thought was to organise all
Polish elements in France to carry on the struggle, and a Polish
Army of over 80,000 men presently took its station on the French

171

fronts. This Army fought with the utmost resolution in the disastrous battles of 1940. Part fought its way out in good order into Switzerland and is to-day interned there. Part marched resolutely to the sea and reached this Island. Here General Sikorski had to begin his work again. He persevered unwearied and undaunted. The powerful Polish Forces which have now been accumulated and equipped in this country and in the Middle East, to the latter of which his last visit was paid, now await with confidence and ardour the tasks which lie ahead.

General Sikorski commanded the devoted loyalty of the Polish people, now tortured and struggling in Poland itself. He personally directed that movement of resistance which has maintained a ceaseless warfare against German oppression in spite of sufferings as terrible as any nation has ever endured, and this resistance will grow in power until, at the approach of liberating Armies, it will exterminate the German ravagers of the homeland.

I was often brought into contact with General Sikorski in these years of war. I had a high regard for him, and I admired his poise and calm dignity amid so many trials and baffling problems. He was a man of remarkable pre-eminence, both as statesman and as soldier. His agreement with Marshal Stalin of 30th July, 1941, was an outstanding example of his political wisdom. Until the moment of his death he lived in the conviction that all else must be subordinated to the needs of the common struggle, and in the faith that a better Europe will arise in which a great and independent Poland will play an honourable part. We British here and throughout the Commonwealth and Empire, who declared war on Germany because of Hitler's invasion of Poland and in fulfilment of our guarantee, feel deeply for our Polish Allies in their new loss. We express our sympathy to them, we express our confidence in their immortal qualities, and we proclaim our resolve that General Sikorski's work as Prime Minister and Commander-in-Chief shall not have been done in vain. The House would, I am sure, wish also that their sympathy should be conveyed to Madame Sikorski, who dwells here in England and whose husband and daughter have both been simultaneously killed on duty.

The House has also sustained a personal loss in the death of two more of our Members, the hon. and gallant Member for Chippenham (Colonel Cazalet) and the hon. and gallant Member for Buckingham (Brigadier Whiteley), for whom many of us cherished warm feelings of friendship and who were held in respect by all. The list of Members who have given their lives in this second struggle against German aggression is lengthening, but when our House of Commons is rebuilt we shall take care to inscribe their names and titles on its panels to be an example to future generations not unworthy of those we have ourselves received from former times.

A Call to the Polish Forces

A MESSAGE BROADCAST IN THE POLISH TRANSMISSION
OF THE B.B.C.
JULY 14, 1943

[July 14, 1943

AT the invitation of the President and Government of Poland, who are our guests in London, I speak these words to Poles all over the world; to the armed forces of Poland in Britain and the Middle East; to Poles in exile in many foreign countries; to Poles in German prison camps, and Poles forced to labour for the enemy; and particularly to the inhabitants of Poland itself, who are enduring with unlimited fortitude the worst that an enemy of unexampled brutality can do to them.

I mourn with you the tragic loss of your Prime Minister and Commander-in-Chief, General Sikorski. I knew him well. He was a statesman, a soldier, a comrade, an ally, and, above all, a Pole. He is gone; but if he were at my side I think he would wish me to say this — and I say it from my heart — soldiers must die, but by their death they nourish the nation which gave them birth. Sikorski is dead, but it is in this sense that you must think of your dead Prime Minister and Commander-in-Chief.

Remember that he strove for the unity of all Poles — unity in a single aim, the defeat and punishment of the German despoilers of Poland. He strove, too, unceasingly, for that larger unity of all the European peoples, for the closest collaboration in the common struggle with Poland's allies in the West and in the East. He knew that in such partnership lies the surest hope of Poland's speedy liberation and lasting greatness.

His efforts and your sacrifices shall not be in vain. Be worthy of his example. Prepare yourselves to die for Poland — for many

A Call to the Polish Forces, July 14, 1943

of you to whom I speak must die, as many of us must die, and as he died, for his country and the common cause. In the farewell to your dead leader let us mingle renewed loyalties. We shall not forget him. I shall not forget you. My own thoughts are with you and will be with you always.

The Call to the Italian People

A JOINT MESSAGE BY MR. WINSTON CHURCHILL AND
PRESIDENT ROOSEVELT BROADCAST TO ITALY
BY ALGIERS RADIO
JULY 16, 1943

July 7.   *General Giraud arrived in Washington for conferences with President Roosevelt.*

July 8.   *Russians counter-attacked in Orel-Kursk sector
and regained lost ground. Announced that 1,843
tanks and 810 aircraft had been lost to the Germans in four days.*

July 9.   *General Giraud reached agreement in Washington
for the equipment of a French Army of 300,000.*

July 10.   *The Invasion of Sicily. British, American and
Canadian forces landed on 100 miles front on the
South-East corner of the island. The Axis H.Q. at
Taormina was smashed by American bombing.*

July 11.   *Allied troops consolidated their positions on the
beaches in Sicily, captured three aerodromes, and
began their triumphant push inland.*

July 12.   *Allied forces captured ten Sicilian towns, including the important port of Syracuse.
Second week of the German offensive in Russia
opened with Russian artillery holding German
tank attacks.*

July 14.   *Allied armies in Sicily continued to make steady
progress, and the British Eighth Army advanced on
Catania, while the Americans penetrated towards
the centre of the island.*

July 15.   *Soviet Armies launched a counter-offensive north
and east of Orel.*

July 16.   *Mr. Churchill and President Roosevelt made a
joint appeal to the Italian people to capitulate.*

THIS is a message to the Italian people from the President of
he United States of America and the Prime Minister of Great
Britain.

At this moment the combined armed forces of the United
States, Great Britain, and Canada, under the command of General
Eisenhower and his deputy, General Alexander, are carrying
the war deep into the territory of your country. This is the
direct consequence of the shameful leadership to which you have
been subjected by Mussolini and his Fascist regime.

Mussolini carried you into this war as the satellite of a brutal
destroyer of peoples and liberties.

Mussolini plunged you into a war which he thought Hitler
had already won. In spite of Italy's great vulnerability to attack
by air and sea, your Fascist leaders sent your sons, your ships,
your air forces, to distant battlefields, to aid Germany in her
attempt to conquer England, Russia, and the world.

This association with the designs of Nazi-controlled Germany
was unworthy of Italy's ancient traditions of freedom and culture
– traditions to which the peoples of America and Great Britain
owe so much.

Your soldiers have fought not in the interests of Italy but for
Nazi Germany. They have fought courageously, but they have
been betrayed and abandoned by the Germans on the Russian
front and on every battlefield in Africa from Alamein to Cape
Bon.

To-day Germany's hopes for world conquest have been blasted
on all fronts. The skies over Italy are dominated by the vast air
armadas of the United States and Great Britain. Italy's sea coasts
are threatened by the greatest accumulation of British and Allied
sea power ever concentrated in the Mediterranean.

The forces now opposed to you are pledged to destroy the
power of Nazi Germany, that power which has ruthlessly been
used to inflict slavery, destruction, and death on all those who
refuse to recognise the Germans as the master race.

The sole hope for Italy's survival lies in honourable capitulation to the overwhelming power of the military forces of the United Nations.

If you continue to tolerate the Fascist regime which serves the evil power of the Nazis, you must suffer the consequences of your own choice. We take no satisfaction in invading Italian soil and bringing the tragic devastation of war home to the Italian people. But we are determined to destroy the false leaders and their doctrines which have brought Italy to her present position.

Every moment that you resist the combined forces of the United Nations — every drop of blood that you sacrifice — can serve only one purpose; to give the Fascist and Nazi leaders a little more time to escape from the inevitable consequences of their own crime.

All your interests and all your traditions have been betrayed by Nazi Germany and your own false and corrupt leaders: it is only by destroying both that a reconstituted Italy can hope to occupy a respected place in the family of European nations.

The time has now come for you, the Italian people, to consult your own self-respect and your own interests, and your own desires for a restoration of national dignity, security, and peace. The time has come for you to decide whether Italians shall die for Mussolini and Hitler — or live for Italy and for civilisation.

The Liberal Ideal

July *17.*   *American troops captured Agrigento, principal
city of southern Sicily. More than 500 bombers
battered Naples.*

July *18.*   *General Alexander was appointed Military Gov-
ernor of Sicily and head of an organisation known
as AMGOT (Allied Military Government of Occupied Territory).*

July *19.*   *First Air Raid on Rome was made by a strong
force of American bombers, great care being taken
to avoid damage to historic monuments.*
        Hitler and Mussolini met in Northern Italy.

July *22.*   *Allied forces gained control of the whole of Western Sicily.*
        *Russians captured Bolkov, north of Orel, and
announced that in ten days fighting in that sector
more than 50,000 of the enemy were killed and
6,000 taken prisoner.*

[July 22, 1943

Y OUR Chairman has said that this is in some ways a unique
occasion. But I must confess that it seems to me very like old
times. I am very greatly honoured to have been invited here
to-day and to sit again beside my old colleague in several ad-
ministrations, Lord Crewe, whose broad, consistent outlook has
been a help to many in the troublous years through which we
have passed, and to receive at the hands of the National Liberal

Club, with apparently the full authority of all its members, the very great compliment of seeing unveiled a portrait which has survived alike the vicissitudes of politics and the violence of the enemy.

Naturally my mind goes back to the days of my earlier life when I first found effective political contact with the Liberal Party. In those days they gained, after a lapse of many years, political power, and at that time — I am talking of 1906 — it seemed that many of the causes which had brought Liberalism into being as a political force had already been achieved. The shackles had been struck off the slaves, careers were open to talent, the barriers of class and privilege were being struck down with great rapidity, or had indeed already been removed. The rights of small nations and the principles and traditions which animate nationalities all over the world were receiving an ever greater measure of respect.

In many ways, when the Liberal Government of 1905–06 came into power, it surveyed a scene in which many of the great tasks with which Mr. Gladstone had been associated had already been achieved, and then it was that that Government came forward and, under the active inspiration and energy of Mr. Lloyd George, brought forward that long succession of social laws, of insurance of all kinds, of old age and invalidity pensions, of labour exchanges, trade boards, in all that great field of social legislation in which Liberalism found a most fertile and practical work to do — a work which has gone steadily forward all through the entire life of the people of this country, and will continue.

It is not finished yet, and has a still greater and finer scope to take. There was a very remarkable fact, that the Liberal forces in this country, when for the moment the principles of liberty seemed to be well established, turned to this warmer, more practical sphere of social reform; and they undoubtedly gave to the whole legislation and life of our land an entirely new and beneficent character.

Time passed, and terrible wars swept across the world, wars utterly abhorrent to all the conceptions of Victorian days, wars not to be conceived in their horror, in their brutality, in their grim, inevitable ruthlessness, by the statesmen of the last century. But these wars, as they have moved in their course, have thrown the Liberal Party back upon its earliest inspiration — upon human liberty and duty — the inescapable duty of free men to defend the soil on which they live and to govern themselves in accordance with their desires, conceptions, and traditions. And thus the flame of liberty has burned, and thus the Liberal Party has entered most fully into this struggle with that flame burning, with that torch going on ahead, that torch of freedom which we shall never allow to be extinguished.

Not only is the sword drawn in a generous cause, commanding the efforts of all; not only is the liberation of all these subjugated and enslaved countries a cause for which every man in whose breast liberal instincts are implanted burns — not only does that cause move forward, but we see that in days to come, and even at the present time, much more exact definitions will be needed of the rights of the individual and of the relations of the individual to the great framework of the State, which, as I hold, must have as its highest purpose the safeguarding of those individual rights, and the reconciling of the freedom of each with the broad general interests of the community.

Therefore it seems to me that across these vicissitudes and storms which we have lived through, which we have survived, which a large part of this building has successfully withstood, after all these shocks and violences and through them all, there has run a steady theme of Liberalism which has broadened out among other parties, and which has given to those who have followed it all their lives a feeling of continuous fruitful exercise and effort. And it seems to me that after this war is over there will be other tasks to do. There will be great tasks of rebuilding. There will be great tasks of securing the advance of ideas, and not letting it be swept back by mere tides of lassitude, exhaustion, or reaction. A steady advance of rising ideas, cultivated and regimented and brought forward, must be maintained, and among them an exact definition of the relations of the individual to the State will play a part in which Liberal conceptions must exercise a most important sway.

From this rebuilding of the country nobody, in my opinion, has a right, except on grounds of intellectual or moral scruple, to stand aside; nobody should content himself with a purely critical attitude, taking the form of throwing brickbats at the toiling workers; and I look forward in the future not only to the Liberal theme, but to Liberal activities, playing a great part in the reconstruction of our country and the consolidation of the gains which we shall have made through this hard and long trial.

I must tell you that I feel greatly moved by your kindness to me, and greatly honoured that my portrait should be hung on these walls along with men I have known and worked with in formative years of British political life. Your welcome to me and the generous kindness with which you have treated me and my wife will ever be gratefully cherished in my memory.

Mussolini's Downfall

July 23.   *American troops captured Palermo, Sicily's largest city.*

July 24.   *R.A.F. dropped more than 2,000 tons of bombs on Hamburg.*

   Stalin declared that the Germans, in 18 days of their summer offensive in Russia, had lost 70,000 men killed, 2,900 tanks, 1,039 guns and 1,392 planes.

July 25.   *Mussolini resigned, and the Fascist regime in Italy ended after 21 years. The King of Italy took supreme command of the Italian forces and appointed as Prime Minister Marshal Badoglio, who declared that the war would continue.*

July 26.   *Italy was placed under martial law. A new cabinet was formed with Dr. Guariglia as Foreign Minister.*

July 27.   *Mr. Churchill told the House of Commons that the choice for Italy was between surrender and an avalanche of fire.*

   R.A.F., continuing a day and night assault on Hamburg, dropped 2,300 tons of bombs in 45 minutes.

[*July 27, 1943*

THE House will have heard with satisfaction of the downfall of one of the principal criminals of this desolating war. The end of Mussolini's long and severe reign over the Italian people undoubtedly marks the close of an epoch in the life of Italy. The keystone of the Fascist arch has crumbled, and, without attempting to prophesy, it does not seem unlikely that the entire Fascist edifice will fall to the ground in ruins, if it has not already so fallen. The totalitarian system of a single party, armed with secret police, engrossing to itself practically all the offices, even the humblest, under the Government, with magistrates and courts under the control of the executive, with its whole network of domestic spies and neighbourly informants — that system, when applied over a long period of time, leaves the broad masses without any influence upon their country's destinies and without any independent figures apart from the official classes. That, I think, is a defence for the people of Italy — one defence — although there can be no really valid defence for any country or any people which allows its freedom and inherent rights to pass out of its own hands.

The external shock of war has broken the spell which in Italy held all these masses for so long, in fact for more than twenty years, in physical and even more in moral subjection. We may, therefore, reasonably expect that very great changes will take place in Italy. What their form will be, or how they will impinge upon the forces of German occupation and control, it is too early to forecast. The guilt and folly of Mussolini have cost the Italian people dear. It looked so safe and easy in May, 1940, to stab falling France in the back and advance to appropriate the Mediterranean interests and possessions of what Mussolini no doubt sincerely believed was a decadent and ruined Britain. It looked so safe and easy to fall upon the much smaller State of Greece. However, there have been undeceptions. Events have taken a different course. By many hazardous turns of fortune and by the long marches of destiny, the British and United States Armies, having occupied the Italian African Empire, the North of Africa, and the bulk of Sicily, now stand at the portals of the Italian mainland armed with the powers of the sea and the air, and with a very large land and amphibious force equipped with every modern weapon and device.

What is it that these masterful forces bring to Italy? They bring, if the Italian people so decide, relief from the war, freedom from servitude, and, after an interval, a respectable place in the new and rescued Europe. When I learn of the scenes enacted in the streets of the fine city of Palermo on the entry of the

United States Armies, and review a mass of detailed information with which I have been furnished, I cannot doubt that the main wish of the Italian people is to be quit of their German taskmasters, to be spared a further and perfectly futile ordeal of destruction, and to revive their former democratic and parliamentary institutions. These they can have. The choice is in their hands. As an alternative, the Germans naturally desire that Italy shall become a battle ground, a preliminary battle ground, and that by Italian sufferings the ravages of war shall be kept as far away as possible for as long as possible from the German Fatherland. If the Italian Government and people choose that the Germans shall have their way, no choice is left open to us. We shall continue to make war upon Italy from every quarter; from North and South, from the sea and from the air, and by amphibious descents, we shall endeavour to bring the utmost rigour of war increasingly upon her. Orders to this effect have been given to all the Allied commanders concerned.

A decision by the Italian Government and people to continue under the German yoke will not affect seriously the general course of the war. Still less will it alter its ultimate result. The only consequence will be that in the next few months Italy will be seared and scarred and blackened from one end to the other. I know little or nothing of the new Government. I express no opinion, but it is obvious that so far as their own people are concerned they have a very important decision to take. Meanwhile I am anxious that the various processes by which this decision is reached should be allowed to run their course under no other pressure than that of relentless war. This operation may well take some time. There may be several stages of transition. Past experience shows that when great changes of heart and character take place in the government of a nation, very often one stage is rapidly succeeded by another. I cannot tell. So far, we have had no approaches from the Italian Government, and therefore no new decisions are called upon from us, except those which are connected with the bringing of the maximum avalanche of fire and steel upon all targets of military significance throughout the length and breadth of Italy.

However, I must utter a word of caution. We do not know what is going to happen in Italy, and now that Mussolini has gone, and once the Fascist power is certainly and irretrievably broken, we should be foolish to deprive ourselves of any means of coming to general conclusions with the Italian nation. It would be a grave mistake, when Italian affairs are in this flexible, fluid, formative condition, for the rescuing Powers, Britain and the United States, so to act as to break down the whole structure and expression of the Italian State. We certainly do not seek to reduce Italian life to a condition of chaos and anarchy, and to find ourselves without any authorities with whom to deal. By so doing, we should lay upon our Armies and upon our war effort the burden of occupying, mile by mile, the entire country, and of forcing the individual surrender of every armed or coherent force in every district into which our troops may enter. An immense task of garrisoning, policing and administering would be thrown upon us, involving a grievous expenditure of power, and still more of time.

We must be careful not to get ourselves into the kind of position into which the Germans have blundered in so many countries — that of having to hold down and administer in detail, from day to day, by a system of gauleiters, the entire life of very large populations, thereby becoming responsible under the hard conditions of this present period for the whole of their upkeep and well-being. Such a course might well, in practice, turn the sense of liberation, which it may soon be in our power to bestow upon the Italian people, into a sullen discontent against us and all our works. The rescuers might soon, indeed, be regarded as tyrants; they might even be hated by the Italian people as much or almost as much as their German allies. I certainly do not wish, in the case of Italy, to tread a path which might lead to execution squads and concentration camps, and above all to having to carry on our shoulders a lot of people who ought to be made to carry themselves.

Therefore, my advice to the House of Commons, and to the British nation, and to the Commonwealth and Empire, and to our Allies may, at this juncture be very simply stated. We should let the Italians, to use a homely phrase, stew in their own juice for a bit, and hot up the fire to the utmost in order to accelerate the process, until we obtain from their Government, or whoever possesses the necessary authority, all our indispensable requirements for carrying on the war against our prime and capital foe, which is not Italy but Germany. It is the interest of Italy, and also the interest of the Allies, that the unconditional surrender of Italy should be brought about wholesale and not piecemeal. Whether this can be accomplished or not, I cannot tell, but people in this country and elsewhere who cannot have the necessary knowledge of all the forces at work, or assign true valuations to the various facts and factors, should, I think, at this juncture be restrained in speech and writing, lest they should add to the tasks, the toils and the losses of our Armies, and prolong and darken the miseries which have descended upon the world.

In all these affairs, we are, of course, acting in the closest concert with the United States, our equal partner and good and gallant comrade in this new tremendous Mediterranean enterprise. Our Russian friends are also being kept regularly informed. The Allied Commanders in the Mediterranean theatre are in the closest accord on the very difficult problems produced in such circumstances by the inseparable interplay of military and political elements; and the British and the United States Armies under their leadership are working as if they were the Army of one single nation, an Army, I may remind the House, which has just shown itself capable of little less than a prodigy of intricate organisation. The two Governments are in continuous consultation and association through the Foreign Office, and I correspond personally almost every day, under the authority of the War Cabinet, with the President of the United States. I conceive that His Majesty's Government have the right to ask for the solid and sustained confidence of Parliament. After years of extreme difficulty and danger, we are conducting increasingly successful war and policy, and we feel sure that the House would not wish us to be deprived of the fullest freedom to act in the name and interest of the nation as we think fit, at this particular and swiftly-moving juncture. It is extremely important that full latitude should continue to be accorded to the Government by the House, that no diminution of the responsibility of the Executive should be attempted, and that no untimely or premature explanations should be sought in respect to business of such consequence and complications.

Questions have been addressed to my right hon. Friend the

Leader of the House about a Debate. It may be possible for me
to make some further statement, not only on the Mediterranean
position but on the war as a whole, before the House rises. I
should be quite willing if this were possible, but I cannot at
present promise to do so, because I do not know whether any
point will be reached in the next week from which a general
survey could usefully be made. Very complete, vivid and excellent
accounts are appearing in the newspapers of all the operations.
An immense army of correspondents move with the troops and
carry their cameras into the heat of the fight, and an immense
volume of material of the deepest interest and of a very high level
of quality and accuracy fills the public Press from hour to hour;
and there is at present very little which I could add to this, except, of course, to set matters in proportion as I and my colleagues view them, and to place the proper emphasis, or what we
conceive, with our fallible judgment, to be the proper emphasis,
upon the various facts and factors.

I will venture to offer another word of caution, and I do not
think it is inappropriate to do so in a period when, not un-
naturally, our spirits run high. What is Italy as a war unit? Italy
is, or rather she was, perhaps about one-tenth of the power of
Germany. The German tyranny is being violently assailed and
beset on every side. Mighty battles on the Russian front, far exceeding in scale any of the operations in which we and the
United States have hitherto been engaged on land, have in the
month of July inflicted further deep injuries upon the German
army. The systematic shattering of German cities continues remorselessly and with ever-growing weight. The spirit of revolt
rises higher in all the subjugated lands. The German rule is
maintained from the North Cape in Norway to the Island of
Crete only by hideous and ruthless cruelty, reprisals and massa-
cres. The German hopes of the U-boat warfare turning the tide
of war are sinking as fast as the U-boat themselves. The whole
outlook of the Nazi party and regime, their whole ideological
outlook, as it is called, will be disturbed and darkened by the
events which have happened and are going to happen in Italy,
and the overthrow and casting-down in shame and ruin of the
first of the dictators and aggressor war lords strikes a knell of
impending doom in the ears of those that remain.

Nevertheless, let us not allow this favourable inclination of our fortunes to blind us to the immensity of the task before us, nor to the exertions still to be made and the privations and tribulations still to be endured and overcome. The German national strength is still massive. The German armies, though seriously mauled by the three Russian campaigns, are still intact and quite unbroken. Hitler has under his orders over 300 German divisions, excluding the satellites. Three-quarters are mobile and most of them continue to be well equipped. We are fighting some of these divisions in Sicily at this moment, and, as we see, they offer a stubborn resistance in positions well adapted to defence. The authority of the central Government in Germany grips and pervades every form of German life. The resources of a dozen lands are in their hands for exploitation. The harvest prospects are reported to be fairly good. This Nazi war machine is the hateful incubus upon Europe which we are resolved utterly to destroy, and the affairs of Italy must be handled with this supreme object constantly in view. Both our strategy and our policy, I venture to claim, have been vindicated by events, and I look forward to offering to Parliament, as the months unfold, further convincing proof of this assertion; but we cannot afford to make any large mistake which we can by careful forethought avoid, nor can we afford to prolong by any avoidable mismanagement the sombre journey in which we shall persevere to the end.

U.S. Ships for Britain

A STATEMENT TO THE HOUSE OF COMMONS
AUGUST 3, 1943

July 28.	*President Roosevelt broadcast that Mussolini and other Fascist leaders would be punished.*
July 29.	*A decree issued in Rome announced that all prominent Fascists were being kept under arrest "for the sake of public order."*
	R.A.F. dropped another 2,300 tons of bombs on Hamburg.
July 30.	*Great Britain and the United States warned neutral countries against sheltering war criminals.*
July 31.	*General Eisenhower broadcast to the Italians that raids would begin again unless Italy surrendered.*
	General Giraud was appointed Commander-in-Chief of the French Forces, and General de Gaulle head of a new Committee of National Defence.
August 1.	*Two hundred American bombers attacked the Ploesti oilfields in Rumania, causing heavy damage.*
August 2.	*R.A.F. made another heavy attack on Hamburg, and it was estimated that in ten days and nights the city had received as great a tonnage of bombs as London in the whole of the 1940–1941 attack.*

[August 3, 1943

I WILL, with the permission of the House, read a letter which I have received recently from the President: —

190

THE WHITE HOUSE,
WASHINGTON.

Dear Mr. Prime Minister,

When you were with us during the latter part of December, 1941, and the first few days of 1942, after we had become active participants in the war, plans for a division of responsibilities between your country and mine became generally fixed in certain understandings. In matters of production, as well as in other matters, we agreed that mutual advantages were to be gained by concentrating, in so far as it was practicable, our energies on doing those things which each of us was best qualified to do.

Here in this country in abundance were the natural resources of critical materials. Here there had been developed the welding technique which enables us to construct a standard merchant ship with a speed unequalled in the history of merchant shipping. Here there was waiting cargo to be moved in ships to your Island and to other theatres. If your country was to have carried out its contemplated ship construction programme, it would have been necessary to move large tonnages of the raw materials that we have here across the Atlantic to your mills and yards, and then in the form of a finished ship to send them back to our ports for the cargo that was waiting to be carried.

Obviously this would have entailed a waste of materials and time. It was only natural for us then to decide that this country was to be the predominant cargo-ship-building area for us both, while your country was to devote its facilities and resources principally to the construction of combat vessels.

You, in your country, reduced your merchant shipbuilding programme and directed your resources more particularly to other fields in which you were more favourably situated, while we became the merchant shipbuilder for the two of us, and have built, and are continuing to build, a vast tonnage of cargo vessels.

Our merchant fleet has become larger, and will continue to grow at a rapid rate. To man its ever increasing number of vessels will, we foresee, present difficulties of no mean proportion. On your side, the British merchant fleet has been diminished, and you have in your pool as a consequence trained seamen and licensed personnel. Clearly it would be extravagant were this body of experienced men of the sea not to be used as promptly as possible. To fail to use them would result in a wastage of man-power on your side, a wastage of man-power on our side, and what is of equal importance, a wastage of shipping facilities. We cannot afford this waste.

In order that the general understanding that we reached during the early days of our engagement together in this war may be more perfectly carried out, and in order, as a practical matter, to avoid the prodigal use of man-power and shipping that would result from pursuing any other course, I am directing the War Shipping Administration, under appropriate bareboat arrangements, to transfer to your flag for temporary wartime duty during each of the suggested next ten months a minimum of 15 ships. I have, furthermore, suggested to them that this be increased to 20.

We have, as you know, been allocating to the British services on a voyage-to-voyage basis large numbers of American-controlled ships. What I am now suggesting to you, and what I am directing the War Shipping Administration to carry out, will be in the nature of a substitution, to the extent of the tonnage transferred, for the American tonnage that has been usually employed in your war programme. The details of the arrangements we can properly leave to the national shipping authorities for settlement through the Combined Shipping Adjustment Board, whose function it is to concert the employment of all merchant vessels, and who will, in accordance with its usual practice, do so in connection with these particular ships.

Always sincerely,

(*Signed*) FRANKLIN D. ROOSEVELT.

In my discussions with the President, which were furthered in great detail by the Minister of War Transport, we confined ourselves purely to the war period, leaving arrangements suitable to peace-time settlements to be discussed at a future date. The transfer to our Flag of 150 to 200 ships has already begun, and will be spread over ten months. It will absorb our reserves of trained seafaring population, and the resources of both countries will be economically and providently applied to the main purpose.

It gives me much pleasure to read to the House this letter from the President, which I have received his permission to make public. I think it shows a deep understanding of our problems, and of the general problems of the war, by the Head of this most powerful State, and the intimate and sympathetic relationships prevailing between our two Allied Governments. This will I am sure be a source of keen satisfaction to the House and to the country, and certainly a powerful factor towards the abridgment of this period of war and destruction.

I should add that the Canadian Government are making a similarly generous arrangement in connection with ships built in Canada.

Asked whether the vessels to be transferred were the "Liberty" or "Victory" type, Mr. Churchill said: —

I could not give the classes of ships, but they are new ships which are being built in the United States. As to the exact proportion in which the different types are mingled, I have not been informed at present. There is no financial arrangement. The method we work on is that we use all things to the common advantage.

I think that whichever type they are we shall be very glad to put some of our sailors, who are accumulating in surplus, and our good engineers and so forth, who are already trained for the sea, on them. These men are very eager to pursue again their dangerous avocation.

War Decorations

[August 3, 1943

I HAVE some statements to make to the House, on a subject which I regard as agreeable, but about which there will be many differences of opinion. As has already been announced, His Majesty has decided to commemorate the victory in North Africa by the creation of the Africa Star, and at the same time to institute the 1939–43 Star as a reward for those in the Services who have taken part in hard fighting elsewhere during the first four years of war. The Merchant Navy will be included. No individual will qualify for both Stars. I must explain that Stars are given in a war, and medals only at the end. There will be Clasps to the Africa Star for the Eighth and First Armies. There will also be a Clasp to the 1939–43 Star for the Navy, the Air Force and the Merchant Navy for services in connection with the North African campaign.

The manufacture of the Stars themselves will be postponed until after the war. The ribbons will be made now, and issued as soon as supplies are ready. In addition the Clasps will be denoted by Emblems on the ribbon. These Emblems will be an Arabic "8" or an Arabic "1" or a "silver rose," as the case may be.

The King has also approved a bronze Emblem to denote Mention in Dispatches which can be worn on the coat in the place where a single Medal ribbon would be worn or immediately after any Medal ribbons, and has authorised the institution of Wound Stripes and Chevrons for years of war service.

The Wound Stripes and Chevrons will be awarded, not only in the Armed Forces, but also in the Merchant Navy, Civil Air Transport, the Police, the National Fire Service, in specified Civil Defence services, and, in addition, in the Fire Guard and to

194

Nurses in Government or Local Authority Hospitals or in the recognised Voluntary Hospitals.

Further details of these matters are contained in a White Paper which will shortly be available to hon. Members in the Vote Office. It is an extremely elaborate Paper, and I have personally devoted a very great deal of time to settling the various difficulties. As I say, there can be no doubt that different views will prevail upon this, but I believe it will be found that we have good grounds for the various decisions we have formed.

Offensive in Sicily

[*August 3, 1943*]

OUR general offensive in Sicily began to develop on Sunday afternoon, and all yesterday was passed in full battle. The report I have received says that the operations have opened well. The 78th Division has captured Centuripe after some very bitter fighting in the streets. The 51st Division are making progress on their right. To the left the Canadians have captured Regalbutto, where the opposition has been particularly fierce. Farther North the American Seventh Army are reported to have captured Troina yesterday evening. On the coast road the advance continues, in the face of extensive enemy demolitions. I should like to explain that during the last week, when things have seemed to be rather quiet, large reinforcements have been moved up to the fighting front, which has been properly garnished with artillery and supplies of every kind. A certain delay was necessary while the American Seventh Army on the Northern flank marched Eastward, driving the enemy before it and taking up its position on the flank of our Eighth Army. Between the two the Canadian Forces are stationed. These two Armies constitute what is called the Fifteenth Group of Armies, and this Fifteenth Group of Armies, I should explain, has been throughout commanded by General Alexander. He has under him, in the Seventh Army, General Patton, of the United States, a most distinguished officer, and on the other flank, General Montgomery, in command of the Eighth Army. He is himself conducting the battle, and I think we may feel sure that our affairs are in good hands.

War on the U-Boats

A STATEMENT ISSUED JOINTLY BY MR. CHURCHILL
AND PRESIDENT ROOSEVELT
AUGUST 15, 1943

[August 15, 1943

DURING July very poor results were obtained by U-boats from their widespread efforts against Allied shipping. The steady flow of Transatlantic supplies on the greatest scale has continued unmolested, and such sinkings as have taken place in distant areas have had but an insignificant effect on our conduct of the war. In fact July was probably our most successful month, because imports have been high, shipping losses moderate, and U-boat sinkings heavy.

Before the descent on Sicily an armada of warships, troop transports, supply ships, and landing-craft proceeded through Atlantic and Mediterranean waters with scarcely any interference. Over 2,500 vessels were involved, and the losses are only about 80,000 tons. The U-boats which attempted to interfere suffered severe losses.

Our offensive operations against submarines continue most favourably in all areas. During May, June and July we have sunk at sea a total of over 90 U-boats.

The decline in effectiveness of the U-boats is illustrated by the following figures: In the first six months of 1943 the number of ships sunk per U-boat operating was only half that in the last six months of 1942, and only a quarter of that in the first half of 1942.

The tonnage of shipping in the service of the United Nations continues to show a considerable net increase. During 1943, new ships completed by the Allies exceed all sinkings from all causes by upwards of 3,000,000 tons.

But it must be remembered that the enemy still has large

U-boat reserves, completed and under construction. It is necessary, therefore, to prepare for intensification of the battle both at sea and in the shipyards, and to use our shipping with the utmost economy to strengthen and speed the general offensive. We can expect continued success only if we do not relax our efforts in any way.

A Denial

DURING HIS VISIT TO QUEBEC FOR HIS CONFERENCE WITH
PRESIDENT ROOSEVELT IN AUGUST, 1943, MR. CHURCHILL
ISSUED THE FOLLOWING STATEMENT

THE Prime Minister of Great Britain denies that he ever made the statement attributed to him that the war would be over in six months. He would like the widest possible publicity given to that denial.

To the King

ON AUGUST 18, 1943, THE KING SENT A MESSAGE TO THE PRIME MINISTER CONGRATULATING HIM ON THE VICTORY IN SICILY AND ASKING HIM TO CONVEY HIS GRATITUDE TO ALL WHO WERE ENGAGED IN THE TASK OF PLANNING AND EXECUTING THE CAMPAIGN. THIS WAS THE PRIME MINISTER'S REPLY

[*August 19, 1943*

S IR,
   I shall be proud to convey Your Majesty's gracious message to all concerned both at home and overseas in the organisation and planning of the invasion and conquest of Sicily.

Your Majesty's congratulations will be received by those to whom they are addressed with the liveliest pleasure. They would, I know, wish me to convey to Your Majesty an expression of their gratitude for this gracious message and their determination to undertake with all possible energy whatever further tasks may lie ahead.

With my humble duty, I remain
Your Majesty's most faithful and devoted servant,

WINSTON S. CHURCHILL.

The Quebec Conference

A JOINT STATEMENT ISSUED IN QUEBEC BY MR. CHURCHILL
AND PRESIDENT ROOSEVELT

AUGUST 24, 1943

August 4.   *Russians recaptured Orel, one of Germany's most important bases on the Eastern Front.*

August 5.   *After more than two weeks of fierce fighting the Eighth Army captured Catania.*

    Marshal Stalin announced that the Red Army had retaken Byelogorod.

    Officially revealed that Allied aircraft operating from Britain had dropped a record total of 12,000 tons of bombs on Germany and occupied territory in the last week of July.

August 6.   *Soviet armies launched a new offensive in the direction of Kharkov.*

August 7.   *For the first time since the fall of Mussolini, R.A.F. heavily bombed Milan, Turin and Genoa.*

August 8.   *Political as well as military leaders attended conferences held at Hitler's headquarters.*

August 10.   *Announced that Mr. Churchill, accompanied by Chiefs of Staff, had arrived in Canada for conferences with President Roosevelt and the Canadian Cabinet.*

    In Sicily, British and United States armies linked up between Brontë and Cecaro.

August 11.   *Kharkov–Poltava railway, the main route for enemy communications with Kharkov, cut by the Red Army.*

August 12.   *Enemy evacuation of Sicily in full swing as American Seventh Army advanced to take key town of Randazzo.*

August 13.   *Randazzo, key enemy town in Sicily, fell to the U.S. Seventh Army.*

August 14. U.S. bombers made their first raid on Austria, attacking Wiener Neustadt, big industrial centre south of Vienna.

August 16. British Eighth Army captured Taormina, enemy G.H.Q. in Sicily, and U.S. Seventh Army reached Milazzo on the North Coast.

British and American Chiefs of Staff held consultations in Quebec.

August 17. Officially announced that all organised enemy resistance in Sicily had ended.

R.A.F. struck hard at a new target in Germany, dropping 1,500 tons of bombs on the research centre at Peenemunde on the Baltic coast.

August 19. Powerful air blows were struck in the Far East, 215 Japanese aircraft being destroyed in two days in New Guinea. In Europe, R.A.F. Mosquitoes continued regular night raids on Berlin.

August 20. U.S. naval forces occupied the Mediterranean islands of Lipari and Stromboli.

August 21. U.S. and Canadian forces occupied Kiska, the last of the Aleutian Islands in Japanese hands.

Russia claimed that the Germans had lost 1,000,000 men on the Eastern Front since the start of the summer offensive on July 5.

August 23. Russians captured Kharkov and also advanced through the Donetz basin toward Voroshilovgrad.

R.A.F. made the heaviest raid so far on Berlin — twice as heavy as the previous record raid in March. More than 1,700 tons of bombs were dropped in 50 minutes, 58 planes being lost.

August 24. A joint statement by Mr. Churchill and President Roosevelt at the end of the Quebec Conference showed that the war against Japan had figured largely in their discussions.

Fires were still blazing in Berlin when R.A.F. Mosquitoes raided the city again.

THE Anglo-American war conference, which opened at Quebec on August 11, under the hospitable auspices of the Canadian Government, has now concluded its work.

The whole field of world operations has been surveyed in the light of the many gratifying events which have taken place since the meeting of the President and the Prime Minister in Washington at the end of May, and the necessary decisions have been taken to provide for the forward actions of the fleet, the army, and the air forces of the two nations.

Considering that these forces are intermingled in continuous action against the enemy in several quarters of the globe, it is indispensable that entire unity of aim and method should be maintained at the summit of the war direction. Further conferences will be needed, probably at shorter intervals than before, as the war effort of the United States and the British Commonwealth and Empire against the enemy spreads and deepens.

It would not be helpful to the fighting troops to make any announcement of the decisions which have been reached. These can only emerge in action. It may, however, be stated that the military discussions of the Chiefs of Staff turned very largely on the war against Japan and the bringing of effective aid to China. Mr. T. V. Soong, representing Generalissimo Chiang Kai-shek, was a party to the discussions. In this field, as in the European, the President and the Prime Minister were able to receive and approve the unanimous recommendations of the Combined Chiefs of Staff. Agreement was also reached upon the political issues underlying or arising out of military operations.

It was resolved to hold another conference by the end of the year between British and American authorities, in addition to any tripartite meetings which it may be possible to arrange with Soviet Russia. Full reports of the decisions, as far as they affect the war against Germany and Italy, will be furnished to the Soviet Government.

Consideration has been given during the conference to the question of relations with the French Committee of Liberation, and it is understood that an announcement by a number of Governments will be made in the latter part of the week.

Answers in the House of Commons

[*June 24, 1943*

[BEVERIDGE REPORT]

Replying to a member who asked the Prime Minister to "allay public anxiety" by making a statement on the Government's attitude towards the Beveridge Report, Mr. Churchill said: —

I DO not think there is any public anxiety on this subject.

I have already made a statement on this subject, with other Members of the Government, and we have made our position perfectly clear. There is no intention of reconsidering our position.

I should be very glad to assist my hon. Friend in making some selections from the Ministerial declarations on this subject which he can use in reply to the people who approach him.

I think it would be very disastrous if so far-reaching a scheme were to be carried through in an atmosphere which appears to show intolerance of the careful examination of details.

[*July 1, 1943*

[EUROPE'S ECONOMIC SERVITUDE]

Replying to a member who asked for a statement on Germany's financial and industrial penetration of Europe, Mr. Churchill said: —

HIS Majesty's Government are well aware of the penetration of European industry and finance by Nazi Germany, and in particular by the Hermann Goering Trust. His Majesty's Government joined with the other Allied Governments chiefly concerned in making a Declaration on 5th January of this year which emphasised their intention to defeat all methods of dispossession practised by the enemy Powers in territories under their occupation or control. As a result of this Declaration, the text of which is contained in Command Paper 6148, an Inter-Allied Committee of Experts was set up in London to prepare the way for further action by a study of the relevant law, and by the collection of the necessary information on what the enemy has done and is still doing. The Governments of the United States of America, the Union of Soviet Republics, China, and the Governments of the European Allies are all represented on this Committee, which is assembling much valuable material. This information, together with information from other sources, including, of course, relevant reports published by the United States Office of War Information, will naturally be taken into full account in framing the future plans of the United Nations.

I cannot at present forecast these plans in detail, nor the arrangements which will follow the unconditional surrender of the enemy; but my hon. Friend can be assured that one of the aims of His Majesty's Government and the Governments of the United Nations will be to ensure that Europe shall be totally purged from the economic servitude which Nazi Germany has forced upon her.

[THE FRENCH IN NORTH AFRICA]

In reply to a member who asked for a statement on the position of the French National Committee in North Africa and also on General Eisenhower's control over the French political organisations there, Mr. Churchill said: —

I assume that the hon. Member for Seaham (Mr. Shinwell) has in mind recent Press messages from Washington on this subject. The facts are these. In view of the prolonged discussion between the French leaders in Algiers on questions involving the character and control of the French Armed Forces, and the serious effect which this might have on the furtherance of the war effort and the safety of the Allied Armies in North Africa, the Allied Commander-in-Chief, with the authority of the

United States Government and His Majesty's Government, on 19th June asked General Giraud and General de Gaulle for an assurance that there should be no important change in the French command in North Africa at the present time, and that General Eisenhower might be satisfied that the French military organisation was such that the French Commander-in-Chief had effective and proper control of the French Forces in this area. This representation was made on military grounds, and implied no decision to invest General Eisenhower with full control over the political organisation in North Africa.

I would take this opportunity to deprecate giving any undue attention to the personality aspect of the new French organisation. I informed the House on 8th June that we all rejoiced when agreement was made and the French Committee of National Liberation was set up and constituted as the single and sole authority for all Frenchmen seeking to free France from the German yoke, and I added that our dealings, financial and otherwise, would henceforward be with this Committee as a whole. The Committee is working on the basis of collective responsibility, and it is our hope that all its members will merge their personal and individual interests for the common good of France. His Majesty's Government have consistently encouraged the Union of all Frenchmen in the fight against the Axis and for the liberation of France. It has never been their policy to take sides between Frenchmen who fall in this category, and it is not their policy to support any one member of the Committee of National Liberation rather than another.

Taking a longer view, I would say that it is not the policy of the United States and British Governments that their Armies, upon whom the main burden must rest, or French Forces equipped by them, shall be used to impose upon France, directly or indirectly, any particular military leader, but rather to make sure that the broad and settled will of the masses of the French people, expressed under conditions of freedom, shall decide upon the future Government of their country.

Replying to a member who asked whether the Prime Minister was satisfied that unity and co-operation would develop under the new system, Mr. Churchill said: —

I think that would be to convict myself of undue optimism.

When another member asked whether the British Government was always consulted on political matters in North Africa and nothing was done without their consent, Mr. Churchill said:—

No, I should not put it as high as that, but my right hon. Friend the Member for Stockton (Mr. Harold Macmillan) has the fullest confidence of General Eisenhower. He lives in the closest association with the United States authorities and with the French authorities of every hue, he sees them continually, and very often reports to us several times a day. Of course, the main direction of the campaign in North Africa is, as I explained to the House earlier in the year, under the United States authorities, but we are also in frequent communication with the American Government, and personally I am in the closest accord with the President upon all the steps that are taken.

Another member asked whether it was not very difficult to distinguish between the political and military aspects of French conversations, and the Prime Minister replied:—

That, no doubt, is one of those difficulties which tax to the utmost the abilities of the distinguished officers involved.

When another member asked whether the House was to understand that in order to ensure the safety of the Allied troops it was necessary that General Giraud should remain in command of the French military forces, Mr. Churchill replied:—

I certainly consider that that is necessary at the present time.

[CONTROL OF INDUSTRY]

Replying to a member who asked whether the Government had decided who should control industry after the war and which major industries were scheduled for State enterprise and free enterprise respectively, Mr. Churchill said:—

I should not dream of embarking on such political and party controversies at the present time.

When the member then pointed out that one of the Prime Minister's colleagues had ventured into "this area of controversy" and added that it had caused a great deal of dissatisfaction, Mr. Churchill replied: —

All the more desirable is it that I should not swell the chorus.

[TRADES DISPUTES ACT]

Replying to a member who asked whether he would consider amending the Trades Disputes Act, Mr. Churchill said: —

This matter raises many controversial issues, and I am not in a position at present to make any statement.

I give it my constant personal attention, and the last thing in the world I want to see is quarrels breaking out between people who are working so very solidly together in the common line of defence.

[July 6, 1943

[MINISTERS' SALARIES]

Replying to a member who drew attention to the fact that Ministers who are members of the House of Commons cannot claim, for Income Tax purposes, against their salaries as Ministers the expenses which are deductible against their salaries as M.P.'s, Mr. Churchill said: —

THIS matter was discussed by the House during the Debates on the Ministers of the Crown Bill, 1937. Undoubtedly, the position as stated by my hon. Friend discloses a case requiring consideration, in respect of junior Ministers. The Government have not, up to the present, felt themselves able to make any recommendation to the House.

Mr. Emanuel Shinwell asked: "Is not being in the Government sufficient recompense for excessive Income Tax?" the Prime Minister said: —

I hope that is personal experience.

[A MINISTER FOR WALES]

Replying to a member who urged the appointment of a Secretary of State for Wales, Mr. Churchill said: —

I think that we have a tendency to have too many Ministers. One must look very jealously at new claimants.

This is a large topic to be dealt with at Question Time. I am well aware of the sentiments cherished by the people of Wales, and also of the very warm desire to gratify those sentiments which is the instinct of the English and Scottish peoples. At the same time, to create this entirely new Department in present circumstances would not, I think, be practicable.

[DOMESTIC SERVICE]

Replying to a member who asked which members of the Government were responsible for deciding the balance between the domestic service requirements of the civilian population and those of the Services, Mr. Churchill said: —

All questions relating to the balance between the man-power requirements of the civil population as against those of the Services are decided by the War Cabinet, which, of course, obtains advice from the Minister of Labour and National Service and other Ministers concerned. If a particular issue were raised by Question or in Debate, there would be no difficulty in selecting the Minister to deal with it.

[July 13, 1943

[RAILWAY CHARGES]

Replying to a member who asked him to appoint a Select Committee to consider equalised rates of freight charges for railways as a means of encouraging the economic rehabilitation of the countryside and the redistribution of industry, Mr. Churchill wrote: —

THE present system of railway rates provides for scales of charges per ton per mile which taper as the distance increases, and also for the application of exceptional rates where circumstances warrant them. While I do not think that it would be opportune or advisable to appoint a Select Committee to consider the introduction of flat rates irrespective of distance, the effect of railway charges upon the distribution of our economic activities will be borne in mind by His Majesty's Government in their consideration of future transport policy.

[*July 14, 1943*

[ELECTORAL REFORM]

Replying to a member who asked for a Parliamentary Committee of Inquiry into such questions of electoral reform as age qualification for ex-servicemen and women, reduction of cost of elections, further restrictions on the activities of outside agencies, variation in amount of deposit, use of conveyances for taking voters to the poll, use of loud speakers, and methods of voting, Mr. Churchill said: —

THE first point raised in this Question has been carefully considered, and it has been decided not to reduce the age qualification below 21 for the next General Election in respect of Service or ex-Service men and women, since any such step would operate harshly on those other young persons who, by virtue of their essential war work, have been unable to join the Forces. Since the other points raised will be open for discussion during the opportunity to be afforded to Parliament to discuss questions of electoral reform in good time before the next General Election, I do not consider it necessary for these matters to be investigated at this time by a Parliamentary Committee of Inquiry.

[ATLANTIC CHARTER]

Replying to a member who asked whether the Atlantic Charter, which had not been ratified by the United States, had any binding force on the United States or Great Britain, Mr. Churchill said: —

The so-called Atlantic Charter, indeed, the well-called Atlantic Charter, was not a treaty requiring ratification or any formal endorsement of a constitutional character on the other side of the Atlantic. It was a statement of certain broad views and principles which are our common guide in our forward march.

When the member then suggested that the first two clauses of the Atlantic Charter bound the Allied Powers in a way that might be perilous for them when peace came to be discussed, Mr. Churchill said: —

We have lots of worse troubles than that ahead.

[TRANSPORT AIRCRAFT]

Asked whether the General Staff were alive to the potentialities of large capacity transport and cargo aeroplanes for speeding-up operational tempo, Mr. Churchill said: —

Yes, Sir. My hon. Friend can be assured that co-operation between the Staffs and Services is such as to ensure that our resources of transport aircraft are used to the best advantage.

[POST–WAR SURPLUS MATERIALS]

Asked which Department was charged with planning the disposal of surplus material after the war, Mr. Churchill said: —

Future policy in regard to the disposal of surplus stocks is being considered through the machinery for the study of reconstruction problems under the guidance of my right hon. and learned Friend the Minister without Portfolio. Meanwhile, the responsibility in this matter lies with the Supply Departments, the Board of Trade and the Minister of Works, according to the kind of goods or material concerned.

[SERVICE PRISONS]

Asked for the names of the members of the Court of Inquiry into detention barracks and the terms of reference, Mr. Churchill said: —

THE Hon. Mr. Justice Oliver has consented to be Chairman of the inquiry. The other members will be the Right Rev. the Lord Bishop of Reading and Lord Moran. The House will note that these three distinguished men, though belonging to very different vocations, all gained the M.C. for gallantry in the last war, and are therefore acquainted with military matters. The following are the terms of reference: —

"To inquire into and report on the treatment of men under sentence in Naval and Military Prisons and Detention Barracks in the United Kingdom, and whether it is in accordance with modern standards and satisfies war-time requirements.

"The investigation will cover *inter alia* the supervision and administration of discipline, medical care, training, welfare accommodation, feeding, and the suitability and adequacy of the staff."

On full consideration the Government consider that, in order to give it the widest possible scope and freedom, the inquiry should be held in private and not under the Tribunals of Inquiry Act, 1921. It is the intention, however, that the Report shall be published.

Asked whether suitable protection would be given to witnesses serving in the Army or other Services, Mr. Churchill said: —

It would be intolerable if any witnesses giving evidence before a court of inquiry of this kind should be victimised.

Asked whether any member of the Court of Inquiry had ever been incarcerated, Mr. Churchill said: —

That has never yet been made an indispensable condition for membership of a public inquiry.

[CANADIANS IN SICILY]

When a member drew attention to a statement by the Prime Minister of Canada regarding the lack of recognition of the part played by Canadian troops in the Sicilian operations, Mr. Churchill said: —

As I understand it, the point of the Canadian Prime Minister's remarks to which my hon. Friend refers was that in the initial draft communiqué prepared by the Allied Headquarters in North Africa for issue as soon as news of the landing in Sicily could be released, reference was made only to "Allied" Forces. On seeing this draft the Canadian authorities asked that at the earliest possible date reference should be made to the fact that Canadian Forces were taking part in the landing. Despite some possible security objections, this was at once agreed to by General Eisenhower, and the initial communiqué when issued referred to United Kingdom, United States and Canadian Forces. Owing to the greater distance of London from Ottawa and the six hours difference in time between them, information to this effect reached Ottawa from Washington sooner than from London. But this was not due to any slothfulness or want of appreciation on the part of any British authority.

Since then, as I think the House will agree, the fullest tribute has been paid in all public statements here and elsewhere to the valiant and successful part which the Canadian First Division is taking in this great enterprise. Our hearts also go out to the rest of the powerful Canadian Army in this country, who have for more than three years guarded the centre of the Empire from invasion. I may add that I have had a very agreeable interchange of telegrams with Mr. Mackenzie King on this matter, and the misunderstanding, for which nobody is to blame, can now be regarded as cleared away.

When another member suggested that, in future, military communiqués should refer to "Allied" forces only, Mr. Churchill said: —

It was exactly that point to which the Canadian Government objected. They objected to the expression "Allied" Forces and wished for the individual mention of their own contingents — a very reasonable wish — and it was immediately granted.

I think that the use of the expression "Allied" Forces is perfectly justifiable in many cases, just as the expression "United Kingdom" is justifiable, but that does not mean that the name of Wales should be entirely suppressed.

[July 21, 1943

[VICTORIA CROSS PENSIONS]

When a member urged that the £10 a year grant to holders of the Victoria Cross should be increased, Mr. Churchill said: —

THE normal pensions payable to recipients of the Victoria Cross may be increased in cases of need to £75. This figure was fixed in 1921. Further inquiries have been made, but they do not show any evidence of general complaint as to the adequacy of this special provision. I do not think any change in this well-established practice is called for.

I do not think this is a matter to be settled entirely on a money basis, and I do not propose to advise the House to make any change.

If we were to compute these matters by money values, I should be strongly in favour of much larger sums; but I think that would alter the character of these awards.

[ADMINISTRATION OF SICILY]

Asked what principles would be followed in the administration of occupied Sicily and the foundation of a democratic regime in place of Fascism, Mr. Churchill said: —

All these matters have been the subject of inter-Allied consideration extending over several months. The administration of Sicily, as explained in General Alexander's Proclamation, which has been published in the Press, is an Allied military administration, in which no political activities by the inhabitants can be countenanced. The Proclamation makes it clear, however, that one of the guiding principles of the administration is the elimination of the doctrines and practices of Fascism, and it is the earnest hope of His Majesty's Government that, when thus delivered from the Fascist regime, the people of Sicily will, of their own accord, turn towards liberal and democratic ideals. The word "liberal" in this case is spelt with a small "l."

Very lengthy preparations have been made both here and in the United States to provide a body of acceptable gentlemen who can assist in these matters, and one hopes that as time goes on the people of the liberated regions will be very sensible of the mitigation of their lot.

[A DE GAULLE DOCUMENT]

A member asked whether the Prime Minister had considered the document, a copy of which had been sent to him, purporting to have been officially prepared to acquaint British officials and the British Press with the views of the Prime Minister on the subject of General de Gaulle, and what steps the Prime Minister was taking to put a stop to the dissemination of mis-statements liable to prejudice the relations of this country with the United Nations. In reply Mr. Churchill said: —

Contrary to the statement in my hon. Friend's Question, no document has been received from him, but only a cutting from a newspaper which refers to a document. I take full responsibility for this document, the text of which was drafted personally by me. It is a confidential document. I am not prepared to discuss it otherwise than in Secret Session, and then only if there were a general desire from the House to have a Secret Session.

In regard to confidential documents, there sometimes occur breaches of confidence. Leakages take place, and so forth. When these take place in a foreign country — I will say in another country — certainly I do not feel that any alteration in our course of action is necessary.

[WOMEN'S SERVICES AFTER THE WAR]

Asked whether the Government would carry out the suggestion in the Report on Women's Services that members of the Auxiliary Services should form part of the Armed Forces for work in Europe and elsewhere after the war, Mr. Churchill said: —

THE future organisation of the Women's Services after general demobilisation cannot be considered apart from that of the Armed Forces as a whole, and the time has not yet come to determine policy on this whole question. The Government can, however, state that for some time after hostilities have ceased in any area the Women's Auxiliary Services will still be needed. In particular, members of the Auxiliary Services will be needed to accompany the Forces of Occupation so soon as conditions permit of their being sent overseas.

Members of the Women's Auxiliary Services and of the Civil Defence Services, when and in so far as they can be spared, will be given opportunities to volunteer for appointments in the administration of liberated territories during the period of military control. In so far as opportunities may arise under the proposed United Nations' Relief Organisation, members of these Services, in common with suitable candidates from other sources, will be eligible to volunteer for appointments, provided they can be spared from their Services. The number of appointments, both during the period of military control and under the proposed relief organisation, is likely to be very small.

[*July 28, 1943*

[BOMBING OF ROME]

Asked whether there had been official reply to the request to the Italians to capitulate, and also whether he was satisfied that "the apologies for bombing Rome serve any useful purpose," Mr. Churchill said: —

NO official reply has been received to the message in the name of the President and myself, unless the disappearance of Mussolini is to be construed as his own reply to it. As regards the second part of the Question, His Majesty's Government have not made any apology for bombing the marshalling yards near Rome. On the contrary, if they are repaired, and hostile military traffic is resumed, they will no doubt have to be bombed again.

Asked for information regarding the political, military and social consequences of the recent air raids on Rome, Mr. Churchill said: —

All my information on this subject is highly encouraging.

[CADET CORPS TRAINING]

Asked whether there was any committee for co-ordinating the training of the three Cadet Corps, Mr. Churchill said: —

The Inter-Services Cadet Committee is responsible for all matters of common interest and for co-operation between the three Cadet Corps. This Committee has under it a training sub-committee, to which are referred any training matters requiring detailed investigation. It is at present considering a common syllabus for basic training in the three Cadet Forces. It is not proposed to include combined operations in this syllabus, but where members of the three Forces are in the same camp they carry out some of their training together.

When a member suggested that the grants for the three Corps should be unified, Mr. Churchill said: —

That is a matter that should be considered by the Inter-Services Cadet Committee. It is for them to make recommendations to the various Ministers, and through them, if necessary, to submit them to me as Minister of Defence.

[WAR AGAINST JAPAN]

Asked whether assurances had been given by Allied European Governments represented in this country and at present at war with Japan, that they would give every aid to the war against Japan in the event of the war against Germany and Italy being previously concluded, Mr. Churchill said: —

Yes, Sir. Under the United Nations Declaration each of the Allied European Governments represented in this country and at war with Japan has undertaken to employ its full resources, military or economic, against those members of the Tripartite Pact and its adherents with which such Government is at war, and not to make a separate armistice or peace with the enemy.

[August 3, 1943

[ADMINISTRATION OF SICILY]

Asked who was responsible for the selection of the personnel for AMGOT (Allied Military Government for Occupied Territory), Mr. Churchill said: —

THE military government of Sicily is a Joint Anglo-American Government carried out under the direction of the Supreme Commander, General Eisenhower, who is responsible through the Combined Chiefs of Staff to the Government of Great Britain and the Government of the United States. The War Office is the Department in this country responsible for selecting the British officers required for this service.

Asked by another member whether General Eisenhower had issued any general directions to AMGOT and whether Parliament could inspect them, Mr. Churchill said: —

The hon. Gentleman has not appreciated what I said in my answer — has not taken it in. I said that the military government of Sicily is a Joint Anglo-American Government, carried out under the direction of the Supreme Commander, General Eisenhower, who is himself responsible through the Combined Chiefs of Staff at Washington to our two Governments. Broadly speaking, complete agreement has been reached between the two Governments, and General Eisenhower acts within the limits of that.

[DEFENCE REGULATION 18B]

Asked to give an assurance that the Government would not bring in an Act of Indemnity after the war with reference to the detention of persons under Defence Regulation 18B, Mr. Churchill said: —

I know of no matters in connection with the administration of Defence Regulation 18B which necessitate an Act of Indemnity, but I have little doubt that at the end of the war consideration will have to be given to legislation such as was passed at the end of the last war to grant indemnity in respect of acts done in good faith and in the execution of duty or for the defence of the realm or the successful prosecution of the war. If such legislation is proposed, it will, of course, be subject to debate in the usual way.

[ITALY'S NEXT GOVERNMENT]

Asked whether the Allies would recognise an Italian Government consisting of Socialists and other Left opinion expressing a desire to negotiate peace, Mr. Churchill said: —

His Majesty's Government will be prepared, in consultation with their principal Allies, to deal with all situations as they arise.

Asked to be more explicit, Mr. Churchill said: —

I have nothing to add to what I have said, which I think is explicit and, I think, has the additional merit of being comprehensive.

[August 4, 1943

[MALTA ENLISTMENTS]

Asked whether, as a recognition of the gallantry of the people of Malta, he would agree to the relaxation of the rules applying to the enlistment in the Services of literate Maltese educated in Malta, Mr. Churchill said: —

HIS Majesty's Government fully recognise the gallant part played in the war by the people of Malta, but I do not think it necessary to make any alteration in the practice governing the entry of Maltese into the Armed Forces. As my hon. and gallant Friend is doubtless aware, the Maltese have made a substantial contribution in man-power to the Fighting Services during the war.

[MINISTER OF WORKS]

Asked whether he was aware of the apprehension that had been aroused that the Ministry of Works would continue as a Department after the war emergency period, Mr. Churchill said: —

I am not aware of any considerable apprehension on this matter. The functions relating to Government lands and buildings previously discharged by the Office of Works, and now assigned by Statute to the Ministry of Works, are of course permanent, as is the legislation establishing the Ministry, unless repealed by Parliament. The powers relating to control of building materials, licensing of non-Government building and the like, which are now exercised by the Ministry by virtue of Orders in Council under the Emergency Powers (Defence) Acts will automatically fall to be reviewed when these Acts expire; any arrangements which may then seem necessary will require the sanction of Parliament. But hon. Members will realise that as indicated in the White Paper on Training for the Building Industry (Cmd. 6428) that industry will occupy a special position in the Government's plans for reconstruction and employment after the war.

When a member then suggested that in a House of Commons debate there had been almost universal condemnation of the actions of the present Minister (Lord Portal), Mr. Churchill said: —

I think it would be most unjust if that were so, because I have rarely had the pleasure of working with a more competent minister than the present Minister of Works.

When a member urged that the emergency powers of Regulation 18B should no longer be exercised solely by the Home Secretary but should be transferred to a properly constituted legal tribunal, Mr. Churchill said: —

The issue raised by my hon. Friend has been debated in the House on more than one occasion, and it has been pointed out that the responsibility for deciding whether circumstances of suspicion exist warranting the restraint of some individual on grounds of public security, could not properly be placed on a legal tribunal. So long as exceptional powers are needed in the interests of national security they must be exercised by a Minister responsible to Parliament.

When another member asked: "Does not the Prime Minister acknowledge that it is the duty of this House to protect the liberties of British citizens?" Mr. Churchill replied: —

Yes, Sir, but I think the House is as good a judge of its own duty as the hon. Gentleman.

The Call for a Three-Power Talk

August 25.	*Lord Louis Mountbatten was appointed supreme Allied Commander South-East Asia, for operations based on India and Ceylon.*
August 26.	*British, United States and Canadian Governments recognised the authority of the de Gaulle-Giraud French Committee of National Liberation.*
August 28.	*King Boris of Bulgaria's death was announced, but no details were given and many rumours circulated.*
August 29.	*Fighting broke out in Denmark and martial law was declared. Eight Danish warships reached Sweden.*
August 30.	*Germans took over full control of Denmark. Russians captured Taganrog.*
August 31.	*Russians launched opening attack in the battle for Smolensk.*

[August 31, 1943

A T the beginning of July I began to feel the need for a new meeting with the President of the United States and also for another conference of our joint staffs. We were all delighted when, by a happy inspiration, President Roosevelt suggested that Quebec should be the scene, and when the Governor-General and the Government of Canada offered us their princely hospitalities. Certainly no more fitting and splendid setting could have been chosen for a meeting of those who guide the war policy of the two great Western democracies at this cardinal moment in the Second World War than we have here in the Plains of Abraham, the Château Frontenac, and the ramparts of the Citadel of Quebec, from the midst of which I speak to you now.

Here at the gateway of Canada, in mighty lands which have never known the totalitarian tyrannies of Hitler and Mussolini, the spirit of freedom has found a safe and abiding home. Here that spirit is no wandering phantom. It is enshrined in Parliamentary institutions based on universal suffrage and evolved through the centuries by the English-speaking peoples. It is inspired by the Magna Carta and the Declaration of Independence. It is guarded by resolute and vigilant millions, never so strong or so well armed as to-day.

Quebec was the very place for the two great Powers of sea and of the air to resolve and shape plans to bring their large and growing armies into closer contact and fiercer grips with the common foe. Here above all, in the capital and heart of French Canada, was it right to think of the French people in their agony, to set on foot new measures for their deliverance, and to send them a message across the ocean that we have not forgotten them, nor all the services that France has rendered to culture and civilisation, to the march of the human intellect and to the rights of man. For forty years or more I have believed in the greatness and virtue of France, often in dark and baffling days I have not wavered, and since the Anglo-French Agreement of 1904 I have always served and worked actively with the French in the defence of good causes.

It was therefore to me a deep satisfaction that words of hope, of comfort and recognition should be spoken, not only to those Frenchmen who, outside Hitler's clutches, march in arms with us, but also to the broad masses of the French nation who await the day when they can free and cleanse their land from the torment and shame of German subjugation. We may be sure that all will come right. We may be sure that France will rise again free, united, and independent, to stand on guard with others over the generous tolerances and brightening opportunities of the human society we mean to rescue and rebuild.

I have also had the advantage of conferring with the Prime Minister of Canada, Mr. Mackenzie King, that experienced statesman who led the Dominion instantly and unitedly into the war, and of sitting on several occasions with his Cabinet, and the British and Canadian Staffs have been over the whole ground of the war together. The contribution which Canada has made to the combined effort of the British Commonwealth and Empire in these tremendous times has deeply touched the heart of the Mother Country and of all the other members of our widespread family of States and races.

From the darkest days the Canadian army, growing stronger year by year, has played an indispensable part in guarding our British homeland from invasion. Now it is fighting with distinction in wider and ever-widening fields. The Empire Air Training Organisation, which has been a wonderful success, has found its seat in Canada, and has welcomed the flower of the manhood of Great Britain, of Australia, and New Zealand to her spacious flying-fields and to comradeship with her own gallant sons.

Canada has become in the course of this war an important seafaring nation, building many scores of warships and merchant ships, some of them thousands of miles from salt water, and sending them forth manned by hardy Canadian seamen to guard the Atlantic convoys and our vital life-line across the ocean. The munition industries of Canada have played a most important part in our war economy. Last, but not least, Canada has relieved Great Britain of what would otherwise have been a debt for these munitions of no less than $2,000,000,000.

All this, of course, was dictated by no law. It came from no treaty or formal obligation. It sprang in perfect freedom from sentiment and tradition and a generous resolve to serve the future of mankind. I am glad to pay my tribute on behalf of the people of Great Britain to the great Dominion, and to pay it from Canadian soil. I only wish indeed that my other duties, which are exacting, allowed me to travel still farther afield and tell Australians, New Zealanders, and South Africans to their faces how we feel towards them for all they have done, and are resolved to do.

I mentioned just now the agreement Britain made with France almost forty years ago, and how we have stood by it, and will stand by it, with unswerving faithfulness. But there is another great nation with whom we have made a solemn treaty. We have made a twenty-years' treaty of good will and mutual aid with

Soviet Russia. You may be sure that we British are resolved to do our utmost to make that good with all our strength and national steadiness.

It would not have been suitable for Russia to be represented at this Anglo-American conference, which, apart from dealing with the immediate operations of our intermingled and interwoven armed forces in the Mediterranean and elsewhere, was largely, if not mainly, concerned with heating and inflaming the war against Japan, with whom the Soviet Government have a five years' treaty of non-aggression.

It would have been an embarrassing invitation for us to send. But nothing is nearer to the wishes of President Roosevelt and myself than to have a threefold meeting with Marshal Stalin. If that has not yet taken place, it is certainly not because we have not tried our best, or have not been willing to lay aside every impediment and undertake further immense journeys for that purpose. It is because Marshal Stalin, in direct command of the victorious Russian Armies, cannot at the present time leave the battle-fronts upon which he is conducting operations of vital consequence — not only to Russia, which is the object of ferocious German attack, but also to the common cause of all the United Nations.

To judge by the latest news from the Russian battle-fronts, Marshal Stalin is certainly not wasting his time. The entire British Empire sends him our salutes on this brilliant summer campaign, and on the victories of Orel, Kharkov, and Taganrog, by which so much Russian soil has been redeemed and so many hundreds of thousands of its invaders wiped out.

The President and I will persevere in our efforts to meet Marshal Stalin, and in the meantime it seems most necessary and urgent that a conference of the British, United States, and Russian Foreign Ministers, or their responsible representatives, should be held at some convenient place, in order not merely to explore the various important questions connected with the future arrangements for world security, but to carry their discussions to a point where the heads of States and Governments may be able to intervene.

We shall also be very glad to associate Russian representatives with us in the political decisions which arise out of the victories the Anglo-American Forces have gained in the Mediterranean. In fact, there is no step which we may take, or which may be forced upon us by the unforeseeable course of this war, about which we should not wish to consult with our Russian friends and allies in the fullest confidence and candour. It would be a very great advantage to us all and indeed to the whole free world, if a unity of thought and decision upon practical measures for the longer future, as well as upon strategic problems, could be reached between the three great opponents of the Hitlerite tyranny.

We have heard a lot of talk in the last two years about establishing what is called a Second Front in Northern France against Germany. Anyone can see how desirable that immense operation of war would be. It is quite natural that the Russians, bearing the main weight of the German armies on their front, should urge us ceaselessly to undertake this task, and should in no way conceal their complaints and even reproaches that we have not done it before.

I do not blame them at all for what they say. They fight so well, and they have inflicted such enormous injury upon the military strength of Germany, that nothing they could say in honest criticism of our strategy, or the part we have so far been able to take in the war, would be taken amiss by us, or weaken our admiration for their own martial prowess and achievement.

We once had a fine front in France, but it was torn to pieces by the concentrated might of Hitler; and it is easier to have a front pulled down than it is to build it up again. I look forward to the day when British and American liberating armies will cross the Channel in full force and come to close quarters with the German invaders of France. You would certainly not wish me to tell you when that is likely to happen, or whether it be soon or late; but whenever the great blow is struck, you may be sure that it will be because we are satisfied that there is a good chance of continuing success, and that our soldiers' lives will be expended in accordance with sound military plans and not squandered for political considerations of any kind.

I submit to the judgment of the United Nations, and of history, that British and American strategy, as directed by our combined Chiefs of Staff, and as approved and to some extent inspired by the President and myself, has been the best that was open to us in a practical sense. It has been bold and daring, and has brought into play against the enemy the maximum effective forces that could have been deployed up to the present by Great Britain and the United States, having regard to the limitations of ocean transport, to the peculiar conditions of amphibious warfare, and to the character and training of the armies we possess, which have largely been called into being since the beginning of the war.

Personally, I always think of the Third Front as well as the Second Front. I have always thought that the Western democracies should be like a boxer who fights with two hands and not one. I believe that the great flanking movement into North Africa, made under the authority of President Roosevelt and of His Majesty's Government, for whom I am a principal agent, will be regarded in the after time as quite a good thing to do in all the circumstances.

Certainly it has reaped rich and substantial results. Africa is cleared. All German and Italian armies in Africa have been annihilated, and at least half a million prisoners are in our hands. In a brilliant campaign of 38 days Sicily, which was defended by over 400,000 Axis troops, has been conquered.

Mussolini has been overthrown. The war impulse of Italy has been destroyed, and that unhappy country is paying a terrible penalty for allowing itself to be misled by false and criminal guides. How much easier it is to join bad companions than to shake them off! A large number of German troops have lately been drawn away from France in order to hold down the Italian people, in order to make Italy a battleground, and to keep the war as distant and as long as possible from German soil. By far the greater part of the German Air Force has been drawn off from the Russian front, and indeed is being engaged and worn down with ever-growing intensity, by night and day, by British and American and Canadian airmen.

More than all this, we have established a strategic initiative and potential — both from the Atlantic and from the Mediterranean — of which the enemy can neither measure the weight nor foresee the hour of application. Both in the Mediterranean and in our air assaults on Germany the war has prospered. An immense diminution of Hitler's war-making capacity has been achieved by the air bombardment, and of course that bombardment will steadily increase in volume and in accuracy as each successive month passes by.

I readily admit that much of all this would have been impossible in this form or at this time, but for the valiant and magnificent exertions and triumphs of the Russian Army, who have defended their native soil against a vile and unprovoked attack with incomparable vigour, skill, and devotion, and at a terrible price in Russian blood.

No Government ever formed among men has been capable of surviving injuries so grave and cruel as those inflicted by Hitler upon Russia. But under the leadership of Marshal Stalin, and thanks also to the stand made by the British peoples when they were all alone, and to abundant British and American ammunition and supplies of all kinds, Russia has not only survived and recovered from these frightful injuries, but has inflicted, as no other force in the world could have inflicted, mortal damage on the German army machine.

Most important and significant events are taking place in the Balkans as a result of the Russian victories, and also, I believe, of the Anglo-American campaign against Italy. Thrice in the last thirty years the Bulgarian people, who owed their liberation and existence to Russia, have been betrayed against their interest, and to a large extent against their wishes, and driven by evil rulers into disaster. The fate of Boris may serve other miscreants with the reminder that the wages of sin is death.

This is also the time to remember the glorious resistance to the invaders of their native lands of the peoples of Yugoslavia and of Greece, and of those whom Mr. Gladstone once called "the heroic Highlanders of Montenegro." The whole of the Balkans is aflame, and the impending collapse of Italy as a war factor will not only remove from the scene the most numerous of their assailants, but will also bring help nearer to those unconquerable races. I look forward with confidence to the day when Yugoslavia and Greece will once again be free — free to live their own lives and decide their own destiny. I take this opportunity to send a message of encouragement to these peoples and their Governments, and to the Kings of Greece and Yugoslavia, who have never faltered for one moment in their duty, and whom we hope to see restored to their thrones by the free choice of their liberated peoples.

Let us then all go forward together, making the best of ourselves and the best of each other; resolved to apply the maximum forces at our command without regard to any other single thought than the attack and destruction of those monstrous and evil dominations which have so nearly cost each and all of us our national lives and mankind its future.

Of course, as I told you, a large part of the Quebec discussions was devoted to the vehement prosecution of the war against Japan. The main forces of the United States and the manhood of Australia and New Zealand are engaged in successful grapple with the Japanese in the Pacific. The principal responsibility of Great Britain against Japan at present lies on the Indian front and in the Indian Ocean. The creation of a Combined Anglo-American Command over all the forces — land, sea, and air — of both countries in that theatre, similar to what has proved so successful in North-West Africa, has now been brought into effect.

A Supreme Commander of the South-East Asia front has been chosen, and his name has been acclaimed by British, American, and Chinese opinion. He will act in constant association with Generalissimo Chiang Kai-shek. It is true that Lord Louis Mountbatten is only 43. It is not often under modern conditions and in established military professions that a man gets so great a chance so early. But if an officer having devoted his life to the military art does not know about war at 43, he is not likely to learn much more about it later on. As Chief of Combined Operations, Lord Louis has shown rare powers of organisation and resourcefulness. He is what — pedants notwithstanding — I will venture to call "a complete triphibian," that is to say, a creature equally at home in three elements — earth, air, and water — and also well accustomed to fire. We all wish the new Command and its commander full success in their novel, varied, and certainly most difficult task.

I have been asked several times since I crossed the Atlantic whether I think the Germans will give in this year or whether they will hold out through another — which will certainly be worse for them. There are those who take an over-sanguine view. Certainly we see all Europe rising under Hitler's tyranny. What is now happening in Denmark is only another example. Certainly we see the Germans hated as no race has ever been hated in human history, or with such good reason. We see them sprawled over a dozen once free and happy countries, with their talons making festering wounds, the scars of which will never be effaced. Nazi tyranny and Prussian militarism, those two loathsome dominations, may well foresee and dread their approaching doom.

We cannot measure the full force of the blows which the Russian armies are striking and are going to strike. We cannot measure, though we know it is enormous, the havoc wrought in Germany by our bombing; nor the effects upon a population who have lived so long by making wars in the lands of others, and now, for the first time for more than a century, are having blasting and desolating war brought to their hearths and homes. We cannot yet measure what further results may attend the Anglo-American campaign in the Mediterranean, nor what depression the marked failure, for the time being, of the U-boat warfare on which German hopes were set, or the consequences of the shattering blows which are being struck, may engender in the German mind.

We pass here into the sphere of mass psychology, never more potent than in this modern age. Yet I consider that there are dangers in allowing our minds to dwell unduly upon the favourable circumstances which surround us, and which are so vividly and effectively brought to our notice every day by Press and broadcast.

For myself, I regard all such speculation as to when the war will end as at this moment vain and unprofitable. We did not undertake this task because we had carefully counted the cost, or because we had carefully measured the duration. We took it on because duty and honour called us to it, and we are content to drive on until we have finished the job. If Almighty God in his mercy should lighten or shorten our labours and the torment of mankind, all his servants will be thankful. But the United Nations feel conscious, both as States and as hundreds of millions of individuals, of being called to a high duty, which they will unflinchingly and tirelessly discharge with whatever strength is granted to them, however long the ordeal may last.

See how those who stray from the true path are deceived and

punished. Look at this wretched Mussolini and his son-in-law and accomplice Ciano, on whom the curse of Garibaldi has veritably fallen. I have heard that Ciano, explaining one day why Mussolini had plunged his dagger into the back of falling France and dreamed himself already among the Cæsars, said that such a chance would not occur again in 5,000 years. Certainly in June, 1940, the odds and omens seemed very favourable to Fascist ambition and greed.

It is not given to the cleverest and the most calculating of mortals to know with certainty what is their interest. Yet it is given to quite a lot of simple folk to know every day what is their duty. That is the path along which the British Commonwealth and Empire, the great Republic of the United States, the vast Union of Soviet Socialist Republics, the indomitable and innumerable people of China — all the United Nations — that is the path along which we shall march till our work is done and we may rest from our labours, and the whole world may turn with hope, with science, with good sense, and dear-bought experience, from war to lasting peace.

Anglo-American Unity

A SPEECH ON RECEIVING AN HONORARY DEGREE
AT HARVARD UNIVERSITY
SEPTEMBER 6, 1943

[September 6, 1943

THE last time I attended a ceremony of this character was in the spring of 1941, when, as Chancellor of Bristol University, I conferred a degree upon the United States Ambassador, Mr. Winant, and *in absentia* upon President Conant, our President, who is here to-day and presiding over this ceremony. The blitz was running hard at that time, and the night before, the raid on Bristol had been heavy. Several hundreds had been killed and wounded. Many houses were destroyed. Buildings next to the University were still burning, and many of the University authorities who conducted the ceremony had pulled on their robes over uniforms begrimed and drenched; but all was presented with faultless ritual and appropriate decorum, and I sustained a very strong and invigorating impression of the superiority of man over the forces that can destroy him.

Here now, to-day, I am once again in academic groves — groves is, I believe, the right word — where knowledge is garnered, where learning is stimulated, where virtues are inculcated and thought encouraged. Here, in the broad United States, with a respectable ocean on either side of us, we can look out upon the world in all its wonder and in all its woe. But what is this that I discern as I pass through your streets, as I look round this great company?

I see uniforms on every side. I understand that nearly the whole energies of the University have been drawn into the preparation of American youth for the battlefield. For this purpose all classes and courses have been transformed, and even the most sacred vacations have been swept away in a round-the-year and almost round-the-clock drive to make warriors and technicians for the fighting fronts.

Twice in my lifetime the long arm of destiny has reached across the oceans and involved the entire life and manhood of the United States in a deadly struggle. There was no use in saying "We don't want it; we won't have it; our forebears left Europe to avoid these quarrels; we have founded a new world which has no contact with the old." There was no use in that. The long arm reaches out remorselessly, and every one's existence, environment, and outlook undergo a swift and irresistible change. What is the explanation, Mr. President, of these strange facts, and what are the deep laws to which they respond? I will offer you one explanation — there are others, but one will suffice. The price of greatness is responsibility. If the people of the United States had continued in a mediocre station, struggling with the wilderness, absorbed in their own affairs, and a factor of no consequence in the movement of the world, they might have remained forgotten and undisturbed beyond their protecting oceans: but one cannot rise to be in many ways the leading community in the civilised world without being involved in its problems, without being convulsed by its agonies and inspired by its causes.

If this has been proved in the past, as it has been, it will become indisputable in the future. The people of the United States cannot escape world responsibility. Although we live in a period so tumultuous that little can be predicted, we may be quite sure that this process will be intensified with every forward step the United States make in wealth and in power. Not only are the responsibilities of this great Republic growing, but the world over which they range is itself contracting in relation to our powers of locomotion at a positively alarming rate.

We have learned to fly. What prodigious changes are involved in that new accomplishment! Man has parted company with his trusty friend the horse and has sailed into the azure with the eagles, eagles being represented by the infernal (loud laughter) — I mean internal — combustion engine. Where, then, are those broad oceans, those vast staring deserts? They are shrinking beneath our very eyes. Even elderly Parliamentarians like myself are forced to acquire a high degree of mobility.

But to the youth of America, as to the youth of Britain, I say

"You cannot stop." There is no halting-place at this point. We have now reached a stage in the journey where there can be no pause. We must go on. It must be world anarchy or world order. Throughout all this ordeal and struggle which is characteristic of our age, you will find in the British Commonwealth and Empire good comrades to whom you are united by other ties besides those of State policy and public need. To a large extent, they are the ties of blood and history. Naturally I, a child of both worlds, am conscious of these.

Law, language, literature — these are considerable factors. Common conceptions of what is right and decent, a marked regard for fair play, especially to the weak and poor, a stern sentiment of impartial justice, and above all the love of personal freedom, or as Kipling put it: "Leave to live by no man's leave underneath the law" — these are common conceptions on both sides of the ocean among the English-speaking peoples. We hold to these conceptions as strongly as you do.

We do not war primarily with races as such. Tyranny is our foe, whatever trappings or disguise it wears, whatever language it speaks, be it external or internal, we must forever be on our guard, ever mobilised, ever vigilant, always ready to spring at its throat. In all this, we march together. Not only do we march and strive shoulder to shoulder at this moment under the fire of the enemy on the fields of war or in the air, but also in those realms of thought which are consecrated to the rights and the dignity of man.

At the present time we have in continual vigorous action the British and United States Combined Chiefs of Staff Committee, which works immediately under the President and myself as representative of the British War Cabinet. This committee, with its elaborate organisation of Staff officers of every grade, disposes of all our resources and, in practice, uses British and American troops, ships, aircraft, and munitions just as if they were the resources of a single State or nation.

I would not say there are never divergences of view among these high professional authorities. It would be unnatural if there were not. That is why it is necessary to have plenary meeting of principals every two or three months. All these men now know each other. They trust each other. They like each other, and most of them have been at work together for a long time. When they meet they thrash things out with great candour and plain, blunt speech, but after a few days the President and I find ourselves furnished with sincere and united advice.

This is a wonderful system. There was nothing like it in the last war. There never has been anything like it between two allies. It is reproduced in an even more tightly-knit form at General Eisenhower's headquarters in the Mediterranean, where everything is completely intermingled and soldiers are ordered into battle by the Supreme Commander or his deputy, General Alexander, without the slightest regard to whether they are British, American, or Canadian, but simply in accordance with the fighting need.

Now in my opinion it would be a most foolish and improvident act on the part of our two Governments, or either of them, to break up this smooth-running and immensely powerful machinery the moment the war is over. For our own safety, as well as for the security of the rest of the world, we are bound to keep it working and in running order after the war — probably for a good many years, not only until we have set up some world arrangement to keep the peace, but until we know that it is an arrangement which will really give us that protection we must have from danger and aggression, a protection we have already had to seek across two vast world wars.

I am not qualified, of course, to judge whether or not this would become a party question in the United States, and I would not presume to discuss that point. I am sure, however, that it will not be a party question in Great Britain. We must not let go of the securities we have found necessary to preserve our lives and liberties until we are quite sure we have something else to put in their place which will give us an equally solid guarantee.

The great Bismarck — for there were once great men in Germany — is said to have observed towards the close of his life that the most potent factor in human society at the end of the nineteenth century was the fact that the British and American peoples spoke the same language. That was a pregnant saying. Certainly it has enabled us to wage war together with an intimacy and harmony never before achieved among allies.

This gift of a common tongue is a priceless inheritance, and it may well some day become the foundation of a common citizenship. I like to think of British and Americans moving about freely over each other's wide estates with hardly a sense of being foreigners to one another. But I do not see why we should not try to spread our common language even more widely throughout the globe and, without seeking selfish advantage over any, possess ourselves of this invaluable amenity and birthright.

Some months ago I persuaded the British Cabinet to set up a committee of Ministers to study and report upon Basic English. Here you have a plan. There are others, but here you have a very carefully wrought plan for an international language capable of a very wide transaction of practical business and interchange of ideas. The whole of it is comprised in about 650 nouns and 200 verbs or other parts of speech — no more indeed than can be written on one side of a single sheet of paper.

What was my delight when, the other evening, quite unexpectedly, I heard the President of the United States suddenly speak of the merits of Basic English, and is it not a coincidence that, with all this in mind, I should arrive at Harvard, in fulfilment of the long-dated invitations to receive this degree, with which President Conant has honoured me? For Harvard has done more than any other American university to promote the extension of Basic English. The first work on Basic English was written by two Englishmen, Ivor Richards, now of Harvard, and C. K. Ogden, of Cambridge University, England, working in association.

The Harvard Commission on English Language Studies is distinguished both for its research and its practical work, particularly in introducing the use of Basic English in Latin America; and this Commission, your Commission, is now, I am told, working with secondary schools in Boston on the use of Basic English in teaching the main language to American children and in teaching it to foreigners preparing for citizenship.

Gentlemen, I make you my compliments. I do not wish to exaggerate, but you are the head-stream of what might well be a mighty fertilising and health-giving river. It would certainly be a grand convenience for us all to be able to move freely about the world — as we shall be able to do more freely than ever before as the science of the world develops — be able to move freely about the world, and be able to find everywhere a medium, albeit primitive, of intercourse and understanding. Might it not also be an advantage to many races, and an aid to the building-up of our new structure for preserving peace? All these are great possibilities, and I say: "Let us go into this together. Let us have another Boston Tea Party about it."

Let us go forward as with other matters and other measures similar in aim and effect — let us go forward in malice to none and good will to all. Such plans offer far better prizes than taking away other people's provinces or lands or grinding them down in exploitation. The empires of the future are the empires of the mind.

It would, of course, Mr. President, be lamentable if those who are charged with the duty of leading great nations forward in this grievous and obstinate war were to allow their minds and energies to be diverted from making the plans to achieve our righteous purposes without needless prolongation of slaughter and destruction.

Nevertheless, we are also bound, so far as life and strength allow, and without prejudice to our dominating military tasks, to look ahead to those days which will surely come when we shall have finally beaten down Satan under our feet and find ourselves with other great allies at once the masters and the servants of the future. Various schemes of achieving world security while yet preserving national rights, traditions and customs are being studied and probed.

We have all the fine work that was done a quarter of a century ago by those who devised and tried to make effective the League of Nations after the last war. It is said that the League of Nations failed. If so, that is largely because it was abandoned, and later on betrayed: because those who were its best friends were till a very late period infected with a futile pacifism: because the United States, the originating impulse, fell out of the line: because, while France had been bled white and England was supine and bewildered, a monstrous growth of aggression sprang up in Germany, in Italy and Japan.

We have learned from hard experience that stronger, more efficient, more rigorous world institutions must be created to preserve peace and to forestall the causes of future wars. In this task the strongest victorious nations must be combined, and also those who have borne the burden and heat of the day and suffered under the flail of adversity; and, in this task, this creative task, there are some who say: "Let us have a world council and under it regional or continental councils," and there are others who prefer a somewhat different organisation.

All these matters weigh with us now in spite of the war, which none can say has reached its climax, which is perhaps entering for us, British and Americans, upon its most severe and costly phase. But I am here to tell you that, whatever form your system of world security may take, however the nations are grouped and ranged, whatever derogations are made from national sovereignty for the sake of the larger synthesis, nothing will work soundly or for long without the united effort of the British and American peoples.

If we are together nothing is impossible. If we are divided all will fail. I therefore preach continually the doctrine of the fraternal association of our two peoples, not for any purpose of gaining invidious material advantages for either of them, not for territorial aggrandisement or the vain pomp of earthly domination, but for the sake of service to mankind and for the honour that comes to those who faithfully serve great causes.

Here let me say how proud we ought to be, young and old alike, to live in this tremendous, thrilling, formative epoch in the human story, and how fortunate it was for the world that when these great trials came upon it there was a generation that terror could not conquer and brutal violence could not enslave. Let all who are here remember, as the words of the hymn we have just sung suggest, let all of us who are here remember that we are on the stage of history, and that whatever our station may be, and whatever part we have to play, great or small, our conduct is liable to be scrutinised not only by history but by our own descendants.

Let us rise to the full level of our duty and of our opportunity, and let us thank God for the spiritual rewards he has granted for all forms of valiant and faithful service.

A Call to Marshal Badoglio

A JOINT MESSAGE FROM MR. CHURCHILL AND PRESIDENT
ROOSEVELT TO MARSHAL BADOGLIO AND THE PEOPLE OF
ITALY, ISSUED FROM THE WHITE HOUSE, WASHINGTON
SEPTEMBER 11, 1943

[September 11, 1943

MARSHAL: —

It has fallen to you in the hour of your country's agony to take
the first decisive steps to win peace and freedom for the Italian
people, and to win back for Italy an honourable place in the
civilisation of Europe. You have already freed your country from
Fascist servitude. There remains the ever-more important task of
cleansing the Italian soil from the German invaders.

Hitler, through his accomplice Mussolini, has brought Italy to
the verge of ruin. He has driven the Italians into disastrous
campaigns in the sands of Egypt and the snows of Russia. The
Germans have always deserted the Italian troops on the battlefield, sacrificing them contemptuously in order to cover their own
retreats. Now Hitler threatens to subject you to all the cruelties
he is perpetrating in so many lands.

People of Italy:

Now is the time for every Italian to strike his blow. The
liberating armies of the Western world are coming to your rescue.
We have very strong forces, and are entering at many points.

The German terror in Italy will not last long. They will be
extirpated from your land, and you, by helping in this great
surge of liberation, will place yourselves once more among the
true and long-proved friends of your country from whom you
have been so long and wrongfully estranged.

Take every chance you can. Strike hard and strike home. Have
faith in your future. All will come well. March forward with
your American and British friends in the great world movement
toward freedom, justice, and peace.

The War: Past and Future

A SPEECH IN THE HOUSE OF COMMONS
SEPTEMBER 21, 1943

September 2.	*R.A.F. planes smashed the lock gates on the Hansweert Canal.*
September 3.	*British and Canadian troops of the Eighth Army invaded the Toe of Italy on the fourth anniversary of the war.*
	Allied bombers blocked the Brenner Pass.
September 4.	*R.A.F. dropped 1,000 tons of bombs on Berlin in 20 minutes.*
September 5.	*Forty miles of Italy's Calabrian coast in the hands of Allied troops.*
September 7.	*The whole of the industrial area in the Donetz Basin was cleared of the enemy, and the Russians reached Stalino.*
September 8.	*General Eisenhower announced the unconditional surrender of Italy, following an armistice secretly signed on September 3. Italian sailors were advised by Admiral Cunningham to sail for Allied ports.*
September 9.	*British and American troops landed at points in the Bay of Naples.*
September 10.	*Germans seized Rome and key points in Northern Italy, while British forces occupied the important naval base of Taranto in the south.*
September 12.	*It was revealed that German paratroops had liberated Mussolini.*
September 14.	*Continuing their retreat on the Russian front, the Germans evacuated Bryansk.*
September 16.	*Russians captured Novorossisk, on the Black Sea.*

September 17.   *Eighth and Fifth Armies continuing their advances in Italy linked up near Salerno.*

         President Roosevelt warned that the United Nations were still a long way from victory.

September 18.   *Mussolini broadcast an account of his liberation by the Germans, and announced the formation of a Republican Fascist Party.*

         Mr. Churchill arrived back in London from his visit to the United States and Canada.

September 19.   *German troops evacuated Sardinia, while other German forces in Corsica were attacked by French patriots who were aided by French Commando troops.*

September 21.   *Sir Kingsley Wood, Chancellor of the Exchequer since 1940, died suddenly in London.*

         Germans began looting and destroying Naples as the Allied armies advanced towards the city.

         Mr. Churchill reviewed the entire war situation in a speech to the House of Commons.

[September 21, 1943

I HAVE to go some way back, in order to place the whole broad scene before the House. At my conference with the President at Washington in June, 1942, a decision was taken to send an American Army and a strong British contingent to occupy French North-West Africa. Later on, 8th November, 1942, was fixed for the descent. I was very much in favour of this for a variety of reasons, most of which are now well known. I have never regarded this African operation as a substitute for a direct attack across the Channel upon the Germans in France or the Low Countries. On the contrary, the opening of this new fronin the Mediterranean was always intended by its authors to be an essential preliminary to the main attack upon Germany and her ring of subjugated and satellite States.

At that time, over fifteen months ago, no decision was taken beyond the occupation of North Africa. There followed almost immediately, in fact while I was in Washington, in June, 1942, the disaster at Tobruk and the retreat, with the loss of 80,000 men, of our Desert Army, of more than 400 miles to the approaches of Cairo and Alexandria. This raised very grave issues, the Delta, the Nile Valley and the Suez Canal all being in jeopardy. At the same time the German attack through the Caucasus was developing in a way which seemed to menace the Caspian basin and the vital oilfields of Baku, Iraq, and Persia. At Moscow, Premier Stalin was able to speak to me with confidence of his ability to withstand the German attack, and he told me beforehand of the counter-strokes by which he intended to relieve Stalingrad, and, if possible, destroy the German forces before it. At Cairo, Generals Alexander and Montgomery were placed in command, and very substantial reinforcements, which had been sent out from Britain several months before, arrived to strengthen the Desert Army. Plans were made to resist Rommel's impending attack, and thereafter to regain the initiative by a major battle. These plans proved successful. Almost exactly a year ago, on 23rd September, began the heavy action which resulted in Rommel's decisive repulse. A month later the Desert Army won the hard and prolonged Battle of Alamein and set forth upon its immortal march, a march not yet concluded. From that time on for a whole year we and our great Allies have had almost unbroken success by land, by sea and in the air. I cannot recollect anything so complete and prolonged as the series of victories which have attended our Allied Arms in almost every theatre. In the same time that the Desert Army has been making its great march and that the conquests of North-West Africa and Sicily have taken place, the Russian Armies have advanced on a front of 1,000 miles from the Volga almost to the Dnieper, a distance in many places of more than 500 miles, driving before them with prodigious slaughter the hordes of Germans that had invaded their country and inflicted so many indescribable barbarities upon its inhabitants.

When I next met the President, in January, 1943, and the combined Anglo-American Staffs went into their protracted conference at Casablanca, the whole scene of the war was already transformed. No decision had hitherto been taken by us to go beyond North Africa. But now the advance of the Desert Army, which already stood before the gates of Tripoli, brought another quarter of a million men into play, and enabled us to carry out the policy which I mentioned in my broadcast in November last of using North Africa not as a seat but as a springboard. We resolved, therefore, to complete the conquest of Tunisia, and meanwhile to make all preparations for invading Sicily. The final victories in Tunisia were obtained in May, and the whole of the enemy forces in North Africa, then little short of half a million strong, were destroyed or captured.

When I visited the President again in Washington, in May, 1943, during and after the victory in Tunisia, the British and American Armies had great results to display. We therefore extended our review, and set before ourselves as our principal objective the knocking of Italy completely out of the war this year. No one in attempting to frame a time-table for this task would have expected it would be so rapidly achieved. On 10th July British and American Armies, on the scale of perhaps half a million men, the first wave of whom were carried, as the House knows, in upwards of 2,700 ships and landing-craft, began their attack upon Sicily, and in a campaign of 38 days the entire island was conquered, with a loss to the enemy of 165,000 in killed, wounded and prisoners, or more than four times our Allied losses in the operation.

In order to have the correct perspective and proportion of events, it is necessary to survey the whole chain of causation, the massive links of which have been forged by the diligence and burnished with the devotion and skill of our combined Forces and their commanders until they shine in the sunshine of to-day, and will long shine in the history of war.

This same year of victory on land has been accompanied by an ever-increasing mastery of the air by the British, Americans and Russians over the enemy in Europe. Speaking particularly of our own air power, the weight of bombs discharged by the Royal Air Force on Germany in the last twelve months is three times that of the preceding twelve months. The weight of bombs discharged in the last three months is half as great again as that of the preceding three months. There has also been a great improvement in accuracy, owing to technical devices. The percentage of loss for the first eight months of 1943 is less than in the same period last year, and the morale and ardour of our bombing crews are very high. The almost total systematic destruction of many of the centres of German war effort continues on a greater scale and at a greater pace. The havoc wrought is indescribable, and the effects upon the German war production in all its forms and upon U-boat building are matched by those wrought upon the life and economy of the whole of the guilty organisation. There has been an enormous diversion of German energy from the war fronts to internal defence against air attack, and the offensive power of the enemy has been notably crippled thereby. The German Air Force has been driven increasingly on to the defensive. The attacks we have had in this island, though marked by occasional distressing incidents, are at present negligible compared with the vast scale of the war. The enemy is increasingly compelled to concentrate on building fighter aircraft and night fighter aircraft for home defence at the expense of bomber production. He is also forced to save his strength as far as possible on all the fighting fronts, and is, therefore, restricted to a far lower rate of activity than we and our Allies maintain. This throws the burden increasingly upon his fully occupied ground forces. The Royal Air Force is at present maintaining in action throughout the war scene in all the theatres nearly 50 per cent. more first line aircraft than Germany. That is the Royal Air Force alone, apart from Russia.

On top of this already heavy preponderance comes the whole rapidly expanding weight of the United States Air Forces building up ceaselessly in this country, and already in action on a great scale both here and in the Mediterranean. The American system of daylight bombing gives great accuracy on special targets, and it is also accompanied by severe fighting, producing heavy losses among the enemy's fighter aircraft and notably diminishing the increase which they are seeking to make. Many superb actions of courage and daring have been fought by the great American Air Forces which are developed here and in the

Mediterranean, and a high spirit of fellowship and generous emulation subsists between them and their British comrades. The British and American Air Forces are fed by an ever-broadening supply of new aircraft, which together exceeds the corresponding German supply by more than four to one. The continued progress of Anglo-American air preponderance, which can certainly be expected month after month, opens possibilities of saturating the German defences both on the ground and in the air, in spite of the desperate efforts which the enemy is making and will certainly continue to make to strengthen those defences in proportion to the mounting weight of our attack. Now, this word "saturation" comes to have particular significance in the general field of the air war. If a certain degree of saturation can be reached, and we can be sure that this will only be won after a hard-fought and bitter struggle with the enemy air defences, reactions of a very far-reaching character will be produced. We shall, in fact, have created conditions in which, with very small loss to ourselves, the accurate, methodical destruction by night and by day of every building of military significance in the widest sense will become possible. Complete strategic air domination of Germany by the Anglo-American Air Forces is not necessarily beyond our reach even in 1944, with consequences, if it were attained, which cannot be measured but must certainly be profound.

All this must be considered in relation to the gigantic struggle proceeding ceaselessly along the 2,000-mile Russian front, from the White Sea to the Black Sea, where the Russian Air Force is already at many points superior in strength to that which the Germans have been able to leave there in the face of the hard pressures from the West and from the South.

We must not in any circumstances allow these favourable tendencies to weaken our efforts or lead us to suppose that our dangers are past or that the war is coming to an end. On the contrary, we must expect that the terrible foe we are smiting so heavily will make frenzied efforts to retaliate. The speeches of the German leaders, from Hitler downwards, contain mysterious allusions to new methods and new weapons which will presently be tried against us. It would, of course, be natural for the enemy to spread such rumours in order to encourage his own people, but there is probably more in it than that. For example, we now have experience of a new type of aerial bomb which the enemy has begun to use in attacks on our shipping, when at close quarters with the coast. This bomb, which may be described as a sort of rocket-assisted glider, is released from a considerable height, and is then apparently guided towards its target by the parent aircraft. It may be that the Germans are developing other weapons on novel lines with which they may hope to do us damage, and to compensate to some extent for the injury which they are daily receiving from us. I can only assure the House that unceasing vigilance and the most intense study of which we are capable are given to the possibilities. We have always hitherto found the answer to any of the problems which have been presented to us. At the same time I do not exclude, and no one must exclude from their minds, that novel forms of attack will be employed, and, should they be employed, I should be able to show to the House in detail the prolonged, careful examination beforehand which we have made into these possibilities, and I trust we shall be able to show the measures which will be brought into force against them.

So much for the air. I have dealt with the land. Not less remarkable than of the air or the land, and certainly not less important, is the revolution effected in our position at sea. I have repeatedly stated in this House that our greatest danger in this war since invasion has become so much more remote is the U-boat attack upon our sea communications and upon Allied shipping all over the world. This must be measured by three tests: First: the sinkings of our own ships; secondly, the killings of the enemy U-boats; and, thirdly, the volume of new building. The great victory which was won by our North Atlantic convoys and their escorts in May was followed by a magnificent diminution in sinkings. The monthly statements which are issued on the authority of the President and myself, and about which the Canadian Government, who contribute to the Battle of the Atlantic brave men, planes and escort vessels, are also consulted, deserve close attention. I have little to add to them to-day. But it is a fact that for the four months which ended on 18th September, no merchant vessel was sunk by enemy action in the North Atlantic. The month of August was the lowest month we have ever had since the United States entered the war, and it was less than half the average of British and Allied sinkings in the 15 months preceding the American entry into the war. During the first fortnight in this September no Allied ships were sunk by U-boat action in any part of the world. This is altogether unprecedented in the whole history of the U-boat struggle, either in this war or in the last. Naturally, I do not suggest for a moment that this immunity or anything like it could possibly continue. A new herd of U-boats have been coming out in the last week or so into the Atlantic from their bases in France and Germany, and they have, no doubt, been fitted with what is thought to be the best and latest apparatus. We, for our part, have not been idle, and we await this renewal of the conflict which has in fact already begun with sober confidence. One convoy is being attacked at the present time. If they come and attack the convoys, we shall be able to attack the U-boats.

In spite, however, of the reduced number of U-boats which have been at work since the May massacre, a day rarely passes without our getting one of these ill-starred vessels. Moreover, the United States and British air attacks on the German bases and building yards and on factories where the component parts are made has definitely reduced the rate of production of U-boats in Germany. The high percentage of killings has certainly affected the morale of the U-boat crews, and many of the most experienced U-boat captains have been drowned or are now prisoners in British or American hands.

Thirdly — I said you must look at it from three points of view — the output of new building from the United States has fulfilled all that was ever hoped from it, and more. We build our regular quota in this Island, and the Canadian output, an entirely new development for Canada, is also remarkable. The credit balance of new building over losses of all kinds, including marine risks, since the beginning of the year, the net gain, that is to say, exceeds 6,000,000 tons, and should the present favourable conditions hold, we shall soon have replaced all the losses suffered by the United Nations since the beginning of the war. As set forth in the letter from the President to me which I laid on the Table of the House before we rose, the massive achievement of United States shipbuilding has been shared generously with us on those principles of the division of war-labour in accordance with the highest economy of effort which were from the beginning of our association with the United States in this war our guide, and which are now becoming increasingly our rule. The favourable position now enjoyed has enabled a larger number of faster ships to be built and projected, with all the advantages attaching to speed.

The House will also realise that we have taken full advantage of the lull in the U-boat attack to bring in the largest possible convoys, and that we have replenished the reserves in these Islands of all essential commodities, especially oil fuel, which is almost at its highest level since the outbreak of the war, and we have substantial margins between us and what is called the "danger level," on which we have never trenched even at the worst time.

All this has not come about accidentally. It is the result of the most astonishing and praiseworthy efforts of industry and organisation on both sides of the Atlantic. It is also the result of hard, faithful, unwearying service given by the multitudes of escort vessels of all kinds; and most of all, so far as last year is concerned, it is the result of the startling intervention of the long-range aircraft of the British Empire and the United States, and especially of our Coastal Command. Besides this the large numbers of auxiliary aircraft carriers which are now coming into service are able to give a measure of air protection to convoys, and to conduct an aggressive warfare against U-boats, in those ocean spaces which are beyond the reach even of the very-long-range aircraft, the V.L.R.'s as they are called, of the two countries.

I repeat, as I have always done, and as I am bound to do, my warning that no guarantee can be given of a continuance of these favourable conditions. But on this occasion I will go so far as to say that we could only be defeated by the U-boats if we were guilty of gross neglect of duty in the shipyards and on the sea, and of an inexcusable falling-off in that scientific and technical ability on both sides of the Atlantic which has hitherto stood us in good stead.

I cannot pass from this subject without paying tribute once more to the officers and men of the Merchant Navy, whose losses have been greater in proportion than those even of the Royal Navy. We never call upon them in vain, and we are confident that they will continue to play their part in carrying our men and their equipment and munitions to any place that may be required and under whatever conditions may exist at the time. I must add, also, when these new resources of shipbuilding are coming into view, that every saving made on the sea is immediately demanded by the Fighting Services in their endeavour to intensify and augment our offensive overseas actions. Their appetite keeps far ahead of the supply, even if it increases beyond our expectation. The more ships we have, the more we seem to want.

I have dealt with the land, the air and the Navy, but now I must turn to another part of the world. At the Conference at Quebec much attention was given to the prosecution of the war against Japan. The offensive is already on foot on a considerable scale in various parts of the Pacific, and the main strength of the United States is deployed in that ocean. The main weight of the offensive operations there at present is in the Solomons and New Guinea, where General MacArthur, an officer of outstanding personality, to whom we and our Australian brothers in the Commonwealth are under a measure of debt, is directing a large-scale offensive. The first steps were taken by the eviction of the Japanese from Guadalcanal and from Papua. These were exploited by landings which took place on 30th June on New Georgia also, and on 4th September in Huon Bay, north-east of Lae. New Georgia has been cleared of the enemy, and the twin bases of Salamaua and Lae were reduced in a manner which shows a remarkable development in the use of amphibian and air-borne power, and which furnished, I may say, another opportunity for the Ninth Australian Division to display those qualities to the Japanese which the Germans tasted at Alamein. These operations give great promise for the future, and they will unfold stage by stage as the months pass by.

Then, while we were in Quebec, we also received the news of the eviction of the Japanese from the Aleutian Islands, which are American territory, by the occupation of Kiska, in which Canadian Forces also took part. This was the sequel to the annihilation of the Japanese garrison on the island of Attu, and it is certainly remarkable for the fact that the Japanese, who had occupied Kiska with a garrison of 10,000 men or more, were not prepared to await the assault, but fled beforehand, under cover of darkness, in their ships. Here is a new feature in the resistance of Japan. Hitherto we have reckoned upon their dying to the last man, which they certainly did at Attu, and in which respect we were prepared to serve them as well as we could. But at Kiska, and also to some extent at Salamaua and Lae, a somewhat different mood has seemed to have possessed the enemy. Evacuation and retreat in order to save their lives now seem to have taken place in their methods of fighting. We shall see in due course whether these new tendencies become pronounced. If so, it will not alter the result, but it will save cost and trouble.

The fundamental fact, however, in the war against Japan, is the steady diminution of Japanese shipping in relation to the tasks their war policy has imposed upon them. The wasting process is most marked. Their widely dispersed conquests depend upon a certain minimum shipping supply, without which they cannot possibly hold the vast areas they have occupied. Their losses certainly exceed any means which they have, or can ever obtain, of replacement. This is also true of their Air Force, which can scarcely keep its initial strength, and has long ago been overtaken, and is now increasingly surpassed every month, by the enormous United States expansion. So that in both those vital respects upon which the Japanese conquests depend for their maintenance, a steady process of attrition is at work, and the strength of the enemy must be considered a wasting asset.

I have ventured to dwell upon these favourable aspects of the war against Japan only because I know it is realised throughout the United States that the slightest slackening of effort would destroy all those favourable tendencies, which depend upon a small margin. If that margin is lost by any slackening, and those tendencies cease to operate, we shall get into a static, stagnant condition. We might well find ourselves condemned to a long-term process of futile expenditure of life and treasure which would be marking time and treading water. We should not be getting on. It is the pace that kills; that is what has to be borne in mind in bringing this war to an end.

I now turn to another but cognate aspect of the war which was discussed at Quebec. Considerable progress has been made in the organisation of the South-East Asia Command, which is being set up in India to intensify the war against Japan. The supreme Allied Commander, Admiral Mountbatten, will shortly arrive in India, accompanied by a staff of officers who will form the Combined Allied Headquarters, modelled on that which has been set up under General Eisenhower with so much advantage. This form of Combined Allied Headquarters for the South-East Asia front was absolutely necessary because of the many United States establishments which were growing up separately for many purposes in that area, and particularly in respect of the great air route to China, which is being expanded and manned on an ever-increasing scale. Although there are excellent liaison and good feeling, it is absolutely necessary to have unity of command in this theatre.

Another step which was foreseen when we examined these matters as much as 16 or 17 years ago on the Committee of Imperial Defence, was the separation from the ordinary normal Command in India, the statutory Command in India, of any large extensive campaigns fought on or beyond the frontiers of India. That also has been achieved. The headquarters of the new Command will be set up first in Delhi so as to be in close liaison during the organisational period. They have to be in the closest liaison with the Government of India and with General Auchinleck, the Commander-in-Chief in India. The new Command and the appointment of Admiral Mountbatten have been warmly welcomed by Generalissimo Chiang Kai-shek, and are in full accord with the views of our American Allies. In all these questions, matters have to be so arranged that the men who are chosen to command have the full confidence of all the parties concerned.

A general survey of this amazing and fearful world war is an essential part of any balanced statement. Without it, the events in any one theatre cannot be viewed in their proper setting or proportion. To understand fully any part of this war, one must have at least a broad conception of the whole. I now return, after placing these general considerations before the House, to the more recent events in the Mediterranean theatre which are so fresh and vivid in our minds.

July 25th was a memorable day. Even before we had half completed the conquest of Sicily or had set foot on the Italian mainland, the Dictator Mussolini was overthrown, and the Fascist regime, which had lasted for 21 years, was cast down and vehemently repudiated by the whole mass of the Italian people. The Badoglio Government came into existence with the intention of making peace in accordance with the will of the nation. They were, however, intruded upon at all points and overlaid by the Germans, and they had the greatest difficulty in maintaining themselves against this hateful pressure. We knew nothing about this new regime. Once Fascism was completely overthrown, we were naturally anxious to find some authority with whom we could deal, so as to bring about the unconditional surrender of Italy in the shortest time and with the least possible cost in the blood of our soldiers. It was necessary, as I advised the House, to wait till the position became more definite. We therefore continued our preparation for the invasion in strength of the mainland of Italy and of Europe on which we had resolved at the May Conference in Washington.

Presently feelers were put out by the new Italian Government through various channels, asking for terms, and explaining the deadly character of the difficulties in which they were involved. These difficulties arose from the menacing presence of German armies, police and spies all around them and all among them. We were sympathetic to those difficulties.

At this point Mr. Gallacher (Communist M.P. for Fife) interjected: "You were quick enough."

Wait and see. That is a cheap criticism from people who must be rather hard put to it to find criticisms. I am going to answer it very precisely and exhaustively, even before we break off for brief refreshment. We were sympathetic to those difficulties. But to all advances we made the reply that the surrender must be unconditional. On 15th August, an Italian envoy, an officer with the rank of general, called upon His Majesty's Ambassador at Madrid, the right hon. Member for Chelsea (Sir S. Hoare), with credentials proving that he came with full authority from Marshal Badoglio to say that when the Allies landed in Italy the Italian Government were prepared to join them against Germany; and when could they come?

I was at this time, not entirely by accident, at Quebec, for the Conference, and I was in the closest contact with the President. My right hon. Friend the Secretary of State for Foreign Affairs was with me, and I was also accompanied by an ample cipher staff and secretariat, through which hourly touch could be maintained with my colleagues in the War Cabinet. The President and I were therefore able to act together and to give prompt guidance in any emergency.

With the approval of the War Cabinet, it was decided that General Eisenhower should send an American and a British staff officer to meet the Italian envoy in Lisbon. We at once informed Premier Stalin of what was in progress. On 19th August the meeting in Lisbon took place. The envoy was informed that we could accept only unconditional surrender. The military terms embodying this act of surrender — not so much conditions as directions following on the act of surrender — which had been prepared some weeks earlier, after prolonged discussions between London and Washington and General Eisenhower's headquarters, were now placed before the envoy. He did not oppose these terms, drastic though they were, but he replied that the purpose of his visit was to discuss how Italy could join the United Nations in the war against Germany. He also asked how the terms could be executed in the face of German opposition. The British and American officers replied that they were empowered to discuss only unconditional surrender. They were, however, authorised — and this was a decision which we took at Quebec — to add that if at any time, anywhere, in any circumstances, any Italian forces or people were found by our troops to be fighting the Germans, we would immediately give them all possible aid. On 23rd August, the Italian general departed with the military terms expressing the act of unconditional surrender, and with full warning that the civil and administrative terms would be presented later. He then made his way back to Rome, with great secrecy and danger. He promised to lay the terms before his Government and bring back their answer to General Eisenhower's headquarters by 31 August.

In the interval another Italian general arrived, bringing with him as his credentials no less a person than General Carton de Wiart, V.C., one of our most famous military figures, whom the Italians captured two years ago through a forced landing in the Mediterranean. This second mission, however, did not affect the general course of events, and when General de Wiart realised this he immediately offered to return to captivity. The Italian officer, however, rejected this proposal, and General Carton de Wiart is now safe and free in this country.

On 31st August the Italian envoy returned. He had met General Eisenhower's representatives at Syracuse. The Italian Government were willing to accept the terms unconditionally, but they did not see how they could carry them out in the teeth of the heavy German forces gathered near Rome and at many other points throughout the country, who were uttering ferocious threats and were prepared to resort to immediate violence. We did not doubt the sincerity of the envoy nor of his Government, but we were not able to reveal our military plans for the invasion of Italy, or, as it had now become, the liberation of Italy. The real difficulty was that the Italians were powerless until we landed in strength, and we could not give them the date. We therefore timed the announcement for the moment which we deemed would give us the best military chance, and them the best chance of extricating themselves from the German grip. This meant that the Armistice should be accorded only at the moment of or just before our main descent. We would have done more, had it been possible, to help this unhappy Government, who were beset on every side by insoluble problems, and who have since acted towards us, to the best of their ability, with both courage and good faith. We offered and prepared to land an American air-borne division in Rome at the same time as the Armistice was declared in order to fight off the two German armoured divisions which were massed outside it and to help the Italians. But owing to the German investment of the Rome airfields which took place on the last day or two before the announcement of the Armistice, of which investment the Italian Government warned us, it was not possible to carry out this part of the plan. It was I think a pretty daring plan, to cast this powerful force there into Rome in conditions which no one could measure, and might have led to its complete destruction, but we were quite ready to try it. But at the last moment the warning came, "The airfields are not in our control."

Unconditional surrender of course comprises everything, but not only was a special provision for the surrender of war criminals included in the longer terms, but a particular stipulation was made for the surrender of Signor Mussolini. It was not however possible to arrange for him to be delivered specially and separately before the Armistice and our main landing took place, for this would certainly have disclosed the intentions of the Italian Government to the enemy, who were intermingled with them at every point and who had them so largely in their power. So the Italian position had to be that although an internal revolution had taken place in Italy, they were still the Allies of Germany and were carrying on common cause with them. This was a difficult position to maintain day after day with the pistol of the Gestapo pointing at the nape of so many necks. We had every reason to believe that Mussolini was being kept under a strong guard at a secure place, and certainly it was very much to the interests of the Badoglio Government to see that he did not escape. Mussolini has himself been reported to have declared that he believed that he was being delivered to the Allies. This was certainly the intention, and is what would have taken place but for circumstances entirely beyond our control. The measures which the Badoglio Government took were carefully conceived, and were the best they could do to hold Mussolini, but they did not provide against so heavy a parachute descent as the Germans made at the particular point where he was confined. It may be noticed that Hitler sent him some books of Nietzsche to console or diversify his confinement. The Italians could hardly have refused this civility, and the Germans no doubt were thus pretty well acquainted with where he was and the conditions under which he was confined. But the stroke was one of great daring, and conducted with a heavy force. It certainly shows there are many possibilities of this kind open in modern war. I do not think there was any slackness or breach of faith on the part of the Badoglio Government, and they had one card up their sleeve. The Carabinieri guards had orders to shoot Mussolini if there was any attempt to rescue him, but they failed in their duty, having regard to the considerable German force which descended upon them from the air, and would undoubtedly have held them responsible for his health and safety. So much for that.

The terms were signed at Syracuse on the night of 3rd September, and from that time forth occasional aircraft passed secretly between Rome and the Allied headquarters. This was a difficult matter. Great numbers of guns had to be silenced, particular batteries had to be warned to be silent at a particular moment to allow an aeroplane to pass freely. This again ran the risk of disclosing the secret, on the whole very well kept. The Russian Soviet Government, having studied the terms, authorised General Eisenhower to sign them in their name. Accordingly he did so, not only on behalf of the United States and Great Britain, but on behalf of the Soviet Government, and on behalf of the United Nations.

I have seen it said that forty days of precious time were lost in these negotiations, and that in consequence British and American blood was needlessly shed around Salerno. This criticism is as ill-founded in fact as it is wounding to those who are bereaved. The time of our main attack upon Italy was fixed without the slightest reference to the attitude of the Italian Government, and the actual provisional date of the operation was settled long before any negotiations with them had taken place, and even before the fall of Mussolini. That date depended upon the time necessary to disengage our landing-craft from the beaches of Southern Sicily, across which up to the first week in August the major part of our Armies actually engaged there had to be supplied from day to day. These landing-craft had then to be taken back to Africa. Those that had been damaged — and they were many — had to be repaired, and then reloaded with all their ammunition, etc., in the most exact and complex order before there could be any question of carrying out another amphibious operation.

I suppose it is realised that these matters have to be arranged in the most extraordinary detail. Every landing vessel or combat ship is packed in the exact order in which the troops landing from it will require the supplies when they land, so far as can be foreseen. Every lorry, indeed, is packed with precisely the articles which each unit will require when that lorry comes. Some of the lorries swim out to the ships and swim back. They are all packed exactly in series, with the things which have priority at the top and so on, so that nothing is left to chance that can be helped. Only in this way can these extraordinary operations be carried out in the face of the vast modern fire-power which a few men can bring to bear. Only in this way are they possible. The condition and preparation of the landing-craft were the sole but decisive limiting factors. It had nothing to do with "wasting time over the negotiations," nothing to do with the Foreign Office holding back the generals while they worried about this clause or that clause and so forth. There was never one moment's pause in the process of carrying out the military operations, and everything else had to fit in with that main-line traffic.

When I hear people talking in an airy way of throwing modern armies ashore here and there as if they were bales of goods to be dumped on a beach and forgotten, I really marvel at the lack of knowledge which still prevails of the conditions of modern war. Most strenuous efforts were made by all concerned to speed up our onfall. For instance, I sent a telegram myself to General Alexander on 18th August as follows: —

"You are no doubt informed of the Italian approaches to us and the answer we have sent them. Our greatest danger is that the Germans should enter Rome and set up a quisling Fascist Government under, say, Farinacci. Scarcely less unpleasant would be the whole of Italy sliding into anarchy. I doubt if the Badoglio Government can hold their position until the day fixed for our main attack, so that anything you can do to shorten this period without danger to military success will help very much."

That was on 18th August, long before the Armistice was signed. General Alexander replied on 20th August: —

"Many thanks for your message. Everything possible is being done to carry out the operation at the earliest possible date. All here realise very clearly that every additional hour gives the enemy more time to organise and prepare against our Forces."

The War: Past and Future, September 21, 1943

Most people knowing the character of these generals, Eisenhower, Alexander, Montgomery, would think that good enough. The date, which had originally been the 15th, was, however, in fact brought forward to the 9th — the night of the 8th and 9th. Thus the whole of this operation — this is my answer to the charge of delay, to the word "slothful" which I have seen used in one quarter — the whole of this operation was planned as a result of decisions taken before the fall of Mussolini, and would have taken place, whatever happened in Italy, at the earliest possible moment. The Italian surrender was a windfall, but it had nothing to do with the date fixed for harvesting the orchard. The truth is that the Armistice announcement was delayed to fit in with the attack, and not the attack delayed to fit in with the announcement.

I must say, if I may make a momentary digression, that this class of criticism which I read in the newspapers when I arrived on Sunday morning reminds me of the simple tale which I heard, and which I dare say other Members are familiar with, about the sailor who jumped into a dock, I think it was at Plymouth, to rescue a small boy from drowning. About a week later this sailor was accosted by a woman, who asked, "Are you the man who picked my son out of the dock the other night?" The sailor replied modestly, "That is true, Ma'am." "Ah," said the woman, "you are the man I am looking for. Where is his cap?"

General Montgomery, at the head of the Eighth Army, with whom marched the Canadians — welcome comrades — on 3rd September began to cross the Straits of Messina and land at various points in the Toe of Italy. One could not tell how much would leak out, or what would happen in Rome in the interval before our main attack, nor to what extent the Italian Government would have the power to carry out their undertakings. In this uncertainty I availed myself of the President's invitation to remain with him in the White House.

We may pause for a moment to survey and appraise the act of the Italian Government, endorsed and acclaimed as it was by the Italian nation. Herr Hitler has left us in no doubt that he considers the conduct of Italy treacherous and base in the extreme — and he is a good judge in such matters. Others may hold that the act of treachery and ingratitude took place when the Fascist confederacy, headed by Mussolini — for he was not alone, though now become the absolute dictator of his country's destinies, with the whole nation ground up into his system after nearly a generation of totalitarian rule — when he used his arbitrary power to strike for material gain at falling France and so became the enemy of the British Empire, which had for so many years cherished the cause of Italian liberty, and afterwards became the enemy of the United States, in which six or seven millions of Italians have found a happy home. There was the crime. Though it cannot be undone, and though nations which allow their rights and liberties to be subverted by tyrants must suffer heavy penalties for those tyrants' crimes, yet I cannot view the Italian action at this juncture as other than natural and human. May it prove to be the first of a series of acts of self-redemption. It is possible indeed that I or my right hon. Friend the Foreign Secretary will have a further statement to make on the subject of the Badoglio Government before we separate at the end of this series of Sittings.

The Italian people have already suffered terribly. Their manhood has been cast away in Africa and Russia, their soldiers have been deserted in the field — we have seen that ourselves — their wealth has been squandered, their Empire has been lost — irretrievably lost. Now their own beautiful homeland must become a battlefield for German rearguards. Even more suffering lies ahead. They are to be pillaged and terrorised in Hitler's fury and revenge. Nevertheless, as the Armies of the British Empire and the United States march forward on Italy, as they will march, the Italian people will be rescued from their state of servitude and degradation, and be enabled in due course to regain their rightful place among the free democracies of the modern world.

I cannot touch upon this matter of Italy without exposing myself to the question, which I shall be most properly asked, "Would you apply this line of argument to the German people?" I say, "The case is different." Twice within our lifetime, and also three times in that of our fathers, they have plunged the world into their wars of expansion and aggression. They combine in the most deadly manner the qualities of the warrior and the slave. They do not value freedom themselves, and the spectacle of it in others is hateful to them. Whenever they become strong they seek their prey, and they will follow with an iron discipline anyone who will lead them to it. The core of Germany is Prussia. There is the source of the recurring pestilence. But we do not war with races as such. We war against tyranny, and we seek to preserve ourselves from destruction. I am convinced that the British, American, and Russian peoples, who have suffered measureless waste, peril and bloodshed twice in a quarter of a century through the Teutonic urge for domination, will this time take steps to put it beyond the power of Prussia or of all Germany to come at them again with pent-up vengeance and long-nurtured plans. Nazi tyranny and Prussian militarism are the two main elements in German life which must be absolutely destroyed. They must be absolutely rooted out if Europe and the world are to be spared a third and still more frightful conflict. The controversies about whether Burke was right or wrong when he said, "I do not know the method of drawing up an indictment against a whole people" — these controversies seem to me at the present time to be sterile and academic. Here are two obvious and practical targets for us to fire at — Nazi tyranny and Prussian militarism. Let us aim every gun, and let us set every man who will march, in motion against them. We must not add needlessly to the weight of our task or the burden that our soldiers bear. Satellite States, suborned or overawed, may perhaps, if they can help to shorten the war, be allowed to work their passage home. But the twin roots of all our evils, Nazi tyranny and Prussian militarism, must be extirpated. Until this is achieved there are no sacrifices that we will not make and no lengths in violence to which we will not go. I will add this. Having, at the end of my life, acquired some influence on affairs, I wish to make it clear that I would not needlessly prolong this war for a single day; and my hope is that if and when British people are called by victory to share in the august responsibilities of shaping the future, we shall show the same poise and temper as we did in the hour of our mortal peril.

I have made a considerable but, I think, by no means unnecessary digression into the relations and views which we may form towards the various enemy or satellite countries with whom we may have to deal; and from this digression, and after what

I trust has been a well-spent interlude, I come back to the purely military sphere. The invasion of Italy in the Naples area was the most daring amphibious operation we have yet launched, or which, I think, has ever been launched on a similar scale in war. In North Africa we expected but little resistance and much help from the French. In Sicily we expected that the opposition of the Italians would be lukewarm, and we knew that we greatly outnumbered the Germans. On landing in North-West Africa no serious air power was likely to be encountered. Our descent on Sicily was covered by overwhelming air power and supported over the beaches and battlefields from our own shore bases at Malta and Pantellaria, but in the Gulf of Salerno we were at the extreme range of shore-based fighter aircraft flying from Palermo and from conquered Sicilian fields. Until we gained refuelling stations on land, our single-engined fighter squadrons had but a quarter of an hour's activity over the battle area. They had to go all that way for just a quarter of an hour — a terrible problem for a pilot who engages in action with no more than a few minutes to spare for reaching home across the sea. In order to give continuous protection for the landing on these terms, it was necessary to make demands upon our air strength which even its great numbers could hardly supply. They can be counted in four figures, but, even so, to maintain control of the air continuously under these conditions with rapid reliefs and even with double flights in the day was an immense strain, and the amount of protection was, of course, not very overwhelming, nothing like what we have when we come and go across the Channel these days. We could not, therefore, go farther North than Naples. People have said, "It would have been better to go to the North of Naples." I dare say it would. People have said Spezia, and so on. All these are very attractive propositions. We could not go farther North than Naples unless we dispensed with any aid from shore-based aircraft. Even landing where we did, we were dependent to an important extent upon sea-borne aircraft, in which happily we are also becoming stronger, and shall in the future become much stronger still. To have gone farther North would have deprived our carriers of the support of shore-based aircraft without which they themselves would have been the sole object of the enemy's air attack, thus absorbing their own air power for their own defence instead of using it to help the troops over the beaches. These are the very hard limitations which are imposed at the present time if success is to be securely founded.

All these considerations must have been known to the Germans, with whom alone we had to deal. Although the German forces were not numerous enough to man the whole of the threatened sector of the coast, they could counter-attack within a few hours with a force which at each stage of the build-up of the first week or so was by our estimates at least equal to our own. That is to say, you land on the beach, and after you have deployed you must expect an equal force to come at you which is fully organised with all its artillery placed and established on land. We knew that the Germans certainly had the power to march against us in counter-attack with equal or superior numbers, before we could secure any refuelling points for our aircraft or any harbour facilities, and while in consequence for several days we still had to land and feed our men over the open beaches.

At this stage in the war a disastrous repulse and enforced embarkation would have been particularly vexatious, and no doubt if this had occurred severe criticism might have been levelled at the British and American war direction by some of those who are clamouring for the far more difficult, far larger and more serious operation across the Channel. The enterprise therefore seemed full of hazard, especially as such a long distance — over 150 miles — separated the vanguards of the Eighth Army from our new and major attack. This attack was confided to the commander of the Fifth United States Army, General Clark, an officer of remarkable energy and force, who had under his command an equal number of United States and British divisions, and was supported by ample British and American naval forces, and by our entire combined air forces. If we had been ready to take greater risks, we could, of course, have attacked earlier with a smaller force; we could have attacked much farther to the Northward, relying in that case wholly on sea-borne aircraft; but the enemy's strength would not have been less in the area involved, for no appreciable reinforcement from the North reached or could have reached the Naples area during the period concerned, owing to faulty communications and our interferences with them. I think the case against needless delay is pretty compact and watertight. Indeed, when I survey in retrospect last week's intense fighting, with the battle swaying to and fro, I am bound to say — I make this admission — that it looks as if we had cut it very fine indeed. For what happened?

On the night of the 8th–9th the approach and the landing were successfully effected, but the battle which developed from the second day onwards was most severe and critical. The British and American divisions fought side by side with their backs to the sea, with only a few miles of depth behind them, with their equipment coming in painfully over the beaches, and their landing-craft and supporting squadrons under recurrent enemy air attack. The Germans came at them in well-organized assaults, fighting with their practised skill both in defence and in offence. From day three to day seven the issue hung in the balance, and the possibility of a large-scale disaster could not be excluded. You have to run risks. There are no certainties in war. There is a precipice on either side of you — a precipice of caution and a precipice of over-daring.

General Alexander, in whose group of armies the whole of this operation lay, and later the supreme commander himself, General Eisenhower, proceeded to the scene in person, visited the divisional and brigade headquarters on this fluctuating battlefront, and conferred with General Clark at his battle-post on shore. Every inch of the ground was savagely disputed. The harbour at Salerno was gradually got into working order, and is now discharging supplies on a considerable scale. Reinforcements, of which there is no lack, were poured-in to the utmost limit of our landing-craft and means of supply. But the battle swayed to and fro, and the Germans' hopes of driving us into the sea after a bloody battle on the beaches must at times have risen high. We thought we had their measure, and so it turned out; but one can quite understand that their hopes may have risen high. The British Battle Squadron, some of the finest battleships, joined the inshore squadron in a heavy bombardment, running a great risk, within close range and in narrow waters, from the enemy's aircraft, U-boats, if any, and the glider bombs which inflicted damage on some of the ships — they came straight in and stood up to it at close range, and equalised and restored the artillery battle. These ships had guns which could contend with enemy batteries mounted in very prominent positions. It was right to risk capital ships in this manner, in view of the improvement in naval balance to which I shall refer before I sit down.

The British and American air forces also surpassed all their previous efforts. Almost 2,500 fighter and bomber sorties were flown during the 24 hours at the height of the battle, and 1,400 tons of bombs were dropped on the German forces on the battlefield and on their immediate communications during this same 24 hours' period. Meanwhile the Eighth Army, whose operations had been considered from the beginning as complementary to the blow we were striking with the Fifth Army — the Eighth Army, which had become master at many points in the Toe, the Ball and the Heel of Italy, advanced with giant strides, and on the tenth day of the struggle began to intervene, as it was meant to do, on the enemy's Southern flank and rear.

Yesterday's reports from the battlefield leave no doubt that the enemy has been worsted, that our main forces are firmly ashore, and that the Eighth Army has come into action in a suitable place, that we have recovered the initiative, and that we are able now to advance Northward on a broad front. That operation is now in progress. We must, I think, consider this episode — the landing on the beaches of Salerno — as an important and pregnant victory, one deserving of a definite place in the records of the British and United States Armies fighting together and shedding their blood in a generous cause.

While this struggle was raging, the Armistice with Italy was made public and the Badoglio Government ordered the Italian troops to fulfil its conditions. They also called upon them to resist the Germans when attacked by them. The German Panzer divisions outside Rome broke into the city and drove out the King and Government, who have now established themselves behind our advancing lines.

I will add no more to the excellent accounts, the very vivid accounts, which have been published in the newspapers, which are not only much fuller and much more interesting than the official accounts, but at the same time are, in my opinion, giving a very true picture to the public of what has been taking place. I do not need to add any more to them. Indeed, I find myself at a disadvantage, having had for five or six days to depend entirely upon the official accounts, and not knowing what the newspapers were saying. The House is already fully possessed of fully descriptive passages about this battle. I will, however, emphasize some of the main points that stand out. The first is, that the Italian forces and population have everywhere shown themselves unfriendly or actively hostile to the Germans, and anxious to obey so far as it is in their power the orders of the King of Italy's new Government. The second is that every effort has been made both by that Government and its forces to comply with the Armistice conditions. Fighting has taken place at many points between the Italians and the German intruders, and there is no doubt whatever on which side the sympathy, hopes and efforts of the Italian nation now lie.

In Sardinia, for instance, which a little while ago was considered a major prize in itself, four Italian divisions have driven out the German garrison, and American forces have now landed in their support. The French have landed in Corsica. We had great plans for the invasion of Sardinia and Corsica, great, elaborate plans, all worked out, but we have got these islands in the pick-up merely as a result of sound blows at the central power, at the vital point of the enemy. As I have said, the French have landed in Corsica, and aided by the Italian garrison and all true Frenchmen and Corsicans, are actively attacking the Germans. This is the first time that the French have been in action for the liberation of their home territory. At one time in Bastia Harbour all the batteries were manned by Italians and French, the patriots whom the Italians had been sent there to put down. The fight in the harbour was conducted by Italian destroyers and a British submarine, all of which united in shelling the Germans and driving them out of the place. We feel the power of the encircling arm of a great world movement in what is taking place, and certainly I am not going to do anything to hamper that. For the first time, the French, as I say, have been in action for the liberation of their home territory. A powerful French Army is growing up which will play an increasing part.

The escape of Mussolini to Germany, his rescue by paratroops, and his attempts to form a Quisling Government which, with German bayonets, will try to re-fix the Fascist yoke on the necks of the Italian people, raise, of course, the issue of Italian civil war. It is necessary in the general interest as well as in that of Italy that all surviving forces of Italian national life should be rallied together around their lawful Government, and that the King and Marshal Badoglio should be supported by whatever Liberal and Left-wing elements are capable of making head against the Fascist-Quisling combination, and thus of creating conditions which will help to drive this villainous combinaton from Italian soil, or, better still, annihilate it on the spot. We are coming to the rescue and liberation of Italy —

A member interjected: "You will not get Italian people to rise behind the banner of turncoats."

I think the hon. Gentleman may be not thinking quite sufficiently of the importance of diminishing the burden which our soldiers have to bear. At any rate, in my view it is the duty, in a situation of this kind, of all forces who will make head against the scourge of their nation — the Fascist-Quisling Government of Mussolini, supported by the German invaders — to rally and get together to make the best stand and head they can. This is, of course, without the slightest prejudice to the untrammelled right of the Italian nation to make whatever arrangements they choose for the future government of their country on democratic lines, when peace and tranquillity are restored. If there is any issue on this point — and it is certainly one which will come more pointedly to the front — we must thrash it out and come to a decision, because the Government certainly intend to pursue a policy of engaging all the forces they can to make head against the Germans and drive them out of Italy. We propose to do that, and we are not going to be put off that action by any fear that perhaps we should not have complete unanimity on the subject. Parliament does not rest on unanimity; democratic assemblies do not act on unanimity. They act by majorities. That is the way they act, and I have not the slightest hesitation or doubt as to what will be the view of the House and what will be the view of the country in respect of the policy which I am announcing, and which we are determined to carry through with the utmost vigour.

I wish to make it perfectly clear that we are endeavouring to rally the strongest forces together in Italy to make head against the Germans and the Mussolini-Quisling-Fascist combination. That is what we intend to do, what we are going to do; and we shall do our utmost to explain and justify any course we are taking to Parliament. But we cannot expect to convince everybody. There are some people who run their own ideas to such a point, without the slightest regard to the addition to the difficulties and dangers which our troops have to face, and also, I may say, without giving the slightest consideration to the actual conditions of confusion and anarchy which prevail in Italy, and which at this terrible juncture do require most, you might say, desperate measures in order to make any form of Italian nationality coherent and integral —

Here Mr. Churchill was interrupted by a member who asked whether the exiled Count Sforza would be allowed to go back to Italy and help rouse the people.

I cannot speak for Count Sforza, but I should be glad indeed to see forces of that kind rallied to the Government which must be formed to drive out the Germans. If they are given an opportunity and do not come forward, then, in my opinion, they will be taking a great responsibility, for there are moments in the life of a country when people cannot be more nice than wise. They have to throw in their lot, for what it is worth, with the forces on which depend the existence and identity of their nation. Well, now, is that all right? Nothing that is settled here prejudges or prejudices in any way the free decision of the Italian people as to the form of government which they intend to have. We are coming to the rescue and liberation of Italy. We are prepared to place large armies in Italy, to deploy on a wide and active fighting front against the enemy on whatever line he chooses to stand on, and to maintain an offensive against him with increasing weight and vigour, if need be throughout the autumn and winter and, of course, beyond. It is of great importance to the United States and Great Britain to bring the largest forces they possibly can to bear upon the enemy and to force the fighting to the utmost. We are terribly hampered by the sea, which has been our shield and protection, but which is now a barrier that prevents the employment of those great forces. It is to our interest to force the fighting to the utmost, and to find means, some of them not even the best, of coming into contact with the enemy. Especially is this true of the air, where our superiority in numbers as well as in quality must find full scope. It is to our advantage to lose on equal terms and on worse than equal terms to the enemy, in order to produce that diminution which we can sustain and which he cannot. But, happily, losses still show an advantage upon our side. The enemy lose more heavily than we do, in nearly all air fights, and what a small capital have they with which to face this continuous strain!

I call this front we have opened, first in Africa, next in Sicily, and now in Italy, the Third Front. The Second Front, which already exists potentially and which is rapidly gathering weight, has not yet been engaged, but it is here, holding forces on its line. No one can tell — and certainly I am not going to hint at — the moment when it will be engaged. But the Second Front exists, and is a main preoccupation already of the enemy. It has not yet opened, or been thrown into play, but the time will come. At what we and our American Allies judge to be the right time, this front will be thrown open, and the mass invasion from the West, in combination with the invasion from the South, will begin.

It is quite impossible for those who do not know the facts and figures of the American assembly in Britain, or of our own powerful expeditionary Armies now preparing here, who do not know the dispositions of the enemy on the various fronts, who cannot measure his reserves and resources and his power to transfer large forces from one front to another over the vast railway system of Europe, who do not know the state and dimensions of our fleet and landing-craft of all kinds — and this must be proportionate to the work they have to do — who do not know how the actual processes of a landing take place, or what are the necessary steps to build it up, or what has to be thought out beforehand in relation to what the enemy can do in days or weeks — it is impossible for those who do not know these facts, which are the study of hundreds of skilful officers day after day and month after month, to pronounce a useful opinion upon this operation.

Here Mr. Gallacher interjected: "Does that apply to Marshal Stalin?"

We should not in a matter of this kind take advice from British Communists, because we know that they stood aside and cared nothing for our fortunes in our time of mortal peril. Any advice that we take will be from friends and Allies who are all joined together in the common cause of winning the victory. The House may be absolutely certain that His Majesty's present Government will never be swayed or overborne by any uninstructed agitation, however natural, or any pressure, however well-meant, in matters of this kind. We shall not be forced or cajoled into undertaking vast operations of war against our better judgment in order to gain political unanimity or a cheer from any quarter. The bloodiest portion — make no mistake about it — of this war for Great Britain and the United States lies ahead of us. Neither the House nor the Government will shrink from that ordeal. We shall not grudge any sacrifice for the common cause. I myself regard it as a matter of personal honour to act only with the conviction of success founded upon the highest professional advice at our disposal in operations of the first magnitude. I decline, therefore, to discuss at all the questions when, where, how and on what scale the main assault from the West will be launched, and I am confident that the House will support the Government in this attitude.

I am glad to say that several important arrangements have been made at Quebec, and in consultation with the War Cabinet here, for closer correlation and action between the Soviet Union and Britain and the United States. The difficulties of geography have hitherto proved an insuperable impediment, though various efforts have been made, not only by the United States but by the British Government, to bridge the physical gap by the successive visits to Moscow of Lord Beaverbrook, the Foreign Secretary, and myself, and by the visits of M. Molotov to this country and to the United States. In August, replying to the telegram from President Roosevelt and myself informing the Russians of the Italian peace feelers, Marshal Stalin expressed a wish to have an Inter-Allied Commission set up in the Mediterranean to deal with this and similar problems — the Mediterranean problem, the working of the Italian Armistice, etc., as and when they arose. We were very glad to find this friendly interest taken in our Mediterranean operations by our Russian Allies. The Commission, of course, cannot supersede the authority or diminish the responsibilities of Governments, but its members will be kept fully informed of all that passes, and will have the power of individual and collective representation to their Governments. Our representative will be my right hon. Friend the Member for Stockton (Mr. Harold Macmillan), whose work at General Eisenhower's headquarters is closely connected with this field, and who has discharged his difficult duties with increasing distinction and success. Arrangements have also been made — I must make it quite clear that this does not release the Government from their responsibilities, because that would be contrary to the parliamentary principles on which we rest, and also, of course, the military emergencies dominate everything — arrangements have also been made, as has already been stated, for a tripartite conference between the Foreign Secretaries of the three countries or their representatives. We shall be represented by my right hon. Friend the Foreign Secretary, in whom the House and his colleagues have the completest confidence. The conference will take place at an early date, and no questions will be barred from its discussions. The whole ground will be surveyed, and matters will be carried forward to agreement wherever possible. Where there is a difference, that will be set aside for what I am coming to now. We also have a confident hope of a subsequent meeting before the end of the year between the President of the United States, Marshal Stalin and myself. I need scarcely say that the time and place of this meeting will not be made public until after it has been concluded, and I may add that speculation on such points of detail in the newspaper Press would on the whole be unhelpful. The work that will have to be done on the Foreign Office level between the three countries should prove an invaluable, and it is certainly an indispensable, preliminary to any such meeting of the Heads of Government. I will not say any more on this subject at present except, which I am sure will be the feeling of the House, that no meeting during this war would carry with it so much significance for the future of the world as a meeting between the Heads of the three Governments, for, without the close, cordial, and lasting association between Soviet Russia and the other great Allies, we might find ourselves at the end of the war only to have entered upon a period of deepening confusion.

At Quebec also was settled the question of the recognition of the French Committee of National Liberation. Any differences in the degree of this recognition which may be noted in the documents of the various Powers arise solely from the importance which attaches to preserving full freedom to the French nation as a whole to decide its future destinies under conditions of freedom and tranquillity. Neither Great Britain nor the United States is prepared to regard the French National Committee as other than a provisional instrument, and this view is also fully accepted by the members of the Committee themselves. I am happy to say that a continued improvement of personal relations and fusion of aims has taken place in the last two months within the Committee itself. Personalities have receded, and the collective strength of this body — which I will call the "Trustees of France" during the time of incapacity — has steadily grown. With the exception only of Indo-China, which is still in enemy hands, they administer with success the entire French Empire. They dispose of a considerable fleet, in which the first-class modern battleship *Richelieu* will presently take its place. A French army of three or four hundred thousand men is being steadily organised by the French Committee under the command of General Giraud, in the closest association with his colleague General de Gaulle. This army is being furnished with the most modern equipment, supplied by the United States Government, and it will not be long before we shall again experience the inspiring sense of having French forces alongside us on the battle front. I am very glad to add that both Russia and the United States are agreeable to the French National Committee being represented on the new Commission which is being set up in the Mediterranean, and in this respect it will be the first time that they have taken their place as an equal partner with the three great Powers warring against Germany in Europe.

Although I have not hesitated to express my difference with the various sections of the French National Committee from time to time — I cannot pretend that all has run smoothly and happily — I wish to make it quite clear that I regard the restoration of

France as one of the great Powers of Europe as a sacred duty from which Great Britain will never recede. This arises not only from the sentiments which we hold towards France, so long our comrade in victory and misfortune, but also from the fact that it is one of the most enduring interests of Great Britain in Europe that there should be a strong France and a strong French army. Such a condition could, however, only be reached on the basis of the free self-expression of the French people as a whole. They must themselves be the judges of the conduct of their fellow-Frenchmen in the terrible conditions which followed the military collapse of the summer of 1940. I remain convinced that the highest honour will be accorded to those who never flinched or wavered in the hour of disaster, and that lasting condemnation and, I trust, salutary punishment will be meted out to all prominent persons who have not merely bowed to the force of circumstances, but who, for the sake of personal ambition or profit, have tried to promote the victory of the common foe. [An Hon. Member: "King Victor Emmanuel and Badoglio."] Some people are reduced by our prolonged unbroken success to little more than mocking laughter.

There are three points arising out of the unconditional surrender of Italy and the Armistice that we have granted which require special notice. The first is our prisoners of war. There were nearly 70,000 British prisoners of war and upwards of 25,000 Greek and Yugoslav prisoners in Italian hands. From the very first moment of Mussolini's fall we made it brutally clear to the Italian Government and King that we regarded the liberation of these prisoners and their restoration to our care as the prime, indispensable condition of any relationship between us and any Italian Government, and this, of course, is fully provided for in the terms of surrender. However, many of these prisoners in the North of Italy, and others in the Central and Southern part, may have fallen into the power of the Germans. I have no precise information to give the House to-day, in view of the confusion prevailing in Italy, which only our armies can clarify. The Italian Government, however, have given orders for the release from confinement of all Allied prisoners under their control, and I have no doubt that these will be succoured by the Italian people among whom they are dispersing, in spite of the German threats of punishment to any Italians who show this kind of common humanity. In all these matters we are acting with the greatest vigilance and earnestness, and everything in human power will be done. Everything, however, depends on the movement of the armies in the next few weeks.

The second important feature arising out of the Armistice with Italy is the situation in the Balkans. Here with marvellous and indomitable tenacity the patriot bands of Greeks and Yugoslavs have maintained a formidable resistance to the torturers of their countries. They hold great regions under their control, they fight fierce battles in the mountains, they destroy communications and occupy important towns and points, with a vigour and on a scale which has required no fewer than 47 German, Italian and Bulgarian Divisions — for this is the dirty work Bulgaria does — to be maintained continually in these vast and wild spaces. Of these, upwards of 25 were Italian divisions who, even if unable to turn upon the common foe, will certainly be of no further danger to the patriots, and will indeed be a valuable source of their equipment. This gap will have to be supplied from some quarter or another by the Germans at a time when they are so heavily strained upon the Russian and other fronts. Hitherto we have had no means of helping these unconquerable champions of Greek and Yugoslav freedom except by air-borne supplies and by offers of money. With the control of Southern Italy, to which we confidently look forward in the near future, and with the building-up of our air power in Italy, our entry and perhaps command of the Adriatic should become possible.

All this opens far-reaching vistas of action which also must be surveyed in relation to the conditions and temper of the people in the satellite States of Hungary, Rumania and Bulgaria, each of which is a study in itself, and all of which will be increasingly affected by the advance of the Russian armies and by the development of Anglo-American bombing. In dealing with this subject I must say no more than is already obvious to the enemy. Henceforward we shall see the Germans holding down or trying to hold down the whole of Hitler's Europe by systematic terror. Whenever Hitler's legions can momentarily avert their eyes from the hostile battle fronts which are closing in upon them, they can take their choice either of looking upon ruined cities of the

German homeland or of looking upon what is a not less awful spectacle, the infuriated populations which are waiting to devour them. The first point then is our prisoners, many of whom we hope will be rescued; and the second is this great development in the Balkans, which I cannot pretend to measure exactly, and which in any case is not suitable for public discussion.

There is a third and most tangible advantage which we have gained from the overthrow of Italy. I mean the surrender of the Italian fleet. This was fulfilled in fidelity to the orders of the Italian King and the Badoglio Government. Practically the whole of the Italian Navy, many merchant ships and many submarines, have, under conditions of great risk, strictly executed the conditions of the Armistice and made their way to Malta or other ports under British control. This event has decisively altered the naval balances of the world. Not only have the Allies gained the Italian fleet to use in any way they think most serviceable, but there is also set free the stronger British fleet which was measured against it. We came into two naval fortunes on the same day, or, as we put it in this House, it counted two on a Division! Very large additional naval forces are therefore at our disposal. The United States forces are already dominant in the Pacific. All the disasters have been repaired by new building. Very large additional naval forces have now come into our hands, and since they will not remain idle for one single unnecessary day, I venture to think that the Japanese war lords may soon find themselves confronted at any rate with some serious considerations which were probably not in their minds at the time they ordered the attack upon Pearl Harbour.

I have now finished my survey, and have but one word more to say. The political atmosphere in the United States is not the same as it is over here. The Constitution decrees elections at fixed intervals, and parties are forced to assert and defend their special interests at the elections in a manner which we have under our more flexible system been able to lay aside for the time being. Nevertheless, I was made conscious of the resolve and desire of all parties to drive forward the war on all fronts and against all foes with the utmost determination. I was also conscious of a feeling of friendliness towards Great Britain and the British Commonwealth and Empire such as I have never known before,

and a respect for the war effort of the 46,000,000 in this small
Island and for the conduct of our troops who are the comrades
of the Americans in the hard-fought fields of this war. All this
was very dear and refreshing to my heart. I found also the feeling everywhere that the war was being well managed, that the
central direction made good plans, and that highly competent
and resolute officers were entrusted with their execution in every
part of the globe. It is my hope that this conviction is generally
shared at home, and that the House of Commons will feel no
need to reproach itself for the unwavering confidence it has
given to His Majesty's servants in their discharge of the exceptional burdens which have been thrust upon them.

*A member then asked the Prime Minister to assure the House
that plans made by himself and President Roosevelt were flexible
enough to enable full opportunities to be taken of any new
situation.*

I can readily give that assurance. Of course, frequent conferences are necessary between the great Staffs, but the general on
the spot, the chief command, can at any time propose a change
in the plans to take advantage of the situation, or we can suggest
a change to him. In fact, a lot of things have been done on the
spur of the moment, like Sardinia and Corsica, which were not
even considered feasible last week. I can readily give the assurance that there is that flexibility, but, of course, when you are
dealing with a number of Allies and have to consult a number
of Governments, and very often inform the Dominions, and so
forth, you have not got exactly the same freedom that you have
when you are simply dealing with your own troops. That is one
of the facts which have to be borne in mind. I could well conceive that if all the Forces were now working under one single
control, some things would be done more quickly than they can
now be done; but when one looks at the disadvantages attaching
to alliances, one must not forget how superior are the advantages.

The best method of acquiring flexibility is to have three or
four plans for all the probable contingencies, all worked out with
the utmost detail. Then it is much easier to switch from one to
the other as and where the cat jumps.

The Air Offensive

ON SEPTEMBER 21, 1943, SIR STAFFORD CRIPPS, MINISTER OF AIRCRAFT PRODUCTION, ADDRESSED A MEETING IN LONDON OF 500 AIRCRAFT WORKERS, AND READ THIS LETTER HE HAD RECEIVED FROM MR. CHURCHILL

I UNDERSTAND that you are having a meeting of representatives of the aircraft industry, and I should be glad if you would tell them from me what a supremely important part they are called upon to play in the coming months of our offensive against the Germans and the Japanese. It is impossible to over-emphasize the need for the most efficient and up-to-date aircraft in the greatest possible numbers.

The contribution of the aircraft industry to our war effort has already been very great, but we are expecting even better results in the months ahead. The high quality of our production, due to the ingenuity of our designers and the skill of managements and workers alike, has given us superiority over the enemy in many theatres of war. This superiority we must maintain at all costs, and at the same time we must increase the weight of our offensive against Germany and the occupied territories.

I am sure that the Government and the people of our country can rely upon the aircraft industry to put their backs into it to the utmost, and so shorten the agony of the war.

Sir Kingsley Wood

A TRIBUTE IN THE HOUSE OF COMMONS TO THE
CHANCELLOR OF THE EXCHEQUER, WHO DIED
ON SEPTEMBER 21, 1943
SEPTEMBER 22, 1943

[September 22, 1943

OUR Chancellor of the Exchequer, Sir Kingsley Wood, was a very old Member of the House. He had been here for a quarter of a century. For the last ten years he had been continuously in office amid all the vicissitudes, changes and shocks of that period. Everyone knows how good his work was at the Post Office and the Ministry of Health. He left a mark on the Post Office, and made a very great contribution to building up the prestige of the Ministry of Health to the high point it has attained among the great offices of State. Then, before the war, he was taken to a field in which he had not had previous experience. It was thought necessary that his business and administrative efficiency should be applied to our air production and to our Royal Air Force, and he became Air Minister in those critical years. As between the different Services, while avoiding invidious comparisons, I should certainly say that the outlook of the Royal Air Force upon this war was more closely attuned to the circumstances and conditions as they emerged in painful experience than that of either of the other two Services. The great contribution for which Sir Kingsley Wood's administration of the Air Ministry will always be remembered was the founding and development of the Empire Air Training Scheme in Canada, to which pilots from New Zealand and Australia came in great numbers, to which would-be pilots from the United Kingdom have also been sent in large numbers, and which has produced us a ceaseless flow, numbered by tens of thousands, of those extraordinarily competent and daring men to whom we owe so much of the satisfactory position we have now attained. This Empire Air Training Scheme was a work of great imagination, and all who were concerned in it deserve the greatest possible credit. It was not only a war winner, but an Empire cementer. I imagine that the friendships and comradeships formed by these young men in the vast training-camps of Canada will carry on their beneficent influence long after the older Members of this House have passed away. That was a very great and outstanding act of his administration.

Then, when I was called upon to form this present Government in the height of the great battle that was raging and which turned out so disastrously, he became Chancellor of the Exchequer. This must be regarded as an historic Chancellorship. It represents by far the greatest financial effort in our history. Nothing like it has been seen before, or anything approaching it, but, of course, all our figures are larger now than at any other time. Sir Kingsley Wood made the fullest contribution which finance can make, with other agencies, to stemming the tide of inflation, which is always driving in upon our breastworks and dykes, and, if it ever burst them, would be the beginning of untold evils and demoralisation. He presented three Budgets to the House. The first Budget of a Chancellor is often well received, but the third Budget is the most critical of all, because it is the heir of previous decisions, and it is by that time you can see whether the Chancellor is really master of this great and dominant Department of State.

The last Budget was the most acceptable of all. It was really a triumph, a great personal triumph, not a triumph particularly for the oratorical fireworks, but for the sound lines on which he had been working, which now at this time arrived at fruition, and enabled him to make a statement to the House which was regarded here and in the United States as masterly. It was a balanced Budget with these colossal figures, and out of £5,700,000,000, half was raised by taxation, the most severe taxation ever imposed by a Government or loyally accepted by the taxpayers. When I think of the very keen manner in which the late Mr. Bonar Law used to take pride in the proportion of the money he had raised by taxation as opposed to borrowing in the last war, I find the means of measuring the achievement of the late Chancellor, who very nearly succeeded in doubling the proportion raised out of direct taxation. All the greatest economists, John Stuart Mill at their head, have always spoken of the evils of borrowing for the purposes of war, and have pointed out that as far as possible posterity should be relieved and the cost of what is consumed in the war be met at the time. That is a counsel of perfection, but nobody has ever come nearer to it than the late Chancellor of the Exchequer. The cost of living has been kept within a 30 per cent. increase over pre-war by a most elaborate system which he introduced. The United States have not adopted it, but it is looked upon in many quarters there with very considerable admiration. At any rate, this keeping down of the cost of living is one of the pillars on which the whole defence against inflation rests.

Our rate of borrowing is incredibly low, far lower than it was in the last war. I remember well at the close of the last war that we were urged to subscribe to Government funds under a slogan, "Security and 6 per cent." We have succeeded in borrowing these vast sums in the fifth year of the war at a rate, when the tax is deducted, which does not amount to more than 1½ per cent. I am not comparing quite fairly, because the 6 per cent. was gross and the 1½ per cent. is net. Nevertheless, we have much heavier taxes at the present time, and the fact remains that these vast loans which have been floated do not impose upon posterity the burden of more than 1½ per cent. if you take in the taxation, and 3 per cent. if you do not. In all these respects — these large, salient features — no comparison can be made between the finance conducted by the late Chancellor of the Exchequer and any finance of which we have record in periods of great expenditure and confusion.

At the beginning of the blitz I pressed upon him the vital need of doing something for the poor people whose houses were smashed up and whose businesses were destroyed, and he devised the elaborate insurance scheme, which has come into the fullest possible fruition. At one time, it looked as if the State were taking on a very heavy burden; but trees never grow up to the sky, and, as a matter of fact, not only have individuals been provided for and the loss inflicted by the enemy shared and spread over the shoulders of the whole community, but the scheme has ultimately turned out to be highly profitable to the Exchequer.

Sir Kingsley Wood, September 22, 1943

The extension of the Income Tax to the wage-earners was a very remarkable step. That it should have gained the assent of this House, elected on universal suffrage, is also a remarkable fact, showing how extremely closely the wage-earning masses of the country and those who represent them feel associated with the vital issues now being fought out in the field. Undoubtedly, payment in arrear, when the Treasury accounts are made up, being demanded from the wage-earners, produced many cases of very great hardship, and tended to cause dissatisfaction with a great principle of taxation which was being so very willingly accepted. The Chancellor had given the closing weeks of his life to a most careful study of the "pay-as-you-go" principle, and he was looking forward, on the very day that he died, to making a statement to the House on the subject. That statement has now been made by the Financial Secretary, and the relevant White Paper will soon be in possession of the House; and it is the last contribution which the late Chancellor has made to our affairs. In addition to this, the recasting of the general form and presentation of the Budget and the nation's accounts which has received the approval of the House and commands the approval of those best qualified to judge in all quarters of the House, will take a permanent part in our affairs. All these are milestones in our long financial history, and they will be associated with the financial administration of Sir Kingsley Wood.

One of the most important achievements in these last years of the Chancellor of the Exchequer has been the relations which he established and maintained with the United States. Our finance is most closely interwoven, and all kinds of questions of the utmost difficulty and delicacy have been arising constantly. We have had the ablest Treasury officials over there, and the Chancellor has always had a series of questions of the utmost complexity to raise and to adjust with his opposite number and colleague, Mr. Morgenthau, the Secretary to the Treasury of the United States. I have received a message, which I will read to the House, from Mr. Morgenthau this morning: —

"Permit me to express through you to His Majesty's Government and people my deep sense of personal loss in the death of Sir Kingsley Wood, Chancellor of the Exchequer, whose sincere friendliness and co-operative spirit have done so much to advance the common cause of our two countries. We in the United States, who knew of his great abilities as well as his fine integrity and personal charm, join with you in mourning his departure."

Of course, it is a difficult and thankless task to be Chancellor of the Exchequer, especially in time of war. Everyone would like to see a generous attitude adopted in respect of questions affecting the Armed Forces. Everyone feels the extremely severe, almost confiscatory, character of the taxation imposed. At every point, it strikes upon the intimate life of the people. The few comforts or luxuries that are left to them are charged with the most immense burdens of taxation. At every point he has a disagreeable job to do. One cannot at all wonder that the Chancellor of the Exchequer goes through periods of disparagement and criticism, but all that was overcome by the massive success of his financial schemes, and all that was also overcome by his own personal qualities.

We in this House and still more in the Cabinet were very fond of Kingsley Wood as a man, amiable, experienced, competent, efficient, accessible. He was all that a Minister who is a good House of Commons man should be. He was also a good party man. There is no reason to be ashamed of that, for in many periods of history, democracy expresses itself best through the ebb and flow of parties. He was a good party man in this sense, because these are the qualifications of a good party man — you must know how to put your party before yourself, and you must know the occasions when to put nation before party. In this he fully qualified. We shall not easily fill the gap, and the balance of our affairs is, at the moment, sadly deranged. A new problem and burden is thrown upon me, and I feel that very much. I feel far more the loss of a genial, sincere and faithful friend, with whom I and my colleagues have stood shoulder to shoulder during a period altogether without precedent in our long history. I feel that in expressing these sentiments I carry with me the genuine and unaffected acquiescence and even active agreement of Members of all parties, seated in all parts of the House.

The Women of Britain

A SPEECH TO A GATHERING OF 6,000 WOMEN AT THE
ROYAL ALBERT HALL, LONDON
SEPTEMBER 29, 1943

September 23.	*Russians captured Poltava, German strong point in the Ukraine, and made important new advance towards the Dnieper.*
September 24.	*Sir John Anderson succeeded the late Sir Kingsley Wood as Chancellor of the Exchequer.*
September 25.	*Russians captured Smolensk and fierce fighting developed on the Dnieper.*
	Officially revealed that a new explosive "RDX," discovered by British scientists before the War, is now being used by the United Nations.
September 27.	*The Eighth Army captured Foggia, a leading Italian air base, a feat which President Roosevelt subsequently described as one of the most important strategic successes for the Allies.*

[September 29, 1943

THIS impressive and representative gathering marks a definite recognition of the part which women are playing in our struggle for right and freedom. I remember in 1939, at Manchester, making an appeal for a million women to come forward into the war effort in all its forms. This was thought to be a very extravagant proposal at the time, but it is not a third of what has since been required and of what has been forthcoming.

We are engaged in total war. We are engaged in a struggle for life. Although you cannot say that the peril is as imminent as it was in 1940, during that year when we were all alone, nevertheless, if this war were so handled that the unity of national effort were diminished, that its pace and vigour were slackened, that we fell apart, that apathy overtook us, and if this were typical throughout the Forces of the United Nations, then indeed another set of dangers, not perhaps so catastrophic in their aspect, but none the less deadly in their character, would march upon us. The war would languish, our soldiers would find themselves short of munitions and services just at the time when they would need them most, just at the time when their action was growing to an ever larger scale.

And the enemy — what is their hope? Their hope is that we shall get wearied, that the democracies will faint and falter on the long road, and that now, in the fifth year of the war, there will be doubts, despondencies and slackness; and then they hope that out of this they will be able, consolidated in their central fortress of Europe or in their remote home islands of Japan, to extract from our weariness and from any divisions which might appear among us the means of making terms to enable them to repair their losses, to re-gather their forces, and to open upon the world in, it may be, a decade, another war, even more terrible than that through which we are passing. Therefore, the ideas of total war, of fighting for life, must be continually in your minds.

The war effort of our 46 millions living in Great Britain and Northern Ireland is at the present time justly admired by our Allies. Upon the whole, there is no community engaged in this war which is more smoothly, effectively, and exhaustively organised for war; there is no community which presents so many different sides and varieties of war effort.

We have to guard the seas; we have to bring in our food and materials; we have to guard our homes against the ever-present threat of oversea attacks; we have to be ready to meet intensive and novel forms of air attack at any time; we have to grow a far greater proportion of our own food than we ever did before; we have to carry on all our vast production of munitions; we have to build warships and merchant ships in large numbers; we have to maintain the life of our civilian population, and take care of the sick, the old and the broken. All this has to be done by this community, and I say that it is a spectacle of marvellous organisation which our country presents at the present time.

This war effort could not have been achieved if the women had not marched forward in millions and undertaken all kinds of tasks and work for which any other generation but our own — unless you go back to the Stone Age — would have considered them unfitted; work in the fields, heavy work in the foundries and in the shops, very refined work on radio and precision instruments, work in the hospitals, responsible clerical work of all kinds, work throughout the munitions factories, work in the mixed batteries — I take a special interest in those — most remarkable societies where there are more women than men, and where the weapons are handled with the utmost skill and proficiency. These mixed batteries have saved scores of thousands of strong men from static employment, and set them free for the field armies and the mobile batteries. Nothing has been grudged, and the bounds of women's activities have been definitely, vastly, and permanently enlarged.

It may seem strange that a great advance in the position of women in the world in industry, in controls of all kinds, should be made in time of war and not in time of peace. One would have thought that in the days of peace the progress of women to an ever larger share in the life and work and guidance of the community would have grown, and that, under the violences of war, it would be cast back. The reverse is true. War is the teacher, a hard, stern, efficient teacher. War has taught us to make these vast strides forward towards a far more complete equalisation of the parts to be played by men and women in society.

I said just now that the conditions in this island present an incomparable example, among the United Nations, of unified, concerted war effort. I cannot expect, after four years of war, that there is much slack to take up; but my friend Mr. Bevin, the Minister of Labour, has the greatest possible difficulty in providing for even the approved demands which are made upon him by all the Departments of the State. We are fully extended now, and what we have to do is to hold it, to maintain this effort, through the fifth year of war, or the sixth if need be; for we will never stop until we have achieved our purpose.

In the forthcoming year you will see larger armies fighting, you will see more powerful air forces striking at the heart of the enemy's country; but the actual demands made upon the British population cannot be greatly increased. The augmentation of munitions will follow from the smoother running of the great processes which are already at work, rather than from any multiplication of the human beings engaged in production. We are, as I say, full out, and to hold that and to maintain that is a tremendous task, and one that will require the utmost firmness of character in all His Majesty's subjects, and extreme care, diligence, and vigilance on the part of those who are entrusted with public office in any form. All will be needed in order that we may keep up the tremendous pace at which we are moving, for whatever time is necessary in order to secure the complete, the absolute victory of the good cause.

It is a good cause. No one has any doubt about that. All over the world men and women, under every sky and climate, of every race, creed and colour, all have the feeling that in the casting-down of this monstrous Nazi engine of tyranny, cruelty, greed and aggression — in the casting of it down shattered in pieces, something will have been achieved by the whole human race which will affect in a decisive manner its future destinies, and which will even in our own time be marked by very sensible improvement in the conditions under which the great masses of the people live.

Freedom will be erected on unshakable foundations, and at her side will be Right and Justice; and I am sure of this, that when the victory is gained we shall show a poise and temper as admirable as that which we displayed in the days of our mortal danger, that we shall not be led astray by false guides either into apathy and weakness or into brutality, but that the name of our dear country, our island home, will, by our conduct, by our clairvoyance, by our self-restraint, by our inflexible tenacity of purpose, long stand in honour amongst the nations of the world.

In all this the women of Britain have borne, are bearing, and will continue to bear, a part which excites admiration among our Allies, and will be found to have definitely altered those social and sex balances which years of convention had established.

I have no fear of the future. Let us go forward into its mysteries, let us tear aside the veils which hide it from our eyes, and let us move onward with confidence and courage. All the problems of the post-war world, some of which seem so baffling now, will be easier of solution once decisive victory has been gained, and once it is clear that victory won in arms has not been cast away by folly or by violence when the moment comes to lay the broad foundations of the future world order, and it is time to speak great words of peace and truth to all.

Messages

THE FOURTH ANNIVERSARY

[*September 5, 1943*

[A REPLY TO A MESSAGE FROM GENERALISSIMO CHIANG KAI-SHEK ON THE FOURTH ANNIVER-SARY OF THE OUTBREAK OF WAR BETWEEN GREAT BRITAIN AND GERMANY]

ON behalf of the Government and people of this country I send you my sincere thanks for your Excellency's kind and inspiring message on the occasion of this, the fourth anniversary of the day on which we took up arms against the aggressor.

Since that day, and the anxious times which followed, our arms have been blessed by Providence with ever-increasing success, and we are celebrating this anniversary by new ventures. Though the battle will still be long and hard, we can now look forward more confidently than ever before to victory and the making of a new world, towards the establishment of which your great and dauntless country has made an unforgettable contribution.

CONGRATULATIONS ON THE SURRENDER OF ITALY

[DURING THE MONTH OF SEPTEMBER, MR. CHURCH-ILL RECEIVED MANY CONGRATULATIONS ON THE SURRENDER OF ITALY. AMONG THE REPLIES HE SENT TO THESE MESSAGES WERE THE FOLLOWING]

TO the King of the Hellenes.

The British people remember with admiration the victories won by the Greek forces and the Greek people under Your

Majesty's leadership against the Italian aggressors in 1940 and 1941, and we are proud that now, as then, Greece is associated with us in the prosecution of the war to final victory.

To the King of Saudi Arabia.

Your Majesty's telegram on the surrender of the Italian Government has given me the greatest pleasure, and I thank Your Majesty warmly for your congratulations. Your Majesty has always been so resolute in the dark days, and I share Your Majesty's hope that this is but the first step towards the early defeat of the powers of evil and the establishment of the peace of justice for which the world is eagerly waiting.

Answers in the House of Commons

[LOCAL GOVERNMENT REFORM]

Replying to questions regarding the reform of local govern-
ment and the redistribution of the powers of local authorities,
and asked to give an assurance that it was not intended to trans-
fer the duties of County Councils to a central body, Mr. Churchill
said: —

IT is, I am assured, generally agreed that there is a strong
case for the expansion and improvement of many local government services, and that we should be ready with plans for execution at the end of the war. I am aware of the fears voiced by the
Associations of local government bodies lest the Government, in
putting forward proposals for such changes, should pay insuffi-
cient regard to their cumulative effect upon the existing local
government system.

The Government have given the fullest consideration to the
representations that have been made to them to the effect that
before any important changes in particular services are decided
upon there should be a comprehensive and authoritative inquiry
into the general machinery of local government. It is clear that
such an inquiry would involve the taking of much evidence, and
the consideration of many highly controversial issues going far
beyond those raised by the plans for meeting post-war needs in
regard to particular services. It would consequently occupy much
time, and the results might not in the end find general acceptance.
The delay involved would be highly prejudicial to the success of
our post-war plans, and in the circumstances it is not the intention of the Government to embark on a comprehensive inquiry

into the machinery of local government at the present time.

The Government are, however, very much alive to the need for avoiding any weakening of the structure of local government, and I can give the assurance that in framing any proposals in relation to particular services for submission to this House, they will pay the most careful regard to this factor.

[INOCULATION IN THE SERVICES]

Asked to state that any man or woman in the Services could refuse to be inoculated or vaccinated without suffering any penalty, Mr. Churchill said: —

Inoculation is voluntary in all three Services, and I am assured that this is well known. In the Navy, however, in the interests of the health of ships' companies, it is necessary to refuse to those who have not been inoculated permission to land in ports where there may be danger of contracting any of the diseases against which this treatment is aimed. If individuals who refuse to be inoculated have been threatened in any way, and if my hon. Friend will forward the particulars to the Ministers concerned, the facts will be looked into.

[STATUTORY RULES AND ORDERS]

A member drew attention to the varying practice in different Government Departments in signing Statutory Rules and Orders, stating that in some cases Orders were signed under seal, and in others by officials whose status was indicated or by persons whose status was not indicated. He asked for greater uniformity, and Mr. Churchill replied: —

I am advised that trying to achieve uniformity at the present time would cause more trouble than it is worth.

The Minister is always responsible ultimately, and the Government are always responsible collectively. If the Minister has not himself seen or signed an Order, as certainly sometimes necessarily occurs, he, nevertheless, is responsible, and can be brought to book in this House. There is the great remedy.

It is not a question of making laws, but of administering certain Acts of Parliament which have already received the assent of the House and which are administered under the strict scrutiny of Parliament, and of the hon. Gentleman.

Replying to another member who suggested that Rules and Orders might be written in Basic English, Mr. Churchill replied: —

I hope in simple English, which is not quite the same thing.

[WAR MEDALS]

A statement on September 22 in reply to several questions concerning the issue of the 1939–43 Star and the Africa Star.

Service in Cyprus will not qualify for the Africa Star. Malta alone of the Mediterranean islands is included in the award of this Star, by reason of its heavy action and long ordeal in combination with the operations in Africa. In the Navy the 1939–43 Star takes priority of award over the Africa Star, and no one eligible for the former will receive the latter. The reason for this is that, from the naval point of view, service in the African campaigns cannot be accepted as ranking before the world-wide services performed by the Navy in other areas of operations. Sea-going personnel of the Air-Sea Rescue Service and of the barrage balloons will qualify under the same rules as the Navy. Service on land on the home front presents many difficult borderline cases on which opinion may well mature. When the Africa and 1939–43 Stars are manufactured after the war, they will be given as mementos to the next-of-kin of those who have suffered death as a result of service in a theatre of operations during the periods laid down.

We are going to get on with the giving-out of the medals. We are not going to delay the issue of the ribbons, but the question is whether some others should come in. There are officers and men, some of whom have been fighting for three years continuously, and who, perhaps, have only a decoration for personal gallantry on their breasts. They will value it very much. We must be careful not to destroy the value of the award by making it practically universal. On the other hand, it may well be that some expansion may be permitted from the present conception.

Everyone will recognise the difficulty of the problem, and how easily opinions may differ upon it.

I certainly hope the House will be able to find time to discuss this, because we obviously want to make these awards correspond with the general wish and feeling of the country and of the House, which represents the country, and also to make them in a form which will be acceptable to the far more critical opinion of the Fighting Services.

[ANXIETIES]

Replying to a member who declared that there was "wide-spread anxiety" concerning the Food Conference at Hot Springs (U.S.) and the delay in announcing the long-term policy for encouraging production, Mr. Churchill said: —

We have a lot of anxieties, and one cancels out another very often.

[EMPIRE COLLABORATION]

Asked to state the views of the Government on the Australian Prime Minister's suggestion for an All-Empire Cabinet, Mr. Churchill said: —

Such spacious issues would be appropriate for an Imperial Conference or for a meeting of Dominion Prime Ministers, whenever either of these becomes possible.

I have been trying for the last two years to get a meeting of Prime Ministers. I understand that is more likely to be acceptable than an Imperial Conference at this moment, and I have hopes that we shall succeed in having such a meeting early next year. Of course, each of these Dominions has had, or is going to have, an election, and that has hung over the movements of the Prime Ministers. In Australia and New Zealand, particularly, they are very near the war against Japan. There are great difficulties in this matter, but we are patiently endeavouring to solve them. We regard it as an important and immediate objective to procure a meeting of Empire Prime Ministers.

[MUSSOLINI'S ESCAPE]

Asked why Mussolini's guards failed to carry out orders to shoot him if he attempted to escape, Mr. Churchill said: —

I was not there at the time. Perhaps it was lucky for him.

[ITALIAN ARMISTICE TERMS]

Asked who was responsible for the broadcasting of the Armistice terms with Italy before they had been communicated to the House of Commons, Mr. Churchill said: —

The President and I authorised General Eisenhower to publish the terms of the Armistice signed on 3rd September, leaving it to him to decide the moment of publication in the light of the military situation. Neither Parliament nor the Congress of the United States was in Session at that time.

Tribute to Sir Dudley Pound

A LETTER TO ADMIRAL OF THE FLEET SIR DUDLEY POUND
ON HIS RESIGNATION FROM THE POST OF FIRST SEA LORD
OCTOBER 4, 1943

[October 4, 1943

MY dear Pound, — I am sorry indeed that you have felt it necessary to lay down your charge on account of your health, and that our four years' work together in this war must come to an end. No one knows better than I the quality of your contribution at the Admiralty and on the Chiefs of Staff Committee to the safety of the country and the success of our arms. Your vast and precise knowledge of the sea war in all its aspects, your fortitude in times of anxiety and misfortune, your resourcefulness and readiness to run the risks without which victory can never be won, have combined to make your tenure as First Sea Lord memorable in the records of the Royal Navy.

You leave us at a moment when the control of the Mediterranean is virtually within our grasp, when the Italian fleet has made its surrender in Malta harbour, and when, above all, the U-boat peril has been broken in a degree never before seen in this war. These results have been of measureless value to your country, and your notable share in them sheds lustre on your name. — I remain, your sincere friend,

WINSTON S. CHURCHILL.

"Beating the Life Out of Germany"

MESSAGES OF CONGRATULATIONS ON THE GREAT AIR OF-
FENSIVE AGAINST GERMANY SENT TO LIEUTENANT-GENERAL
JACOB L. DEVERS, COMMANDING GENERAL EUROPEAN THE-
ATRE OF OPERATIONS, UNITED STATES ARMY, AND AIR
CHIEF MARSHAL SIR ARTHUR HARRIS, COMMANDER-IN-
CHIEF, BOMBER COMMAND
OCTOBER 11, 1943

[October 11, 1943

[TO GENERAL DEVERS]

I SHALL be obliged if you will convey to General Eaker and
his Command the thanks of the British War Cabinet for the
magnificent achievements of the Eighth Air Force in the Battle
of Germany in recent days, culminating in their remarkable successes of last week.

In broad daylight the crews of your bombers have fought their
way through the strongest defence which the enemy could bring
against them, and have ranged over the length and breadth of
Germany, striking with deadly accuracy many of the most important hostile industrial installations and ports.

Your bombers and the fighters which support them in these
fierce engagements have inflicted serious losses on the German
Air Force, and, by forcing the enemy to weaken other fronts,
have contributed notably to the successes of the Allied arms
everywhere.

The War Cabinet extend their congratulations also to the
ground crews of the Eighth Air Force, without whose technical
skill and faithful labour these feats of arms would not be possible.

I am confident that with the ever-growing power of the Eighth
Air Force, striking alternate blows with the Royal Air Force

Bomber Command, we shall together inexorably beat the life out of industrial Germany, and thus hasten the day of final victory.

[TO AIR CHIEF MARSHAL HARRIS]

The War Cabinet have asked me to convey to you their compliments on the recent successes of Bomber Command, whose deeds in the first week of October mark yet another stage in the offensive against Germany.

The War Cabinet realise that the results of this campaign are not restricted to damage which can be seen and photographed, but are reflected with equal significance in the extent to which the German Air Force has been forced from the offensive to the defensive, both operationally and in new construction, and compelled to concentrate more and more of its resources on the protection of Germany against bombing attacks from the West, to the benefit of our own and Allied forces on the other European fronts.

Your Command, with the day-bomber formations of the Eighth Air Force fighting alongside it, is playing a foremost part in the converging attack on Germany now being conducted by the forces of the United Nations on a prodigious scale. Your officers and men will, I know, continue their efforts in spite of the intense resistance offered, until they are rewarded by the final downfall of the enemy.

These growing successes have only been achieved by the devotion, endurance, and courage for which Bomber Command is renowned. Airmen and airwomen of Britain, the Dominions, and our Allies have worked whole-heartedly together to perfect the mighty offensive weapon which you wield in a battle watched by the world.

I request you to bring this message to the attention of all members of your Command.

British to Occupy Azores

October 1.	*The Fifth Army entered Naples and continued to chase the retreating Germans.*
	Munich and Wiener Neustadt, near Vienna, bombed for the first time from North Africa.
October 2.	*There were signs that the Germans were preparing to fight a major battle for Rome.*
	Finschafen, in New Guinea, fell to the Australians after 11 days fighting.
October 3.	*The Germans fought back in the Dodecanese with a sea and airborne attack on the island of Cos.*
October 4.	*Eighth Army troops outflanked the Germans by sea, and landed at Termoli, which they captured after fierce fighting.*
	Admiral of the Fleet Sir Dudley Pound resigned his post as First Sea Lord, owing to ill health, and was succeeded by Admiral of the Fleet Sir Andrew Cunningham.
October 5.	*U.S.S.R. announced the destruction of 223 German tanks and 95 aircraft in two days.*
October 6.	*The Fifth Army, pushing north of Naples, reached the Volturno river, where heavy fighting developed.*
	The Germans claimed the capture of Cos.
	U.S. Naval forces heavily attacked the Japanese base on Wake Island.
October 8.	*Hitler and his party chiefs appealed for the maintenance of home front morale.*
October 9.	*U.S. bombers, flying from Britain, attacked targets on the far Eastern boundaries of Ger-*

	many only 250 miles from the Russian battle-front.
October 10.	Russians freed the Caucasian mainland of the enemy by clearing the Taman peninsula.
October 11.	British midget submarines, it was announced, had penetrated a narrow Norwegian fiord and had damaged the Tirpitz, Germany's greatest battleship.
October 12.	Mr. Churchill announced that Portugal had agreed to grant Great Britain facilities in the Azores which would ensure better protection for shipping in the Atlantic.
October 13.	Italy declared war on Germany "in face of the repeated and intensified acts of war committed against the Italians." Britain, the United States and U.S.S.R. accepted Italy's active co-operation as a "co-belligerent."
	The Russians broke through the enemy defences at Melitopol and Zaparozhe.

[*October 12, 1943*

I HAVE an announcement to make to the House arising out of the Treaty signed between this country and Portugal in the year 1373 between His Majesty King Edward III and King Ferdinand and Queen Eleanor of Portugal. This Treaty was reinforced in various forms by Treaties of 1386, 1643, 1654, 1660, 1661, 1703 and 1815, and in a secret declaration of 1899. In more modern times, the validity of the Old Treaties was recognised in the treaties of Arbitration concluded with Portugal in 1904 and 1914. Article I of the Treaty of 1373 runs as follows:

"In the first place we settle and covenant that there shall be from this day forward . . . true, faithful, constant, mutual and perpetual friendships, unions, alliances and needs of sincere affection, and that as true and faithful friends we shall henceforth, reciprocally, be friends to friends and enemies to enemies, and shall assist, maintain and uphold each other mutually, by sea and by land, against all men that may live or die."

This engagement has now lasted for over 600 years, and is without parallel in world history. I have now to announce its latest application. At the outset of the war the Portuguese Government, in full agreement with His Majesty's Government in the United Kingdom, adopted a policy of neutrality with a view to preventing the war spreading into the Iberian Peninsula. The Portuguese Government have repeatedly stated, most recently in Dr. Salazar's speech of 27th April, that the above policy is in no way inconsistent with the Anglo-Portuguese Alliance, which was re-affirmed by the Portuguese Government in the early days of the war.

His Majesty's Government in the United Kingdom, basing themselves upon this ancient Alliance, have now requested the Portuguese Government to accord them certain facilities in the Azores which will enable better protection to be provided for merchant shipping in the Atlantic. The Portuguese Government have agreed to grant this request, and arrangements, which enter into force immediately, have been concluded between the two Governments regarding (1) the conditions governing the use of the above facilities by His Majesty's Government in the United Kingdom and (2) British assistance in furnishing essential material and supplies to the Portuguese armed forces and the maintenance of the Portuguese national economy. The Agreement concerning the use of facilities in the Azores is of a temporary nature only, and in no way prejudices the maintenance of Portuguese sovereignty over Portuguese territory. All British Forces will be withdrawn from the Azores at the end of hostilities. Nothing in this Agreement affects the continued desire of the Portuguese Government, with which His Majesty's Government have declared themselves in full sympathy, to continue their policy of neutrality on the European mainland, and thus maintain a zone of peace in the Iberian Peninsula.

In the view of His Majesty's Government, this Agreement should give new life and vigour to the Alliance which has so long existed between the United Kingdom and Portugal to their mutual advantage. It not only confirms and strengthens the political guarantees resulting from the Treaties of Alliance, but also affords a new proof of Anglo-Portuguese friendship, and provides an additional guarantee for the development of this friendship in the future. On the conclusion of these negotiations the Foreign Secretary, who has, I think, conducted them with the very greatest skill and patience, has exchanged most cordial messages with the Portuguese President of the Council. In his message, he affirmed his conviction that the facilities now granted by the Portuguese Government would greatly contribute to the effective defence of our shipping, and thus prove an important factor in shortening the war. He added that the Agreement would give fresh vitality to the ancient Alliance and enhance the close and friendly relations which have so long subsisted between Portugal and Great Britain. In replying to this message, Dr. Salazar stated that he shared the hope that the facilities granted by Portugal to her Ally would help to bring about greater safety for shipping in the Atlantic, and that he trusted that this new proof of Portugal's loyalty to her traditions would fortify the secular Alliance and serve to draw still closer the bonds of friendship between the two peoples.

I take this opportunity of placing on record the appreciation by His Majesty's Government, which I have no doubt is shared by Parliament and the British nation, of the attitude of the Portuguese Government, whose loyalty to their British Ally never wavered in the darkest hours of the war.

The Coalmining Situation

A SPEECH IN THE HOUSE OF COMMONS
OCTOBER 13, 1943

[*October 13, 1943*

I MUST apologise to the House for intervening in this Debate, because I have not had the advantage of having been on the bench and of listening to it yesterday. But I have read not only the newspaper reports, but the Hansard Report to a very large extent, and I have spent since yesterday a good deal of time discussing the position with various friends and colleagues. I did notice that a request was made that there should be some statement from a War Cabinet Minister, and in deference to that request, I thought perhaps I should say a very few words in order to clarify, so far as possible, the situation.

Of course, I do not intend to go unduly into the technicalities of this problem, because that is not my business at the present time. They have been dealt with by the Minister of Fuel and Power (Major G. Lloyd George) and by his Parliamentary Secretary. They will be dealt with by the Minister again, when he winds up to-day and replies on the special points which have been raised. I would not presume to plunge into them, as the House would naturally know that I had merely had the answers given to me and had not been able to pass them through my mind. I thought however it might help if I reminded the House at the outset of this discussion of the general foundations upon which we stand at the present time. We have a National Coalition Government, which came together to try to pull the nation out of the forlorn and sombre plight into which the action, or inaction, of all political parties over a long period of years had landed it. [HON. MEMBERS: "The Tory Party."] It all depends where you draw the datum line. I stand very well placed in that matter, having been out for eleven years. Perhaps if I had not been out so long, I might have got mixed up in all those compromises which are inseparable from loyal collective action between colleagues. At any rate this National Coalition came together at a moment of very great peril and for that purpose, and I think we have not been altogether unsuccessful in our task.

What is it that holds us together? What holds us together is the conduct of the war, the prosecution of the war. No Socialist, or Liberal, or Labour man has been in any way asked to give up his convictions. That would be indecent and improper. We are held together by something outside, which rivets all our attention. The principle that we work on is: "Everything for the war, whether controversial or not, and nothing controversial that is not *bona fide* needed for the war." That is our position.

We must also be careful that a pretext is not made of war needs to introduce far-reaching social or political changes by a side wind. Take the question of nationalising the coal mines. Those words do not terrify me at all. I advocated nationalisation of the railways after the last war, but I am bound to say that I was a bit affected by the experience of the national control of the railways after the war, which led to the public getting a very bad service, to the shareholders having very unsatisfactory returns, and to one of the most vicious and hazardous strikes with which I have ever been concerned. However, as I say, the principle of nationalisation is accepted by all, provided proper compensation is paid. The argument proceeds not on moral grounds but on whether in fact we could make a better business of the whole thing for ourselves, a more fertile business for the nation as a whole, by nationalisation than by relying on private enterprise and competition. It would raise a lot of argument, a lot of difference of opinion, and it would be a tremendous business to nationalise the coal mines, and unless it could be proved to the conviction of the House and of the country, and to the satisfaction of the responsible Ministers, that that was the only way in which we could win the war, we should not be justified in embarking upon it without a General Election. It would be very difficult to have a General Election at the present time. I do not say it would be impossible. It would certainly not be so difficult as it would have been during the blitz, though perhaps the blitz might recommence, which would add to the gaiety of the proceedings. But still it would be very harmful to the war effort. Moreover such a policy would probably be preceded by a break-up of the present Administration and a separation of parties into the regular lines of political battle. I could not be responsible, as at present advised, for undertaking any further great change, and certainly not a permanent great change, in the mining industry during the war, because that I think would require to be ratified or preceded by a national mandate. Therefore, we must resist all such proposals, and we must ask for the support of the House in so doing.

I must point out that Parliamentary democracy does not proceed only by debate. It proceeds by debate and by division. It is only in this way that the majority can express its views. The majority can dismiss an Administration at any time, unless of course the Administration obtains a Dissolution from the Crown and finds itself sustained by the people. That is the way the Constitution works — and it is greatly admired in many countries — and it is a good thing always to keep that position in mind. As soon as the war is ended, the soldiers will leave off fighting and the politicians will begin. Perhaps that is rather a pity, but at any rate it is not so bad as what goes on in some countries, which I should not venture to name, where the soldiers are fighting abroad and the politicians are fighting at home with equal vigour and ferocity.

Let us see what will happen at the end of the war. It is very difficult indeed to pierce the veil of the future. We do not know how far away the end of the war is, or what condition or mood we shall be in at that time, or what our position will be in relation to the other great Powers. We cannot tell. However, in all this mist, the following seems to stand out very plainly. Either there will be agreement between the parties, or there will be a General Election on party lines. At the present time the latter looks more probable. At that General Election the people will decide which set of gentlemen, which political party, shall constitute the majority in the House of Commons, and the Crown will commission someone to form a Government accordingly. Now in time of war or great public stress and danger a National Coalition, with all parties officially represented in it as parties, not as individuals, gives great strength and unity to the country, as it is doing now. Anyone or any body of men who succeeded in breaking it up in time of war would, I am sure, incur the censure of the vast majority of the people. But in time of peace conditions are different. Party government is not obnoxious to democracy. Indeed, Parliamentary democracy has flourished under party government. That is to say, it has flourished so long as there has been full freedom of speech, free elections, and free institutions. So we must beware of a tyranny of opinion which tries to make one side of a question the only one which may be heard. Everyone is in favour of free speech. Hardly a day passes without its being extolled, but some people's idea of it is that they are free to say what they like, but if anyone says anything back, that is an outrage.

I earnestly hope that it may be possible to preserve national unity after the war, but I say quite frankly that I should not be at all alarmed for the future of this country if we had to return to party government. We may have to do that. But this I will say — and the House will pardon me, I am sure, for saying it — that whatever bitterness or differences or party fighting may have to take place among us, each representing our constituencies and our convictions, things can never be quite the same again. Friendships have been established, ties have been made between the two parties, minglings have taken place, understandings have been established, which, without any prejudice to each man's public duty, will undoubtedly have a mellowing effect on a great deal of our relations in the future; and for my part I must say that I feel I owe a great debt to the Labour Party, who were a most stalwart support to me at the time when I first undertook the burdens which I am still being permitted to bear.

About what happens after the war, we must see how things go and how we feel. However, should agreement unfortunately fail and a party Government be returned after a free election, then will be the time for that Government to make their proposals and to carry them out, and those who are in opposition, whoever they may be — and who can forecast what the choice of the electors will be? — will exercise their critical faculty, I trust with good temper and with the fullest freedom of debate. That is how the matter lies, and how our affairs will have to settle themselves. And one need not be too much alarmed in Britain about these things, because of the good sense of our people and because of our well-tried institutions, which are meant to face all the shocks and difficulties which past years have brought before us. Therefore I must say there is no question of far-reaching changes of a controversial character being made by the present Government, unless they are proved indispensable to the war. Another Government might take a different view, but not this one. We are making every kind of preparation and study, including legislative preliminaries, so that those who are responsible after the war will be able to deal with the many problems of that time under the best conditions.

This present House of Commons, which has so long exceeded its normal constitutional life and will shortly be asking for a renewal of the lease — a matter which does not rest entirely in our hands alone — has no right, except with a very general measure of agreement, to step outside the one function by which its continued existence is justified, namely the prosecution of the war. It is only the continuance of the war and the extraordinary conditions which it imposes and forces upon us all that justifies us in remaining together as a Parliament. I certainly could not take the responsibility of making far-reaching controversial changes which I am not convinced are directly needed for the war effort, without a Parliament refreshed by contact with the electorate.

Within the framework of these general observations, which I trust have been conceived in a spirit of detachment and without desire in any way to cause undue despondency or alarm, or still less to raise tempers, let us come to the present coal situation. What is the position? Fifteen months ago the House, without a Division, agreed to a scheme of reorganisation which aimed at full control over the operation of the mines, and the organisation of the industry on the basis of national service. This organisation was to continue, and is to continue, "pending a final decision by Parliament on the future of the industry." It is barely a year since this organisation came into being. I must submit to the judgment of the House as a whole that, taking it by and large, it has functioned very well. We were assured this time last year that there would be a breakdown in the coal supply for the winter. It is as much my duty to form an opinion upon such matters as it is about whether there will be enough shot and shell or enough shipping or enough petrol. I have to do the best I can to form an opinion, and I have various means of checking the facts and figures, and special means — a statistical department of my own — by which I can test the various statements of the Departments. The Paymaster-General makes a ceaseless examination of all the figures that are rolling out before us, and is entirely free to bring them forward. On the information which was presented to me, I took the opposite view. I thought we should get through, and we certainly did. The prophets of woe — and, the House will pardon me, the would-be profiteers of woe — were confounded by the event, as they have been in other spheres of activity quite a lot during the last twelve months. In fact, we survived last winter. No single factory has had to stop through lack of fuel, and our stocks of fuel, I am informed, are higher — not large, but still, higher now than they were this time last year. We owe this in a great part to the patriotic co-operation of the domestic consumers who responded so well to the Minister's appeal for economy. We hope that the coming year will not induce them to relax at all in their well-doing and self-restraint, or to feel that their share in this, as in other directions, goes unrecognised by Parliament and by the public.

We are told of the great unrest in the mining industry. I think that is a little unjust to the miners. Only 750,000 tons of coal have been lost during the last twelve months out of upwards of 200,000,000 tons which have been produced. The loss by strikes and stoppages has been no more than two-thirds of half of one per cent. We have always to run a great risk in these matters — two-thirds of 0.5 per cent. Neither I nor my father was ever any good at arithmetic. This loss by stoppages compares very favourably with the last war, and I must draw other comparisons outside this country. It must be remembered that we are in our fifth year of war. There is a fifth-year-of-the-war mentality. We perhaps, living rapidly under the pressure of events, all of us exerting ourselves above the normal line, do not realise the changes that are taking place and the strains to which all of us are subjected. We have entered the fifth year of this war, and our people must endeavour to attune themselves to the mood prevailing in that year, and to act harmoniously in regard to all the circumstances which surround us.

I am told that there is a great deal of absenteeism, and some scolding speeches have been made on that. Well, there is no Department which gives so much information of its working to the public as the Ministry of Fuel and Power, and it is natural, and not unhealthy, that a great deal of public attention should be focused on its difficulties. We hear a great deal about the rate of absenteeism among miners. The figure of wilful absenteeism, or voluntary absenteeism as it is euphemistically called, is I am told at this time slightly under 5 per cent. There is also a certain increase in short absenteeism. Not only in the mining trade, but throughout the industries of the country, there are small ailments which I must say I think are not entirely dissociated from the dietary changes to which we have subjected ourselves and the regime under which we live. It is said that a disproportionate amount of this total is due to the younger men. Well, it is for their comrades in the industry and the Army to instill into them by their example as well as by precept the duty which lies upon these young men to do their utmost to be worthy of all the wonderful effort and combination of effort which is proceeding in the country. But even when you take absenteeism through sickness or through accidents and add it to the absenteeism I have mentioned, I am informed that there has been no more loss of tonnage this year than last. A year of extra strain has been added, and many other circumstances are at work which make more difficult the getting of the coal; but the loss of tonnage although increased by a slightly larger proportion of sickness, is not greater than it was the year before.

I am also told that a decay of discipline has set in. I have no doubt that the Minister, when he spoke yesterday, was right in pointing out that conditions are very different when every man is needed to get coal and there is a great scarcity of miners, from what they were in the periods through which we have passed, those unhappy periods when cruel unemployment racked the mining industry. But I think that is rather a bad basis to rest upon. I trust that after the war, or during the war, most careful consideration of the problem by the Mineworkers' Federation and the Mining Association, acting together, may bring about conditions which will make the standard of discipline independent of any fluctuations which may occur in the labour market, and allow it to stand on duty honestly and fairly done by all.

We are told of all these difficulties in the mining industry. I think this is a very valuable two days' Debate, as almost everything stands on coal. It is vital to our war-making capacity. All our refined manufactures of civilisation in time of peace go down to the footing of this intense labour underground by a comparatively small section of our people, the miners. We must not underrate the strain upon the miners. Their average age has increased. Their food is less stimulating and their diet less varied. They do not get the holidays or the leisure to which their exceptionally arduous calling entitled them in the past during the summertime when coal consumption was small. They are now pressed to work just as hard, or harder, in the summertime in order to pile up for the winter and to make good the needs of the war. These are very considerable factors, and no one should underrate them or make them the basis of an indictment against the mining population.

If allowance is made for the fact that not much overtime or Sunday labour is worked in the pits, I am advised it is true to say that miners' earnings do not compare unfavourably with the average in munition industries. Their rates of wages have advanced over 50 per cent. as against an increase in the cost of living of 30 per cent. You must remember that these wages, whatever they may be, are appreciably discounted by the fact that there is so little to buy. The strain on the miners has been severe, and I am not here to-day to make complaints about them. We must rely upon them to do their best for the cause which they so warmly and sternly espouse.

Looking forward to next year, the miners will have the aid of the outcrop coal produced by surface workers, which may well amount to anything from ten to fifteen million tons. Therefore, I do not feel, provided everyone does his duty to the utmost, that we are in any danger of a collapse in coal production in the coming year. It must be a matter of some satisfaction to my hon. and gallant Friend the Member for Buckrose (Major Braithwaite), who was an early advocate of outcrop working and who wrote me several letters on the subject more than a year ago, to see how very substantial is the contribution in time of need which is coming from this source.

Great efforts are being made to increase the labour supply in the mines and to meet the annual wastage — nearly 20,000 a year. I am asked to release large numbers of men from the Army overseas. No new men have been taken for the Forces from mining for over two years. In fact, 11,000 have been returned. Now, in the advent of the bloodiest fighting of the war so far as our people are concerned, I am not prepared to weaken the field forces or the reserves of trained man-power which lie behind them beyond the limited comb-out of older men which was approved by the War Cabinet and which was announced by my right hon. and gallant Friend yesterday. Unless we are relieved by some altogether unexpected collapse on the part of the enemy — which we should be absolute fools to count upon — the worst fighting of the war, so far as the British people are concerned, lies ahead. Our manpower is fully extended, and I believe it is applied to the best advantage. When three months ago we had a series of War Cabinets and inter-Departmental discussions on man-power, a most difficult and painful process began. Departments, all keen on their plans for war and for the greatest effort, required 500,000 more men than existed, and there is no means of repairing such a deficiency in time for them to be of any use in the coming campaign. There was a struggle, and everyone had to face the cutting of dearly-loved and wisely-conceived plans for increasing our war effort. Man-power — and when I say that I include of course woman-power — is at a pitch of intensity at the present time in this country which was never reached before, not even in the last war, and certainly not in this. I believe our man-power is not only fully extended, but applied on the whole to the best advantage. I have a feeling that the community in this Island is running at a very high level, with a good rhythm, and that if we can only keep our momentum — we cannot increase our pace — that very fact will enable us to outclass our enemies and possibly even our friends.

I always assured the House that we should get through our shipping difficulties, although I admit that I had some extremely uncomfortable moments. I cannot see anything in the mining situation which makes me apprehend that this will be found to be the one gloomy failure in our national struggle. But of course in this field much depends on good will and on zeal for the common cause. I hold the opinion that there is nothing in the present coal situation which would justify a violent overturn of our existing system. Even if the overturn were well conceived, which is improbable having regard to the hurried conditions in which it would be born, it would cause more trouble than it was worth, and the reactions engendered might be deeply harmful to our war effort and might well prolong the war. Therefore I submit to the House for its judgment that the case for violent controversial legislation or the reconstruction of the mining industry as an essential to win the war has not in any way been made out, and is not sustained by the actual facts of the situation as it exists.

However, it was promised when the White Paper scheme was approved by Parliament that its workings would be continually reviewed. This is being done by the Minister and the War Cabinet, to whom the Minister has constant access on all matters affecting his Department. We are not prohibited from making any modifications or improvements which we think will yield beneficial results. My right hon. and gallant Friend announced yesterday that he had already made several changes and improvements, and this process is unceasing, and will be conducted, as everything has to be conducted, by consultations between the two sides of this industry. I pay tribute to my right hon. and gallant Friend the Minister for Fuel and Power. He has a very difficult task. There are in the House several Members capable of such a task, but I am sure they would be burdened to the full by it. It is largely a thankless task; he grudges nothing. I think he undertook over a hundred meetings at different pits last year. He spends every scrap of his life and strength upon that task, and I am bound to say that I feel we all owe him a debt.

I have asked myself whether my right hon. and gallant Friend needs any further powers. If he did, or if he does, he has only to ask for them, and if they are thought to be indispensable for the war effort, then, however rough, they will be given to him. If legislation were necessary, I should come without hesitation to the House. We were told, for instance, that there were some owners who obstructed the working of the best seams in order to prolong the life of their mines after the war. Well, I may mention that in not one single case out of the many investigated has this charge been made good. But if it were made good, or even if it were merely shown that there was inefficiency of a serious kind, there is not the slightest reason why the Minister should not use his powers. He has full powers to take over pits, or groups of pits, just in the same way as various firms have been taken over by the Minister of Aircraft Production. The Minister is perfectly free to make examples in any case where obstruction or incompetence of management or of control has been proved. But this has to be proved, and it has certainly not been proved yet.

I am told that the introduction of the new American machinery has in a few cases been delayed by the difficulties of fixing wage rates. This is a complicated question, because the machines are popular with those who use them. The question is complicated, because not only those who use the machines are affected, but those working farther back in the process of the industry. I think the Minister's powers do not extend to the general question of the fixing of wages, which it has long been the practice and custom to settle by agreement between the Mineworkers' Federation and the Mining Association. Yet if it were shown that any such failure to reach agreement about the introduction of these machines stood in the way of the fullest adoption of more modern methods, powers to appoint arbitrators already exist in the hands of the Minister, and they would be used to the full. I attach great importance from a long-term point of view to the increasing use of machinery in the pits. There is no doubt at all that the steady conversion of an ever larger proportion of the miners from human engines to handlers of machines — the steady transition of an increasing proportion to be engineers — will give this industry a much greater hold upon the future of our economic life. It may be that the hard teachings of war are one of the instruments by which these changes are forced upon us.

Though I cannot speak as an expert, I claim to have followed the fortunes of the miners all my life — for a great many years. I introduced the Coal Mines Regulation Bill in 1910 as Home Secretary, and I moved the Second Reading of the Mines (Eight

Hours) Bill, and I remember well the long battles that I fought side by side with Bob Smillie, who will be remembered in this House, in order to establish the very essential feature of pit-head baths. Everyone knows what I have done and where I have stood in the great controversies that have occurred in this country. You may say "1926." I was very much scolded as Chancellor of the Exchequer for providing £16,000,000 in 1925 in the hope that that lamentable breakdown might have been averted by negotiation.

I must make these references to the miners, because I am told and can well realise that anxiety exists among them about what is to happen to them and their industry after the war. They had a very grim experience after the last war, which went on biting away at them for a long period and greatly affected the whole conception that they had of mining as a means of getting their living. I know that there is anxiety. We can all lie awake thinking of the nightmares that we are going to suffer after the war is over, and everyone has his perplexities and anxieties about that time. But I, for one, being an optimist, do not think peace is going to be so bad as war, and I hope we shall not try to make it as bad. After the last war, which I lived through in a responsible position, nearly everyone behaved as badly as they could, and the country was at times almost uncontrollable. We have profited a great deal in this war by the experience of the last. We make war much better than we did, owing to previous experience. We are also going to try to profit to the full by the hard experience of what happened in the last peace. I am casting no reflection on the Government of that day when I say that, armed with their dear-bought experience, we shall make the transition from war to peace in a more orderly and disciplined fashion than we did last time.

But the miners are worried about their future. Who is not? His Majesty's Government give this assurance to them. It was made by my right hon. and gallant Friend yesterday, but I do not know that it made the impression it should have done. This assurance is that the present system of control, plus any improvements that may be made to it, will be continued after the war until Parliament shall decide upon the future structure of the industry. That means either that there will be a settlement by agreement between the great parties, or that there will be a General Election at which the people will be free to choose between political doctrines and political leaders. But anyhow, until all that is over there will be no decisive change in the present structure of the coal industry, or any removal of the many guarantees for the continuity of employment and wages and limitation of profits which are embodied in it. I am so anxious that we should all be together in this. Let us see how this will work out in point of time. It will certainly take three or four months after the war to hold a General Election and assemble a new Parliament. It will then take that Parliament a considerable time to deal with its many problems. In my opinion at least a year of stabilisation, probably a good deal more, under the present war-time White Paper conditions, can be counted on by the mining community. If it will give a further sense of security to the miners, and if they would welcome this, I should be quite ready to arrange for discussions to take place under the Minister of Fuel and Power in order that the uncertainty and harassing fears may be as far as possible allayed, and that the miners may know that there will be full consideration by Parliament and a definite period for reconstruction or transition after the war, and that they need not imagine that such violent changes as followed the end of the last struggle will be brought upon them then before they have had full time to organise their political action, and make sure that their case has been thoroughly examined by the Imperial Parliament. We will go into this matter with pleasure if it will give any satisfaction.

These are the only points of detail which I wish to touch on now, and the House will realise that I am not so well brushed-up in the subject as I have been at other times in my political life; but I thought it right that it should be set in its proper framework. It is only in the proper framework that we can take any decision for the time that lies before us. The task is long, and the toil is heavy. The fifth year of the war in which everyone has given the utmost in him weighs harsh and heavy on our minds and on our shoulders. Do not let us add to our difficulties by any lack of clarity of thinking or any restive wavering in resolve. Upon the whole, with all our faults and the infirmities of which we are rightly conscious, this Island is a model to the world in its unity and its perseverance towards the goal. However intense may be the strain of the fifth year upon us, it will be far worse for our enemies; and we have to continue to show them what they are now beginning reluctantly to realise, that our flexible system of free democratic government is capable alike of pursuing the most complex designs of modern war and of bearing invincibly all the varied strains which come upon our soldiers on the battlefields and upon all of us whose duty lies behind the fighting fronts.

Rebuilding the House of Commons

A SPEECH TO THE HOUSE OF COMMONS
OCTOBER 28, 1943

October 14.	*Allied tanks crossed the Volturno River in Italy.*
	In the Pacific the Allies gained complete control of the New Georgia group.
October 18.	*Mr. Anthony Eden and Mr. Cordell Hull arrived in Moscow for the Three Power Conference with M. Molotov.*
October 21.	*The Russians pushed on with their great drive in the Dnieper Bend and cleared the enemy from the centre of Melitopol.*
October 23.	*The whole German front in Southern Russia became endangered as Soviet troops took Melitopol and made a new break through at Kremenchug.*
October 25.	*Russians captured Dnepropetrovsk.*
October 29.	*President Roosevelt described the relations at the Moscow Conference as "100 per cent. good."*

[October 28, 1943

I BEG to move,

"That a Select Committee be appointed to consider and report upon plans for the rebuilding of the House of Commons, and upon such alterations as may be considered desirable while preserving all its essential features."

On the night of 10th May, 1941, with one of the last bombs of the last serious raid, our House of Commons was destroyed by the violence of the enemy, and we have now to consider whether we should build it up again, and how, and when. We shape our buildings, and afterwards our buildings shape us. Having dwelt and served for more than forty years in the late Chamber, and having derived very great pleasure and advantage therefrom, I, naturally, should like to see it restored in all essentials to its old form, convenience, and dignity. I believe that will be the opinion of the great majority of its Members. It is certainly the opinion of His Majesty's Government, and we propose to support this Resolution to the best of our ability.

There are two main characteristics of the House of Commons which will command the approval and the support of reflective and experienced Members. They will, I have no doubt, sound odd to foreign ears. The first is that its shape should be oblong and not semi-circular. Here is a very potent factor in our political life. The semi-circular assembly, which appeals to political theorists, enables every individual or every group to move round the centre, adopting various shades of pink according as the weather changes. I am a convinced supporter of the party system in preference to the group system. I have seen many earnest and ardent Parliaments destroyed by the group system. The party system is much favoured by the oblong form of Chamber. It is easy for an individual to move through those insensible gradations from Left to Right, but the act of crossing the Floor is one which requires serious consideration. I am well informed on this matter, for I have accomplished that difficult process, not only once but twice. Logic is a poor guide compared with custom. Logic, which has created in so many countries semi-circular assemblies with buildings that give to every Member, not only a seat to sit in, but often a desk to write at, with a lid to bang, has proved fatal to Parliamentary Government as we know it here in its home and in the land of its birth.

The second characteristic of a Chamber formed on the lines of the House of Commons is that it should not be big enough to contain all its Members at once without over-crowding, and that there should be no question of every Member having a separate seat reserved for him. The reason for this has long been a puzzle to uninstructed outsiders, and has frequently excited the curiosity and even the criticism of new Members. Yet is not so difficult to understand if you look at it from a practical point of view. If the House is big enough to contain all its Members, nine-tenths of its Debates will be conducted in the depressing atmosphere of an almost empty or half-empty Chamber. The essence of good House of Commons speaking is the conversational style, the facility for quick, informal interruptions and interchanges. Harangues from a rostrum would be a bad substitute for the conversational style in which so much of our business is done. But the conversational style requires a fairly small space, and there should be on great occasions a sense of crowd and urgency. There should be a sense of the importance of much that is said, and a sense that great matters are being decided, there and then, by the House.

We attach immense importance to the survival of Parliamentary democracy. In this country this is one of our war aims. We wish to see our Parliament a strong, easy, flexible instrument of free Debate. For this purpose a small Chamber and a sense of intimacy are indispensable. It is notable that the Parliaments of the British Commonwealth have to a very large extent reproduced our Parliamentary institutions in their form as well as in their spirit, even to the Chair in which the Speakers of the different Assemblies sit. We do not seek to impose our ideas on others; we make no invidious criticisms of other nations. All the same we hold none the less tenaciously to them ourselves. The vitality and the authority of the House of Commons, and its hold upon an electorate based upon universal suffrage, depend to no small extent upon its episodes and great moments, even upon its scenes and rows, which, as everyone will agree, are better conducted at close quarters. Destroy that hold which Parliament has upon the public mind and has preserved through all these changing, turbulent times, and the living organism of the House of Commons would be greatly impaired. You may have a machine, but the House of Commons is much more than a machine; it has earned and captured and held through long generations the imagination and respect of the British nation. It is not free from shortcomings; they mark all human institutions. Nevertheless, I submit to what is probably not an unfriendly audience on that subject that our House has proved itself capable of adapting itself to every change which the swift pace of modern life has brought upon us. It has a collective personality which enjoys the regard of the public, and which imposes itself upon the conduct not only of individual Members but of parties. It has a code of its own which everyone knows, and it has means of its own of enforcing those manners and habits which have grown up and have been found to be an essential part of our Parliamentary life.

The House of Commons has lifted our affairs above the mechanical sphere into the human sphere. It thrives on criticism, it is perfectly impervious to newspaper abuse or taunts from any quarter, and it is capable of digesting almost anything or almost any body of gentlemen, whatever be the views with which they arrive. There is no situation to which it cannot address itself with vigour and ingenuity. It is the citadel of British liberty; it is the foundation of our laws; its traditions and its privileges are as lively to-day as when it broke the arbitrary power of the Crown and substituted that Constitutional Monarchy under which we have enjoyed so many blessings. In this war the House of Commons has proved itself to be a rock upon which an Administration, without losing the confidence of the House, has been able to confront the most terrible emergencies. The House has shown itself able to face the possibility of national destruction with classical composure. It can change Governments, and has changed them by heat of passion. It can sustain Governments in long, adverse, disappointing struggles through many dark, grey months and even years until the sun comes out again. I do not know how else this country can be governed than by the House of Commons playing its part in all its broad freedom in British public life. We have learned — with these so recently confirmed facts around us and before us — not to alter improvidently the physical structures which have enabled so remarkable an organism to carry on its work of banning dictatorships within this Island, and pursuing and beating into ruins all dictators who have molested us from outside.

His Majesty's Government are most anxious, and are indeed resolved, to ask the House to adhere firmly in principle to the structure and characteristics of the House of Commons we have known, and I do not doubt that that is the wish of the great majority of the Members in this the second longest Parliament of our history. If challenged, we must take issue upon that by the customary Parliamentary method of debate followed by a Division. The question of Divisions again relates very directly to the structure of the House of Commons. We must look forward to periods when Divisions will be much more frequent than they are now. Many of us have seen twenty or thirty in a single Parliamentary Sitting, and in the lobbies of the Chamber which Hitler shattered we had facilities and conveniences far exceeding those which we are able to enjoy in this lordly abode. I am, therefore, proposing in the name of His Majesty's Government that we decide to rebuild the House of Commons on its old foundations, which are intact, and in principle within its old dimensions, and that we utilise so far as possible its shattered walls. That is also the most cheap and expeditious method we could pursue to provide ourselves with a habitation.

I now come to some of the more practical issues which are involved. It is said that we should wait until the end of the war, and I think perhaps that was the point my hon. Friend opposite wished to put. Certainly we must do nothing which appreciably detracts from the war effort, but what we have to do in the first instance is to make up our minds and have a plan and have the preliminary work and survey effectively done, so that at the end of the war, if not earlier, we can start without delay and build ourselves a House again. All this will be a matter for the Committee, which will certainly have more than fifteen Members of the House, representative of the different parties and different points of view. I am, however, not entirely convinced that it may not be found possible to make definite progress with this work even during the course of the war. The First Commissioner of Works has submitted a scheme which would enable the old House of Commons to be reconstructed, with certain desirable improvements and modernisations, accommodation for the Press, the Ladies' Gallery and other prominent features. This scheme would take only 18 months, but it would be prudent — and those concerned with building houses would, I think, feel that it would be prudent — to count on double that period, because everything must be fitted in with war needs, and also because it is the habit of architects and builders to be more sanguine when putting forward their plans than is subsequently found to be justified by the actual facts. The last House of Commons, the one which was set up after the fire in 1834, was promised in six years and actually took 27 years, and so, when I speak of rebuilding the House of Commons in 18 months, it is, of course, without panelling or carving, which can be added as the years pass by. It is simply a Chamber for us to dwell in and conduct our Business as we require to do. The timber must be set aside now if it is to be properly seasoned. The Clipsham Quarry, from which the stone was produced for the maintenance and replacement of the Houses of Parliament is temporarily closed. It would have to be reopened. We must then consider very carefully the strain upon our labour resources. The First Commissioner informs me that for the first six months after the plan has been started, after the word "Go" has been given, only 46 quarrymen and demolition men would be required, of whom half would be over 40 years of age and the other half over 50 years of age. In the second six months 185 men would be required over 40 and an equal number over 50. But of those over 50 years of age 60 would be masons, whose trade has so little work at the present time. In the third six months — and we shall be getting on by then — we shall require 170 men, not additional, over 40 and an equal number over 50. All the 170 over 50 would come from the building trade; the 170 over 40 and under 50 would come from the engineering trade. This last is a much more serious consideration. But there is no need for us, even when the whole scheme is approved and the work has begun, to commit ourselves to the rate of reconstruction. We can fit it in as a stand-by job. It might well be that in a year's time, when we require men from the engineering trade, our affairs might be in such a posture that we shall be looking for jobs rather than men.

However, the House is not asked to commit itself to any decisions of this kind. On the contrary, the Committee has first of all to make its decisions of principle, and then the execution of those decisions must be a matter for the Government to carry out as and when the public interest requires, and strictly within the limits of the war effort. All the same, I must tell you, Mr. Speaker, that it would be a real danger if at the end of the war we found ourselves separated by a long period from the possibility of obtaining a restored and suitable House of Commons Chamber. We are building warships that will not be finished for many years ahead, and various works of construction are going forward for war purposes. But I am bound to say that I rank the House of Commons — the most powerful Assembly in the whole world — at least as important as a fortification or a battleship, even in time of war. Politics may be very fierce and violent in the after-war days. We may have all the changes in personnel following upon a General Election. We shall certainly have an immense press of Business and, very likely, of stormy controversy. We must have a good, well-tried and convenient place in which to do our work. The House owes it to itself, it owes it to the nation, to make sure that there is no gap, no awkward, injurious hïatus in the continuity of our Parliamentary life. I am to-day only expressing the views of the Government, but if the House sets up the Committee and in a few months' time the Committee gives us their Report, we shall be able to take decisions together on the whole matter, and not be caught at a disadvantage in what must inevitably be a time of particular stress and crisis at the end of the war, from a Parliamentary point of view. Therefore, I ask that the Committee should be set up, and I feel sure that it will be able to make a good plan of action, leaving the necessary latitude to the Government as to the time when this action can be taken and the speed at which it can be carried into effect, having regard to the prime exigencies of the war. We owe a great debt to the House of Lords for having placed at our disposal this spacious, splendid hall. We have already expressed in formal Resolution our thanks to them. We do not wish to outstay our welcome. We have been greatly convenienced by our sojourn on these red benches and under this gilded, ornamented, statue-bedecked roof. I express my gratitude, and my appreciation of what we have received and enjoyed, but

> "Mid pleasures and palaces though we may roam,
> Be it ever so humble, there's no place like home."

Answers in the House of Commons

[HELIGOLAND]

Asked whether he would make a condition of peace the hand-ing over of Heligoland to Great Britain, Mr. Churchill said: —

SUCH matters would be more appropriate to the Peace Con-ference than to Question Time.

[BOMBING OF GERMANY]

A member asked whether steps were being taken "to bring up the strength of our Bomber Command and the United States Eighth Army Air Force here so as to enable them to bomb Ger-many to saturation point and thus, by destroying all her main sources of production, bring about her early defeat with a mini-mum loss of man-power?" Mr. Churchill replied: —

Yes, Sir; this seems to express the general idea very cogently.

Asked whether he felt we had reached the point of saturation, Mr. Churchill replied: —

That can only be ascertained by an empirical process.

[CONFIDENTIAL STATEMENTS]

Asked whether, when confidential statements are made by Min-isters to non-official bodies outside Parliament, the members of those bodies are under the same obligations of secrecy as Mem-bers of Parliament in relation to Secret Sessions; what their posi-tion is with regard to the Official Secrets Act; and under what

circumstances they could divulge the information so received,
Mr. Churchill *replied:* —

I cannot give authoritative interpretations of the law, but I am advised, firstly, that the rules of Privilege and the law relating to Secret Sessions would not apply to the circumstances set out in the Question; secondly, that under the Official Secrets Act, if it is made clear that the information is entrusted to the persons concerned in confidence by a person holding office under His Majesty, for example, a Minister of the Crown, its unauthorised communication by them to others, when of a character hurtful to public interest or safety, would be an offence. With regard to the last part of the Question, such information should not be divulged except with the authority of the Minister.

[EX-SERVICE ORGANISATIONS]

Asked to take steps to co-ordinate the work of organisations for the benefit of ex-servicemen and women, Mr. Churchill *replied:* —

These organisations are to a large extent purely voluntary bodies, but it is the policy of the Departments concerned to co-ordinate their efforts so far as possible and to further their efficient administration. I understand that, with the encouragement of the Service Departments, certain of the largest organisations are already directing their efforts to closer co-ordination.

[POST-WAR CONTROL]

Asked whether a speech by the Home Secretary on the future of controls in industry represented the policy of the Government, Mr. Churchill *replied:* —

I have seen some reports of this speech, and of others too. It is common ground that, in the words of the late Chancellor of the Exchequer in this House on 3rd February: —

"a considerable measure of control of our economic life will have to continue after the war."

This is very much what my right hon. Friend the Home Secretary said. In a National Coalition formed to carry on the war, a certain diversity of opinion, or at least of emphasis, is indispensable to political sincerity. I earnestly hope, however, that party controversy will be avoided, at least until we are nearer to our goal. This is a time when all combative impulses should be reserved for the enemy.

[POST-WAR AVIATION]

Asked about arrangements for the holding of an Imperial Conference on post-war civil aviation, Mr. Churchill said: —

Conversations of an informal and exploratory nature are now taking place in London. Besides the United Kingdom, the following are represented: Canada, the Commonwealth of Australia, New Zealand, the Union of South Africa, and India. Newfoundland, Southern Rhodesia, and Burma are represented by observers. The United Kingdom delegation includes the representative of the Secretary of State for the Colonies.

[CIVIL AIR CREWS]

Asked to consider the award of Service medals to the pilots of British Overseas Airways, Mr. Churchill said: —

The awards available for Civil Air Transport air crews are the George Cross, appointment to the appropriate class of the Order of the British Empire, the George Medal, the British Empire Medal, Commendation for valuable service in the air, Wound Stripes, and Chevrons for war service. Bars may be awarded to the George Cross and to both Medals. These air crews are therefore accorded a wide range of appropriate Honours and awards, and I do not think that there is need for any change.

[ITALIAN FLEET'S SURRENDER]

Asked to give details of the surrendered Italian fleet, Mr. Churchill stated in a written reply: —

The major part of the Italian Fleet, totalling over 100 warships of all categories, is in Allied hands. This includes five out of the six battleships in commission, and eight out of eleven cruisers. More than 150,000 tons of merchant ships have so far been accounted for in ports under Allied control. It would not be in the public interest to go into further detail. The position of ships and crews is still under active consideration, but I can assure my hon. and gallant Friend that the ships will be used to the best possible advantage of the United Nations.

[*October 13, 1943*

[POST-WAR AVIATION]

Asked to state the duties of the Lord Privy Seal (Lord Beaverbrook) in relation to post-war air transport, Mr. Churchill said: —

I HAVE asked the Lord Privy Seal to assume responsibility for the co-ordination of post-war civil air transport policy.

We are proceeding by steps. The first thing is, undoubtedly, a family talk, and that will, I think I need scarcely say, have no aim prejudicial to the interests of the United States. Thereafter we shall discuss with them, and of course also with Soviet Russia.

I should think it would be possible to make a very good arrangement for the interests of all parties. Certainly the British Empire has a great deal to give, and we certainly do not wish to obstruct natural and normal healthy development in civil aviation. I have every reason to believe that we shall be able to settle it, first of all among ourselves, and then by full and free discussion with those other great nations, in a manner which will be found satisfactory. At any rate, we will try our best.

[*October 14, 1943*

[ELECTORAL REFORM]

Asked whether he would give the House an opportunity of discussing electoral reform, Mr. Churchill said: —

THE Government are fully conscious of the importance of giving attention to all measures designed to secure that whenever there is an appeal to the country — whether at by-elections or at a General Election — the result shall be fully and truly representative of the views of the people. It will no doubt be the wish of the House, as it is of the Government, that this measure should be passed before the end of the present session. The Home Secretary has also announced the Government's intention to submit to parliament legislation on the subject of redistribution.

In addition, however, to measures of this kind designed to improve the machinery by which the existing Parliamentary franchise is exercised, the Government recognise that full consideration ought to be given to various proposals for changes in the existing franchise law, for controlling the expenditure allowable to candidates, and for other amendments designed to secure the maximum of fairness in the conduct of elections. In the opinion of the Government the best method of securing a full examination of these problems will be by a Conference, presided over by Mr. Speaker, and if the House concurs in the proposal the Government would propose that Mr. Speaker should be invited to undertake this important task in addition to his already onerous duties.

In the first instance, however, as I have already stated, the Government desire that there should be a wide Debate on electoral reform in order to give the House a full opportunity of expressing its opinion. We propose therefore to set apart two days for this Debate early in the new Session.

[*October 19, 1943*

[U.S. SENATORS' REPORT]

Asked to place on record the British view of the report of the five United States Senators who recently visited the fighting areas, Mr. Churchill said: —

S IR, the Report in question was made to Congress in Secret Session, and I am therefore neither fully nor accurately acquainted with its nature. A summary of ten conclusions reached by the Senators has been printed in the Record of the United States Senate. These conclusions bring no charges of the kind referred to by my hon. and gallant Friend. However, apart from the above, many stories have been published purporting to represent what the individual Senators have said. I am well aware of the pain which some of these unfair and probably unauthorised statements have caused. I have carefully considered whether it is my duty to make a public reply. I have come to the conclusion that there would be no advantage in His Majesty's Government taking part in this wordy warfare, especially at a time when the British and United States Armies are engaged shoulder to shoulder in the battles taking place or impending on the Italian front, and when the Royal Air Force and the United States Eighth Air Force in a perfect brotherhood of arms are making heavy sacrifices in their attacks upon Germany. I have however caused a full statement of the facts to be drawn up and kept here for the purposes of record or, if it should become expedient, for publication.

[*October 21, 1943*

[SWORD OF STALINGRAD]

Asked whether M.P.'s would have an opportunity to inspect the Sword of Stalingrad before it was sent to Russia, Mr. Churchill said: —

T HE time likely to be available for the exhibition of the Sword to the public is extremely limited, and we are anxious to use it in such a way as will enable the Sword to be seen as widely and by as many people as possible. This involves complicated arrangements with which I should be reluctant to interfere. As has already been announced, it is the intention that the Sword should be on exhibition in Westminster Abbey on 29th, 30th and 31st of this month. I will endeavour to arrange for special facilities to be given for hon. Members to see it there.

[THE LEA BRIDGE FACTORY]

Asked what reply he had sent to a resolution addressed to him by the Lea Bridge Works Factory Committee demanding the removal from office of the Secretary of State for India, Mr. Churchill said: —

Such matters hardly seem to fall within the province of the Lea Bridge Works Factory Committee, and I have accordingly directed that no answer should be sent to them.

Perhaps if they send me a communication on some subject on which they are specially qualified to express an opinion, I shall have the opportunity, which I should greatly value, of corresponding with them.

[October 26, 1943

[BEVERIDGE REPORT QUESTIONS]

Asked why the Minister without Portfolio now answered questions regarding the implementation of the Beveridge Report, Mr. Churchill said: —

I AM not aware that there has been any change of practice in this matter. I am always prepared to deal with Questions raising major issues of policy, but Questions relating to the Government's work on the Beveridge scheme as a whole, as well as to particular parts of it not falling within the province of any existing Department — such as children's allowances — should continue to be addressed to my right hon. and learned Friend the Minister without Portfolio.

When the member then suggested that questions should not be answered "by a stooge," Mr. Churchill said: —

I certainly am not prepared to answer a Question couched in such very unseemly terms.

[*October 28, 1943*

[A PARLIAMENTARY CONFERENCE]

Asked to make a statement regarding the visit of United States Congress representatives to Ottawa in June and July, Mr. Churchill said: —

I AM very glad to have this opportunity of saying a few words about the Conference which on the invitation of the Canadian branch of the Empire Parliamentary Association recently took place at Ottawa between delegations from the branches of the Association in Canada, the United Kingdom, the Commonwealth of Australia, New Zealand and Bermuda. A notable feature of the meeting to which my hon. Friend has drawn attention, was the presence of members of the Senate and of the House of Representatives of the United States of America.

The informal discussions in Canada, some of which were attended by the United States delegation, afforded a valuable opportunity for the exchange of private and quite unofficial views on matters of great interest, covering both defence and international problems of the British Commonwealth and Empire, and also questions of the relations between members of the Commonwealth and the United States in war and in peace. The United Kingdom delegation also had an opportunity while in Canada of discussions with the Canadian and Provincial Prime Ministers, and of seeing evidences of Canada's war effort both in defence and aggressive operations and in the industrial sphere, for which we express our gratitude. These meetings were followed by a visit of certain members of the delegation to Washington, where they attended the Senate and the House of Representatives, and also met a number of members of Congress personally; and in addition they paid a visit to Bermuda. Everywhere they received the most cordial welcome and generous hospitality.

Apart from its value as a means of personal contact and inter-change of opinion between representatives of the different members of the British Commonwealth, which is of such importance to our mutual relations, this Conference was of historic significance as being the first occasion on which representatives of the United States of America had taken part in such a gathering. I am sure that I am voicing the feelings of the House in expressing our obligations to all those, whether in Canada or in the other countries concerned, who by their organisation of the Conference and their interest in its proceedings helped to contribute to its success, as well as of course to all those who took part in its deliberations. I should also like to express our thanks to all those in both Canada and the United States who accorded such open-handed hospitality to these visitors from overseas. In all these events we can see a happy augury of fellowship and mutual understanding in the days when after victory we face together the problems of peace.

[SERVICE AFTER HOSTILITIES]

Asked to give an assurance that after the conclusion of hostilities men would not be retained in the Services by means of an Order in Council or under the Defence of the Realm Act instead of by a Bill which could be debated in the House of Commons, Mr. Churchill wrote: —

On the conclusion of hostilities no enactment will be immediately necessary to ensure the continuance in service of members of the Armed Forces then serving. There is a general obligation under existing Statutes to continue in service for the period of the present emergency, and that period will not end until its termination is declared by an Order in Council.

Let Vision Guide Our Steps

A SPEECH TO THE BOYS OF HARROW SCHOOL ON
NOVEMBER 5, 1943

October 30.	*Genichesk fell to the Red Army. The Germans flooded the Pontine Marshes in an attempt to stem the drive for Rome.*
November 1.	*Moscow Conference decisions were announced. Full agreement had been reached on measures to hasten the defeat of Germany.*
November 2.	*The Russian vanguard streamed across the Perekop Isthmus.*
November 3.	*More than 400 U.S. heavy bombers made a day attack on targets at Wilhelmshaven. At night the R.A.F. attacked Cologne and Düsseldorf.*
November 4.	*Isernia, first of the German defence lines in Italy, was stormed and captured by the Eighth Army.*
	Marshal Stalin revealed that 900,000 Germans were killed in the great four months' offensive.
November 6.	*Following the capture of Kiev, Russian troops invaded the Crimea from the Caucasus.*
	Marshal Stalin told the world: "Germany is standing on the edge of a catastrophe."

[November 5, 1943

A WHOLE generation has passed through the school since I was here in the winter of 1940. I am quite sure that in those dark and stern hours, from the youngest boy to the oldest master, there was only one sentiment in your breasts. That was that we would stand together and we should come through, and whether we came through or not we would stand together. England, which then stood alone against mighty forces, is now taking her place, one of the leading places, with 32 United Nations, comprising the vast majority of the populations of the globe, equipped with factories and arsenals and training-schools of war and with every form of military endeavour and attribute. We, with this great company, are striding forward.

We cannot doubt, we need not doubt. If we do our duty, victory will be our reward. We shall once again have brought the great British Commonwealth, and all it stands for, safely through one of the greatest convulsions which have ever shaken humanity, without the slightest loss to our possessions or the slightest diminution of our character and our honour.

The path of this war is hard and long, and no one would be so foolish as to try to fix some point at which it would end. However hard, however long, we shall go forward.

No one can tell at what time the resistance of the enemy may break. That is not our affair. That is theirs. That is for them to say. Then when it comes a great responsibility will fall on our country with others, but primarily with us, because we shall have to bear the burden of shaping the future as far as it is in our power or in our duty to do so.

You young men here may be in the battle, in the fields or in the high air. Others will be the heirs to the victory your elders or your parents have gained, and it will be for you to ensure that what is achieved is not cast away either by violence of passion or by sheer stupidity. But let keen vision, courage, and humanity guide our steps, so that it can be said of us that not only did our country do its duty in the war, but afterwards in the years of peace it showed wisdom, poise, and sincerity, which contributed in no small degree to bind up the frightful wounds caused by the struggle.

I hope, if another year comes and we are all intact, you will honour me with another invitation. I hope you will all nurse high thoughts in your minds, and high ambitions.

I can see myself, as it seems but yesterday, sitting a little boy here in these audiences, always feeling the thrill of your songs, and always feeling the glory of England and its history surrounding me and about me, and always praying that the day might come when I should have the honour of doing something to help forward the great association with which our lives have been connected.

[Referring to the songs of the school, "which, I think, I still know as well as most of you, and which have comforted me and have been an inspiration in my walk through life," Mr. Churchill went on to say:

"These Harrow songs are a great possession which the school has and which, I am sure, Malvern [which is sharing the Harrow premises] will enjoy, and of which they will carry away memories. This is a wonderful collection, and the fact that it is sung and known by each generation of Harrow boys is an ever-renewed pleasure to the school."

He remarked that the contribution of Mr. Bowen, in his opinion, gave him a solid claim to inclusion in the ranks of English men of letters and poets.

Mr. Bowen, to whom Mr. Churchill referred, was Mr. Edward Bowen, assistant master at the school in the second half of the last century, and the greatest contributor to the famous Harrow song book. The most famous of his works is "Forty Years On."]

No Time to Relax

A SPEECH AT THE LORD MAYOR'S DAY LUNCHEON
AT THE MANSION HOUSE, LONDON
NOVEMBER 9, 1943

November 8.	Russia forces struck rapidly Westward.
	The Eighth Army captured Casalbordino.
November 10.	The Fifth Army captured Castiglione.
November 11.	Russian bridgeheads on the Kerch peninsula were enlarged.
November 12.	German forces attacked Leros Island, gaining a foothold at some points.
November 13.	Cossack troops swept into Zhitomir.
November 14.	Eighth Army patrols crossed the Sangro.
November 16.	Organised resistance ceased on Leros.
	U.S. bombers attacked the molybdenum mines at Knaben and the power station at Rinkan, Norway.
November 18.	Berlin and Ludwigshafen were targets of simultaneous night raids in which Bomber Command set up a new record.

[November 9, 1943

I THANK you whole-heartedly for your kindness, for the warmth of your welcome, and for all the complimentary terms in which you, my Lord Mayor, have commended His Majesty's Government to the good will of the City of London. This is the fourth of your annual festivals which I have attended since the war began, and I confess that it seems to me they have all been milestones on our journey.

In November, 1940, when we were quite alone in the midst of the blitz, I had occasion to repeat to all the nations that were

overrun by the Germans our British pledge and guarantee that
we would never abandon the struggle until every one of them
had been liberated from the Nazi yoke. I see no reason to modify
that statement to-day. When I came here in 1941 I gave a solemn
warning to the Japanese Government that if they went to war
with the United States we should immediately declare war on
them. Well, there was nothing wrong with that. Last year, in
1942, I thought it right to say that I did not consider it any part
of my duty to liquidate the British Empire. I do not conceal
from you that I hold the same opinion to-day.

Since we were last gathered here, we and our Allies have had
a year of almost unbroken victory in every theatre and on every
front. British, Dominion, and United States armies have cleared
Africa of the enemy. Together the British and United States
forces have conquered Sicily, Sardinia, Corsica, and one-third of
Italy. We have broken the back of the U-boat war, which at
one time had seemed our greatest peril. We have inflicted, and
we are inflicting, shattering damage upon German cities which
are the centres of munitions production, and this has caused an
injury to the German war effort and to the German morale which,
combined with other blows, may well be the precursor of decisive events in the European struggle.

In all these operations, on land, on sea, and in the air, Great
Britain has had the honour to bear the greatest part and to pay
the heaviest price. In the Pacific, where the main forces of the
United States have been deployed, and where Americans, Australians, and New Zealanders are fighting together under the
inspiring leadership of General MacArthur, many brilliant actions have been recorded, and the strength of Japan has been
steadily and remorselessly worn down. But I gladly admit, and
indeed proclaim, that the outstanding event of this famous year
has been the victorious advance of the Russian armies from the
Volga westward across the Dnieper, thus liberating, as Marshal
Stalin has told us, two-thirds of the occupied Russian soil from
the foul invader. In this process the Russian Soviet armies have
inflicted deep and dire injury upon the whole life and structure
of the German military power. That monstrous juggernaut engine of German might and tyranny has been beaten and broken,
outfought and outmanoeuvred, by Russian valour, generalship,

and science, and it has been beaten to an extent which may well prove mortal.

We and our American allies have done, and are doing, our utmost to bring our forces across the seas and oceans into action against the enemy, and I rate the Anglo-American air attacks on Germany as one of the prime causes of the impending ruin of the Hitler regime. But it must never be forgotten that there was not in the whole world, nor could there have been created for several years, any military organism which could ever have given the blows which Russia has given, or survived the losses which Russia has borne. Here, from this City of London at our time-honoured gathering, we salute the Soviet armies and Marshal Stalin.

We have all been cheered by the results of the Moscow Conference, and we look forward to welcoming back in the next week or so our Foreign Secretary from his most successful mission. There is no doubt that the full and frank discussions between the three Foreign Ministers, M. Molotov, Mr. Eden, and that gallant old eagle, Mr. Hull, who flew far on a strong wing, have had the effect of making our Russian friends feel as they have never felt before that it is the heartfelt wish of the British and American nations to fight the war out with them in loyal alliance, and afterwards to work with them on the basis of mutual respect and faithful comradeship in the resettlement and rebuilding of this distracted and tormented world. I have not abandoned the hope that some time or other it may be possible for the Heads of the three Governments to meet together, because all my experience in this war shows that friendly and trustful personal contacts between the responsible leaders are the best foundation for all plans, whether for war or for peace.

In our Grand Alliance of 33 States or Governments constituting the United Nations, we try all we can by correspondence and consultation to preserve harmony and intimacy and to procure concerted action. As you may well imagine, it is not possible to consult with every member about the details of all military movements or plans. These must be confined to as few circles or persons as possible.

The high aims we set before ourselves were first outlined in the Atlantic Charter, and now we have published in Moscow the all-important Four-Power Agreement, which looks to the future foundations of world peace after these storms are over. There are many nations in our thoughts to-day. We hope that France will rise again to her true greatness, and will play a worthy part in shaping the progress of Europe and of the world. I rejoice in every increase of unity and consolidation that I notice in the French National Committee at Algiers, and I also rejoice at the growing power of the French armies which are being recreated and rearmed in North Africa, and which will presently take their share in the liberation of the soil of France from the most hateful form of human bondage. The French National Committee are not the owners but the trustees of the title deeds of France. These must be restored to the French nation when freedom is achieved, for it is only on the will of the people, freely expressed under conditions of reasonable tranquillity, that in France, as in other enslaved countries, any permanent structure can be raised.

A great many people speak as if the end of the war in Europe were near. I hope, indeed, that they may prove right, for certainly every month that this devastating struggle continues carries human society into deeper depths, and adds to the toil, the length, and the burden of recovery. We should, however, be foolish and blameworthy if we allowed our plans and actions to be based on the prospect of an early collapse in Germany. There is danger in anything which diverts the thoughts and efforts of any of the Allied nations from the supreme task which lies before them—namely, that of beating down into dust and ruin the deadly foes and tyrants who so nearly subjugated the entire world to their domination. I am myself proceeding on the assumption that the campaign of 1944 in Europe will be the most severe and, to the Western allies, the most costly in life of any we have yet fought; and we must all brace ourselves for that task and strain every nerve for its successful accomplishment.

This is no time for relaxation or soft thoughts on the joys of peace and victory. Hitler still has 400 divisions under his command or control. He has a party police force which gives him a grip upon the agonised and regimented people of Germany, incomparably stronger than anything that was at the disposal of the late Kaiser. Under this odious Nazi system the children still betray to their teachers, and thus to the police, any incautious remarks that their fathers and mothers may have used in their presence. Hitler and his guilty confederates know that their lives are at stake, and that they at any rate run no extra risks in making other people fight on to the bitter end. The German troops, wherever we have met them, have been found fighting with their veteran skill. The hazards of great land battles lie before us.

We cannot, moreover, exclude the possibility of new forms of attack upon this Island. We have been vigilantly watching for many months past every sign of preparation for such attacks. Whatever happens, they will not be of a nature to affect the final course of the war. But, should they come, they will certainly call for the utmost efficiency and devotion in our fire watchers and Home Guard, and also for a further display of the firmness and fortitude for which the British nation has won renown. This is no time to relax any of our precautions or discourage our splendid auxiliary services. This is no time to divide the unity of the nation by raising fierce party political issues. This is no time for persons who have practical war work to do to dream easy dreams of brave new worlds. We must keep our sense of proportion, even when discussing the incidents of procedure in some of our juvenile courts.

We must not lose for a moment the sense and consciousness of urgency and crisis which must continue to drive us, even though we are in the fifth year of war. We must go forward with unrelenting and unwearying efforts through every living minute that is granted to us. I am the head of a national coalition of all the three British parties, whose leaders are represented here to-day at your board. This Government came together with the sole policy of making war until the victory is won. We cannot to-day exclude from our minds, nor need we do so, the conviction that victory will certainly be won, and that not only Germany, but Japan, with whom the British Commonwealth and Empire have an inexpiable quarrel, will be forced into unconditional surrender.

We have no need to exclude that from our minds. But that does not mean that our war task is done. Another tremendous and practical duty is involved in what is called winning the war. Just as in time of peace plans for war and measures of defence ought to be in readiness for any sudden emergency, so in time of war we must make sure that confusion and chaos do not follow the victories of the armies or stultify an unexpectedly early surrender by the enemy. I regard it as a definite part of the duty and responsibility of this National Government to have its plans perfected in a vast and practical scheme to make sure that in the years immediately following the war food, work, and homes are found for all. No airy visions, no party doctrines, no party prejudices, no political appetites, no vested interests, must stand in the way of the simple duty of providing beforehand for food, work, and homes. These plans must be prepared now during the war, and they must come into action just as general mobilisation is declared when war breaks out. They must come into action as soon as the victory is won.

On this far-reaching work His Majesty's Government are now concentrating all the energies that can be spared from the actual struggle with the enemy. The policy of waging war until victory would be incomplete, and indeed spoiled, if it were not accompanied by a policy of food, work, and homes in the period following the victory for the men and women who fought and won.

I regard this hour as one more hopeful and more stirring than any through which we have passed. It is a reasonable assumption that, unless we make some grave mistakes in strategy, the year 1944 will see the climax of the European war. Unless some happy event occurs on which we have no right to count, and the hand of Providence is stretched forth in some crowning mercy, 1944 will see the greatest sacrifice of life by the British and American armies, and battles far larger and more costly than Waterloo or Gettysburg will be fought. Sorrow will come to many homes in the United Kingdom and throughout the great Republic. British and American manhood — true brothers in arms — will attack and grapple with the deadly foe. This year, 1944, is also election year in the United States — a strange coincidence, but I am sure I speak for all those on both sides of the Atlantic who mean the same thing — and they are numbered by scores of millions — when I say that the supreme duty of all of us, British and Americans alike, is to preserve that good will that now exists throughout the English-speaking world, and thus aid our armies in their grim and heavy task. Even if things are said in one country or the other which are untrue, which are provocative, which are clumsy, which are indiscreet, or even malicious, there should be no angry rejoinder. If facts have to be stated, let them be stated without heat or bitterness. We have to give our men in the field the best chance. That is the thought which must dominate all speech and action. Not only the fortunes of this fearful war, but also the happiness of future generations, depend upon the fraternal association of Great Britain and the United States, without prejudice to the larger world structure that will be erected to secure the peace and freedom of mankind.

Answers in the House of Commons

November 19.   *The Russians withdrew from Zhitomir, but occupied Ovruch.*

November 20.   *A tremendous battle developed in the Dnieper Bend.*

November 22.   *A German counter-offensive in the Kiev salient was held.*

November 25.   *The Russians captured Propolsk, on the River Sozh.*

     The Eighth Army crossed the Sangro and established a substantial bridgehead.

November 26.   *The Russians recaptured Gomel.*

     U.S. heavy bombers attacked Bremen in greater force than ever before in a daylight operation.

     R.A.F. bombers attacked Berlin for the fifth night in succession.

November 27.   *One-third of Berlin was reported wrecked as a result of the tremendous raids.*

[November 4, 1943

[BASIC ENGLISH]

Answering questions regarding Basic English, the Prime Minister said he hoped to receive the recommendations of the Committee of Ministers on the subject before very long. He continued: —

Basic English is not intended for use among English-speaking people, but to enable a much larger body of people who do not have the good fortune to know the English language to participate more easily in our society.

People are quite purblind who discuss this matter as if Basic English were a substitute for the English language.

[ALBANIAN GUERRILLAS]

Replying to a member regarding Guerrillas in Albania, the Prime Minister said: —

Thousands of Albanian guerrillas are now fighting in their mountains for the freedom and independence of their country. From the experience of other occupied countries they have learned that the so-called independence conferred by Germany is a cruel fraud. Some weeks ago the Fascist occupation, which for over four years they had refused to accept, was replaced by German oppression. The Germans are employing all the usual methods by which they seek to subdue warlike peoples; already they have bombed Albanian villages and killed Albanian women and children; but the Albanian guerrillas continue to harass the enemy and to attack his communications.

The British liaison officers who are with these guerrillas have paid high tribute to their fighting qualities. We look to the Albanians to play their part in accordance with their ancient warlike traditions in the future military developments in the Mediterranean area. The policy of His Majesty's Government remains as explained by my right hon. Friend the Secretary of State for Foreign Affairs in his statement on 18th December, 1942; that is to say, we wish to see Albania freed from the Axis yoke and restored to her independence. The frontiers will of course be considered in the Peace Settlement.

[November 10, 1943

[STATE CONTROL OF INDUSTRY]

When a member asked whether a speech made by the Home Secretary on Government control and economic affairs to the Fabian Society represented the policy of His Majesty's Government, the Prime Minister answered: —

MY right hon. Friend the Home Secretary informs me that
he made it clear at the beginning of the speech referred to that
he was speaking as a Socialist to his fellow Socialists of the Fabian
Society. There was no implication in the speech that he was
speaking for the Government.

*Lord Winterton: Will the Prime Minister make it clear that
members of the Coalition Government have a perfect right in
this Government, as in previous Governments, to speak to their
own political Associations as my right hon. Friend does to the
Conservative Association and as Liberals do to the Liberal Association?*

THE PRIME MINISTER: I do not think that any particular
advertisements of these facts are needed from me. In my view
the less divergencies are emphasised the better.

*Major Lloyd asked the Prime Minister whether the views on
State control of industry after the war expressed by the Secretary
of State for the Home Department at a public meeting in the
Caird Hall, Dundee, on 3rd October last, represent the policy
of His Majesty's Government.*

THE PRIME MINISTER: I would refer my hon. and gallant
Friend to the answer which I gave on 12th October last in reply
to a Question by my hon. Friend the Member for South Croydon
(Sir H. Williams), to which I have nothing to add.

*Mr. McKinlay: Is it the intention of the Government to ease
the situation on the other side by making a declaration that it
is the purpose to withdraw the controls immediately the war is
finished?*

THE PRIME MINISTER: No, Sir. This would not be the moment
at which I should be inclined to make any new declaration.

*Mr. Shinwell: Can the Prime Minister say whether the views
of the right hon. Gentleman the Home Secretary are having any
influence on the Government?*

· THE PRIME MINISTER: We derive the greatest advantage from the counsel of the Home Secretary on a great many subjects, and I hope we shall long continue to do so.

Mr. Shinwell: But apart from deriving counsel and guidance, has the right hon. Gentleman any intention of ever applying any of these suggestions?

THE PRIME MINISTER: My hon. Friend is dealing with the speech delivered in the Caird Hall, Dundee, and I should not like to try to unravel this tangled skein at this moment.

Mr. Kirkwood: Will the Prime Minister support the Home Secretary in the statements that he makes?

THE PRIME MINISTER: I am afraid I am a life-long opponent of Socialism.

[*November 11, 1943*

[AID TO CHINA]

Answering a member as to the duties of General Carton de Wiart in Chungking, the Prime Minister said:—

GENERAL CARTON DE WIART will act as my personal representative with Generalissimo Chiang Kai-shek, and he will also be under Admiral Mountbatten's orders as Principal Liaison Officer at Chungking. It is hoped that this additional contact between me and Generalissimo Chiang Kai-shek will be helpful in promoting close relations between us. It has been cordially welcomed by the Generalissimo.

The relations of General Carton de Wiart with General Stilwell will, I trust, be of the greatest comradeship and amity. I cannot make any statement on the forms of military aid that we intend to give to China, except to say that everything in human power is being done.

[THEIR DUTIES ARE VITAL]

Answering a question regarding the Home Defence Services, the Prime Minister said: —

His Majesty's Government attach the highest importance to the work of the Home Guard and the fire-guards, who have played and continue to play so important a part in our home defence. In my speech at the Mansion House I gave reasons why in my opinion this is no time to relax any of our precautions or discourage our Auxiliary Services. On the other hand, I have asked that steps should be taken to ease up, as much as public safety allows, the strain upon efficient members of the Home Guard who are working long hours a day.

The Sword of Stalingrad

November 30.	*The Russians announced that they had evacuated Korosten, in the Kiev salient.*
	Attacking across the Sangro, the Eighth Army penetrated deeply into the enemy's lines.
December 1.	*First announcement that Mr. Churchill, President Roosevelt and Generalissimo Chiang Kai-shek had had a five-day conference in Cairo at which plans were made for prosecuting the war against Japan.*
	Following the conference in Teheran, President Roosevelt, Marshal Stalin and Mr. Churchill issued a joint statement on the plans for hastening victory and establishing an enduring peace.
December 2.	*The Germans fell back in the Sangro sector. Heavy fighting continued in the Dnieper Bend between the Kiev and Kherson areas.*
December 3.	*Further progress was made by the Eighth Army. The Germans admitted evacuating Lanciano.*

[November 29, 1943

In a deeply impressive ceremony the Sword of Stalingrad, tribute of King George VI and the people of Great Britain to the people of Stalingrad, was presented by Mr. Churchill to Marshal Stalin at the Soviet Embassy in Teheran on November 29, 1943. Making the presentation, Mr. Churchill said: —

MARSHAL STALIN — I have the command of His Majesty King George VI to present to you for transmission to the city of Stalingrad the Sword of Honour of which His Majesty himself has approved the design. This blade bears upon it the inscription "To the steel-hearted citizens of Stalingrad, the gift of King George VI, in token of the homage of the British people."

Sixty-Ninth Birthday

[*November 30, 1943*

Mr. Churchill was sixty-nine on November 30, 1943, and his birthday was celebrated in the midst of the historic conference at which the Prime Minister, Marshal Stalin and President Roosevelt met.

Among the many gifts the Prime Minister received were three from the troops doing duty as guards at the Conference. They were a silver cigar-box of Isfahan work "from all ranks of Paiforce" (Persia and Iraq Command), an oval silver tray also of Isfahan work "from the Buffs," and an Imami miniature on ivory in an ivory frame "from the Sikhs."

Acknowledging the gifts, Mr. Churchill said he was a stranger to Paiforce, but he knew what the troops had done and what a worthy part they had played.

I HOPE and trust," he continued, "that the decisions we are making may play their part in shortening the war and enabling you to get back to your homes, East and West, wherever they may be."

349

A Future without Tyranny

[*December 1, 1943*

The following is the official joint statement issued after the Conference of the allied leaders in Teheran: —

W E, the President of the United States of America, the Prime Minister of Great Britain, and the Premier of the Soviet Union, have met these four days past in this capital of our ally Iran and have shaped and confirmed our common policy.

We expressed our determination that our nations shall work together in war and in the peace that will follow.

As to war, our military staffs have joined in our round table discussions, and we have concerted our plans for the destruction of the German forces. We have reached complete agreement as to the scope and timing of the operations which will be undertaken from the East, West, and South.

The common understanding which we have reached guarantees that victory will be ours.

And as to peace, we are sure that our concord will make it an enduring peace. We recognise fully the supreme responsibility resting upon us and all the United Nations to make a peace that will command the good will of the overwhelming masses of the peoples of the world and banish the scourge and terror of war for many generations.

With our diplomatic advisers we have surveyed the problems of the future. We shall seek the co-operation and the active participation of all nations, large and small, whose peoples in heart and mind are dedicated, as are our own peoples, to the elimination of tyranny and slavery, oppression and intolerance. We shall welcome them as they may choose to come into a world family of democratic nations.

No power on earth can prevent our destroying the German

armies by land, their U-boats by sea, and their war plants from the air. Our attacks will be relentless and increasing.

From these friendly conferences we look with confidence to the day when all peoples of the world may live free lives, untouched by tyranny, and according to their varying desires and their own consciences.

We came here with hope and determination. We leave here friends in fact, in spirit, and in purpose.

> Signed at Teheran, December 1, 1943. —
>
> ROOSEVELT, STALIN, CHURCHILL.

December 5.	*The Fifth Army made gains in a new offensive in Italy. The Eighth Army took San Vito.*
	Ground was gained by the Russians West and South of Kremenchug.
December 6.	*Montgomery's men reached the line of the River Moro.*
December 8.	*The Russians gained ground north of Znamenka and inflicted heavy tank losses on the enemy in the Kiev salient.*
December 9.	*A new drive in the Dnieper Bend brought the Russian forces within 17 miles of Kirovograd.*
	Practically the whole of Monte Maggiore was cleared of the enemy.
December 10.	*Marshal Stalin announced the capture of Znamenka.*
	Sofia received its heaviest air raid.
December 13.	*The Eighth Army advanced to the high ground overlooking Ortona.*
December 14.	*Marshal Stalin announced the capture of Cherkasy.*
December 15.	*The Russians continued to stand firm in the Kiev salient and increased the threat to Kirovograd and Smyela.*
December 16.	*The Eighth Army was engaged in heavy fighting along the 15 miles of the Adriatic coast sector.*
	American forces landed on New Britain, in the Pacific.
	First announcement that Mr. Churchill, still abroad, was suffering from pneumonia.

December 18. U.S. troops landed on *New Britain and captured the Arawe peninsula.*

December 19. The Red Army broke through the enemy's defence line south of Nevel on a front of nearly 50 miles.

December 20. Day attacks on Bremen, Innsbruck and Augsburg. Heavy night attack on Frankfort.

December 23. The Eighth Army drove the Germans from all but the North-West end of Ortona.

December 24. Announced that General Eisenhower had been appointed Commander-in-Chief of the Second Front in Europe.

Largest force of American bombers yet sent on a single mission attacked special military objectives across the Channel.

December 26. German battleship Scharnhorst *sunk off Norway by units of the Home Fleet.*

The Russians resumed their offensive West of Kiev and advanced on a front of 50 miles. Radomysl was recaptured.

December 28. The Russians quickened their advance in the Kiev salient.

The Germans admitted evacuating Ortona.

December 29. Announced that three destroyers and a blockade runner had been sunk in the Bay of Biscay.

More than 2,000 bombs were dropped on Berlin in a night raid.

December 30. Marshal Stalin announced that the Russians had advanced 30 to 60 miles in the Kiev salient. Twenty-two enemy divisions were routed and more than 1,000 places liberated.

December 31. The Russians recaptured Zhitomir.

The Fifth Army made a large-scale raid across the Garigliano towards Minturno.

[REPLY TO A MESSAGE FROM GENERALISSIMO CHIANG KAI-SHEK ON THE ANNIVERSARY OF THE OUTBREAK OF THE PACIFIC WAR]

Y OUR Excellency's telegram has been dispatched to me, and I hasten to thank you for your most encouraging and inspiring message on this anniversary. I, and the whole British nation, have long admired the steadfastness and endurance of China, and I am confident that as a result of the decisions of the Conference which has just taken place, the efforts of our two peoples and those of the United States and our other Allies will bear good fruit. With my renewed personal good wishes to yourself and Mme. Chiang Kai-shek.

TO BOMBER COMMAND

[December 21, 1943

[THE PRIME MINISTER, WHO HAD BEEN RECEIVING FULL DETAILS OF AIR OPERATIONS DURING HIS ILLNESS, SENT HIS CONGRATULATIONS TO AIR CHIEF MARSHAL SIR ARTHUR HARRIS, COM- MANDER-IN-CHIEF OF BOMBER COMMAND. SIR ARCHIBALD SINCLAIR, SECRETARY OF STATE FOR AIR, WROTE: –]

T HE Prime Minister has asked me to convey his congratula- tions to crews who have taken part in the series of great battles over Berlin and Leipzig and in the associated attacks.

CHRISTMAS GREETINGS

[December 25, 1943

[CHRISTMAS DAY FOUND THE PRIME MINISTER RE-
COVERING FROM HIS ILLNESS AND GATHERING
STRENGTH. THE FOLLOWING STATEMENT WAS
ISSUED FROM 10, DOWNING STREET.]

THE Prime Minister has been informed of the Christmas greetings sent to him by many friends, known and unknown, both at home and abroad. He had also been cheered by the large number of kind messages received during his illness from all parts of the world. Mr. Churchill looks forward to reading these messages on his return. In the meantime he regrets that he cannot reply personally, but sends his warm thanks to all, and hopes that this message will be accepted as an acknowledgment.

[December 28, 1943

[REPLY TO A MESSAGE OF CONGRATULATIONS
FROM THE PRESIDENT OF MEXICO ON THE
RESULT OF THE TEHERAN CONFERENCE]

I DESIRE to express my warm thanks for the telegram which you, Mr. President, have been so good as to send me on learning of the results of the conversations at Teheran. I feel, with your Excellency, that these conversations enable us to look forward with increased confidence to the creation of an international system of the kind so eloquently described by your Excellency. — Winston Churchill, Prime Minister of Great Britain.

"THIS ADMIRABLE M AND B"

[*December 29, 1943*

[A PERSONAL MESSAGE ISSUED BY THE PRIME MIN-
ISTER DURING HIS CONVALESCENCE AND DATED
FROM 10, DOWNING STREET.]

NOW that I am leaving the place where I have been staying
for "an unknown destination," after more than a fortnight's
illness, I wish to express my deep gratitude to all who have sent
me kind messages or otherwise helped me. I had planned to visit
the Italian front as soon as the conferences were over, but on
December 11, I felt so tired out that I had to ask General Eisenhower for a few days' rest before proceeding. This was accorded
me in the most generous manner.

The next day came the fever, and the day after, when the
photographs showed that there was a shadow on one of my lungs,
I found that everything had been foreseen by Lord Moran. Excellent nurses and the highest medical authorities in the Mediterranean arrived from all quarters as if by magic. This admirable
M and B, from which I did not suffer any inconvenience, was
used at the earliest moment, and after a week's fever the intruders
were repulsed. I hope all our battles will be equally well conducted. I feel a good deal better than at any time since leaving
England, though of course a few weeks in the sunshine are
needed to restore my physical strength.

I did not feel so ill in this attack as I did last February. The
M and B, which I may also call Moran and Bedford, did the
work most effectively. There is no doubt that pneumonia is a
very different illness from what it was before this marvellous drug
was discovered. I have not at any time had to relinquish my part
in the direction of affairs, and there has been not the slightest
delay in giving the decisions which were required from me. I am
now able to transact business fully. I have a highly efficient
nucleus staff, and am in full daily correspondence with London;

and though I shall be resting for a few weeks I shall not be idle, providing of course that we do not have any setbacks.

I thought that some of those who have been so kind as to inquire, or express themselves in friendly terms, about me, would like to have this personal note from me, which they will please take as conveying my sincere thanks.